The New Queensland House

The New Queensland House

Cameron Bruhn
& Katelin Butler

Contents

6   **Foreword**
By David Malouf

8   **Introduction**
By Cameron Bruhn and Katelin Butler

12   **Inside Becomes Outside: Queensland's Domestic Landscape**
By Silvia Micheli and Ashley Paine

20   **C House**
Photo essay by David Chatfield

30   **Houses From a School of Ideas**
By Brit Andresen and Michael Keniger

A life lived outdoors

43   **Chelmer House**
Bligh Graham Architects
Chelmer, Brisbane

51   **Oxlade Drive House**
James Russell Architect
New Farm, Brisbane

59   **Rosalie House**
Owen Architecture
Paddington, Brisbane

67   **Cantala Avenue House**
ME
Miami, Gold Coast

75   **Beck Street**
Lineburg Wang
Paddington, Brisbane

85   **Earl Parade**
Cavill Architects
Manly, Brisbane

93   **La Scala**
Richards & Spence
Bowen Hills, Brisbane

A home in the landscape

105 **Cape Tribulation House**
m3architecture
Cape Tribulation, Daintree National Park

115 **Jule House**
Claire Humphreys and Kevin O'Brien Architects
St Lucia, Brisbane

123 **Planchonella House**
Jesse Bennett Studio
Edge Hill, Cairns

133 **Moonshine**
Brit Andresen Architect
Minjerribah (North Stradbroke Island)

141 **Bellbird Retreat**
Steendijk
Killarney, Southern Downs

149 **Mount Coot-tha House**
Nielsen Jenkins
Mt Coot-tha, Brisbane

159 **Sunrise Studio**
Bark Architects
Doonan, Noosa Valley

Traditions reimagined

169 **Aperture House**
Blight Rayner and Twofold Studio
Highgate Hill, Brisbane

177 **Shutter House**
Kim and Monique Baber
West End, Brisbane

185 **Left Over Space House**
CultivAR Architecture
Paddington, Brisbane

193 **West End House**
KIRK
West End, Brisbane

201 **Camp Hill House**
Twohill & James
Camp Hill, Brisbane

211 **Terrarium House**
John Ellway Architect
Highgate Hill, Brisbane

221 **Annerley House**
Zuzana&Nicholas
Annerley, Brisbane

Suburban ensembles

231 **Keperra House**
Atelier Chen Hung
Keperra, Brisbane

241 **Granny Flat**
Clare Design
Burleigh Heads, Gold Coast

249 **Bath House**
Stephen de Jersey Architect
Hermit Park, Townsville

257 **Auchenflower House**
Vokes and Peters
Auchenflower, Brisbane

265 **Morningside Residence**
Kieron Gait Architects
Morningside, Brisbane

275 **One Room Tower**
Phorm Architecture + Design in collaboration with
Silvia Micheli and Antony Moulis
West End, Brisbane

283 **Channel Street Studio**
Anna O'Gorman Architects
Cleveland, Redland City

292 Pictorial endnote

295 Architects, designers and photographers

296 Artwork credits and acknowledgements

Foreword

David Malouf

Brisbane, from its beginnings, presented a unique urban landscape. Its tin-roofed, one-storeyed weatherboards – protected by verandahs against the subtropical sunlight and raised on wooden stumps to deal with the hilly terrain of one bank of its serpentine river and the recurrent flooding of the other – had more in common with the British and French colonies of the Caribbean and near Pacific than with the Georgian stone terraces and villas of the southern European capitals. This was a necessary response to climate and topography but was also determined by a lack of local sandstone and the ready abundance, in cedar and hoop and bunya pine, of native timber.

The dwellings themselves were simple in form. Their living spaces – a stuffily furnished 'good room', based on the British parlour and opened only on special occasions, and two or three bedrooms open to a verandah – lay on either side of a hallway that ran as a breezeway from front door to back. Behind them a dining room and kitchen, plus a smaller room with a wireless where the family gathered for the evening news, favourite serials and the Lux Radio Theatre, and a piano for family singalongs. This rear of the house, shaded by a mango tree or camphor laurel and a clump of pawpaw, faced the long backyard, which sometimes included a tennis court and always a sizeable vegetable garden and chook house.

The very British family lifestyle of such houses, whose spaces were determined by that life but also helped maintain it, lasted pretty much unchanged through the long years of the Depression and war into the mid-fifties. Then, with the advent of rock-and-roll, the shared cultural life of parents and children fractured; youth culture was born and was soon intensified by the arrival of such new technologies as the transistor radio and the Walkman. At the same time there was a shift in the family's outdoor culture, from a British-style 'watering place' with still water and a pier to the Californian surf culture of what would later be called the Gold Coast, and from traditional 'British' food habits to something more compatible with the climate, the diet and the al fresco dining of the Mediterranean. Olive oil was no longer something you bought from the chemist and took with a spoon.

These changes in lifestyle made the older forms of domestic space outdated and in need of change, but their wider application was slower than might have been expected.

After the brief excitement of being in the front line in the Pacific War, Brisbane went back to being 'sleepy'; it resisted until the early seventies the rush to development of the southern capitals. Then, under the influence of a growing affluence, it took a rapid turn towards expansion: the replacement of the tramway network by buses; new highways, tunnels and flyovers; and skyscrapers that made the City Hall's clocktower no longer the city's highest building. In 1986 Harry Seidler's Riverside Centre, with a plaza that was open to the river, established the river as the focus of the city's orientation and one of its major thoroughfares.

This was the moment too when what had previously been something of an embarrassment was redefined as an 'Old Queenslander', and in being revered at last as 'historic' could also be bypassed.

The 'New Queenslander' opens its interior spaces, via a wooden deck or patio and sliding screens, to the garden: a swimming pool and barbecue area, a pizza oven. Indoors and outdoors become one. It is this blending of spaces and the turn to a variety of new building materials that *The New Queensland House* traces and richly illustrates in twenty-eight houses from 2012, with proper recognition of the imagination and skill of their makers.

David Malouf
David Malouf is the internationally acclaimed author of novels including *Ransom*, *The Great World* (winner of the Commonwealth Writers' Prize and the Prix Femina Etranger), *Remembering Babylon* (winner of the IMPAC Dublin Literary Award), *An Imaginary Life*, *The Conversations at Curlow Creek*, *Dream Stuff*, *Every Move You Make*, along with his autobiographical classic *12 Edmondstone Street* and recent publications *A First Place* and *The Writing Life*. His epic collection *The Complete Stories* won the 2008 Australia-Asia Literary Award. David was born in 1934 and brought up in Brisbane.

Opposite:
Auchenflower House (2016) in Auchenflower, Brisbane, by Vokes and Peters.
Photography: Christopher Frederick Jones.

Introduction

Cameron Bruhn and Katelin Butler

Queensland has a unique historic and contemporary architecture; a bespoke regionalism that has contributed to national and international conversations about the progress of architecture. The residential thread of this story has three distinct parts: a timber and tin tradition with origins in the 19th century; a modest mid-20th century engagement with modernism attaching to the emergence of a sun-drenched lifestyle; and a postmodern condition that diversified and reoriented the local scene toward the end of the 20th century. In this volume, twenty-eight engaging houses from the past decade are presented in detail, describing the architectural atmosphere of Queensland in the early 21st century and exemplifying the ideas, teaching and buildings that have shaped Queensland residential architecture since the late 1970s.

These homes constitute a new chapter in the story of architecture in this part of the world. The latest chapter builds on the past, embraces the opportunities of the present day and offers glimpses of the future. In the past decade the architectural gaze, cultural policy and lifestyle-driven investment have highlighted the residential achievements of Queensland architects and the economic prosperity of the past 30 years has delivered an ambitious body of residential architecture. The new stream in the architectural conversation that emerged at the turn of the century is distinguished by its authentic attention to the pragmatics of the local condition and a studious consideration and acknowledgement of international architectural precedents.

The elevated timber and tin pavilion, perched on the hillside is the historic and enduring image of suburban life in Queensland's hilly cities and towns. The detached Queenslander is a prefabricated, climate-responsive building type that has its origins in the mid-1800s and a century-long stylistic development that extends through to the interwar gabled bungalows of the mid-20th century. They are edged by ethereal verandahs and have cellular rooms that are arranged on either side of a long, piercing corridor that runs right through the building. An enduring and memorable image is the view of a venerable tree deep in a backyard captured in the frame of an open front door. The family tree of this vernacular architecture extends across the cities and towns of the global south, with close connections to colonial buildings across the former British Empire. These buildings have a taut, yet complicated relationship to the landscape. They are an exemplar of architectural adaption, eschewing the terrace house type of building that was adopted in Victoria and New South Wales, creating a new type of building rather than a style of architecture. The connection to the landscape is ever-present in this part of the world. Somewhat paradoxically, before the entertainer's deck and the backyard swimming pool became ubiquitous lifestyle accoutrements in Queensland, the plots these houses sit on could be encountered as an other-worldly jungle of tropical vegetation. The plots were then set to work and given over to food production or left perversely empty with a mat of grass mown with a slight whiff of dendrophobia.

There are three key moments that shape the most recent period of residential architecture in Queensland, and these are captured in texts that provide a contextual and intellectual scaffold to the exemplary built works. The first is a turn-of-the century moment that coalesced the architectural conversations of the region and profoundly set these within an international zeitgeist. Silvia Micheli and Ashley Paine pick up the story in the late 1990s with the emergence of the architecture practice Donovan Hill, led by Brian Donovan and Timothy Hill, and the completion of the landmark C House, a work of such great intellect and rigour that it has become a seminal marker in the story of architecture in Queensland and a wellspring of ideas that continues to shape the local scene. The second of these scene-setting accounts is an essay by Brit Andresen and Michael Keniger. Andresen and Keniger have had a profound influence on the trajectory of architecture in Queensland for more than four decades. Since the late 1970s they have shaped architectural education, completed built works and advocated for the architectural profession. The earliest built works of Donovan Hill, exemplified by the landmark C House announced a typological departure in Queensland houses – from the historic and persistent vernacular cottage to the commodious villa and its international exemplars. This much-loved and well-aged home is captured in an atmospheric photo essay by David Chatfield, reminding us of the calibre of architectural enquiry imbued into every detail. Threads of design inspiration from the C House are evident in the collection of twenty-eight contemporary houses that are profiled.

The buildings are organised with four key themes: a life lived outdoors; a home in the landscape; traditions reimagined; and suburban ensembles. Grouping the selected projects into these broad categories foregrounds the ways in which living in this tropical and subtropical part of the world is special. The unique experience of living in each of the featured houses is described via a series of conversations with the owners ('the lived experience') and these words are paired with a piece of writing that contextualises the architectural approach within the broader Queensland milieu ('the architectural setting').

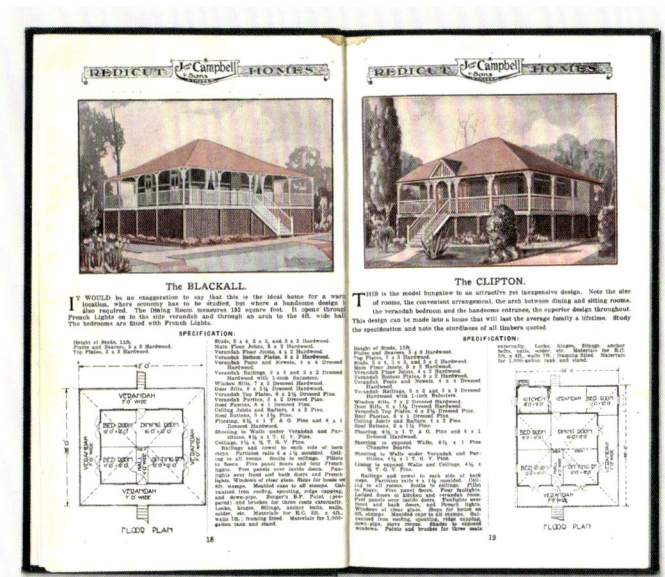

Top:
Spread from *Redicut Homes: from the forest to the finished home*, James Campbell and Sons. 192-. Architecture and Music Library, The University of Queensland.

Bottom:
Embracing the sun-drenched lifestyle: Roadside pool of Santa Fe Apartments, Surfers Paradise, 1964. Photography: John Gollings.

A life lived outdoors is a subversion of the established Australian idea of what constitutes the best room in the house. The idea of 'the good room' is enshrined in contemporary Australian domestic life and has a cultural expression that is popularised and satirised. The unique character of the Australian good room has socio-cultural origins in the polite and stuffy parlours of 19th-century middle-class houses from the Northern Hemisphere and has been shaped and reshaped by the ethnic diversity of Australia's migrant population. A European, colder-climate architectural inheritance shaped the housing built in southern Australia in the 1800s – particularly the iconic terrace houses of Sydney and Melbourne. Conversely, the benign Queensland climatic conditions encourage a more relaxed, holiday-esque lifestyle – or a life lived outdoors. This is a place to gather with neighbours and friends, or it's a place for mindfulness and refuge. Architecturally, this results in buildings that frame an outside space, allowing inhabitants to simultaneously be embedded in nature, yet protected from it. The garden is often the anchor to the plan and acts as the heart of the home, as is the case in projects such as Richards & Spence's La Scala or Earl Parade by Cavill Architects.

In contrast to this idea of garden as a place of refuge is the notion of landscape as a place of prospect and dreaming, buildings at home in the landscape. Queensland's verdant tropical and subtropical landscapes and the gentle, year-round climate of much of the state establishes a special relationship between buildings and their settings. The traditional Queenslander houses are elevated above the ground on stumps in response to the climate and have delicate, screened verandahs that mediate the relationship between inside and outside. Trees and other foliage are important elements for tempering the climate, providing shade and, in some cases, cooling down hot breezes as they pass through. The contemporary response to this landscape is often to defer to the magic of the place and recede into the lush greenery – as seen in the dark-coloured pavilions of the Cape Tribulation House by m3architecture or Moonshine House by Brit Andresen.

Although there is wide-spread nostalgia for the traditional, elevated Queenslander house, climatic performance and a connection to the backyard is often a compromise. Connecting the house and garden by reimagining old traditions and grafting new sections onto old houses is now challenging the previous approach to extensions and reimagining traditions. In the 1980s, the 'raise and build under' extension became the preferred approach to renovating in Brisbane. For dwellings within the council's traditional building character overlay, raising a house (where the new height does not exceed 9.5 m) and building under is considered 'minor building work' and there is no assessment against the planning scheme. This has led to a variety of unfortunate consequences such as the abandonment of the garden as a part of family life. There are, of course, exceptions to this rule – and architect John Ellway has used a steep site to his advantage at Terrarium House. In other cases, new extensions have been grafted onto the back of an existing Queenslander, splicing the interior open to embrace the garden via wide cascading stairs at Left Over Space House by CultivAR Architecture, or extruding into an outdoor terrace at Camp Hill House by Twohill & James.

The historical low density of Queensland's cities and towns – resulting from government and financial instruments that modelled the detached-dwelling, garden-suburb lifestyle – gives rise to an alternative approach for updating an existing Queenslander house that involves a completely detached or semi-detached new structure on site. Taking the form of a garden pavilion like Kieron Gait's Morningside Residence, or a versatile secondary dwelling such as One Room Tower by Phorm Architecture + Design in collaboration with Silvia Micheli and Antony Moulis, these buildings address the urgent need to increase the density and occupation of the suburbs.

Although these four approaches to contemporary residential architecture are connected to place and climate, they are also a product of the increasing number of conversations and alliances between Queensland architects and the wider national and international architectural community. New types of influential media, national conferences and awards programs have all played a part in the evolution of the new Australian residential architecture over the last twenty years. Contextual, joyous and inventive, the approach to design is socially conscious – leading to considered responses to questions of housing affordability, the climate crisis and shifting demographics. Design thinking has expanded to encompass a broader impact on community rather than just focus on the single dwelling itself. This leads to outcomes that address densification strategies in suburban settings, such as secondary dwellings; or schemes that contribute to the broader context of the local area and demonstrate that design interventions can build neighbourhood connectedness. An exploration of economy of materials, scale and cost are strong drivers of design, and leads to making something extraordinary from something ordinary. And finally, informal planning reflects the Australian way of life and allows for inhabitation in a variety of ways.

By 1980, Queensland's population had grown by a staggering 27 per cent in a decade. The carnival atmosphere of Expo 88 attracted more than 15 million visitors to Brisbane's South Bank and was momentous in illustrating the sudden and latent possibility of a public life in the city. Prior to this time, al fresco dining was prohibited, ostensibly on the grounds of health concerns, and the city heart was empty outside of working hours. The national interest in Queensland architecture, and particularly Queensland residential architecture, was clearly heating up in the mid to late 1980s, exemplified by a slew of Robin Boyd Award winners, and this has grown since the turn of the century. Since the inception of the national Houses Awards program in 2011, five Queensland houses have won. Countless covers of magazines have been adorned with Queensland's tall blue skies and verdant subtropical greenery draping over beautifully detailed structures. The opportunities presented by the benign climate is the point of difference between Queensland residential designs and those in other Australian states, where a greater porosity between indoor–outdoor living exists, both in a private sense and in an active public engagement with the streetscape. In writing about the individual buildings, we have sought to inhabit them, providing context and detail, history and lifestyle and this is the invitation of this book – a moment to reflect on the special qualities of place that architecture amplifies and of the joys of daily life in a well-designed home.

Cameron Bruhn
Cameron Bruhn is the Dean and Head of School at the University of Queensland's School of Architecture. Prior to this appointment he was the editorial director of Architecture Media. Bruhn holds a Bachelor of Architecture from the University of Queensland and a practice-based PhD from RMIT University. He was a co-creative director of the 2015 Australian Festival of Landscape Architecture: This Public Life and the 2016 Australian National Architecture Conference: How Soon is Now. In 2016 he initiated Queensland's Asia Pacific Architecture Festival. Bruhn is the editor of *MMXX*, a landmark volume for Thames & Hudson that documents significant architecture in Australia in the first two decades of the 21st century. He is a co-editor of *The Forever House*, *The Terrace House* and *The Apartment House*, also published by Thames & Hudson. Bruhn is a Fellow of the Design Institute of Australia and an Honorary Fellow of the Australian Institute of Architects.

Katelin Butler
Katelin Butler is the editorial director at Architecture Media. Prior to her appointment as editorial director, Katelin was the design portfolio manager at Architecture Media, editor of *Houses* (2010–18) and assistant editor of *Architecture Australia* (2005–09). She has co-edited three books, *The Forever House*, *The Terrace House* and *The Apartment House*, all published by Thames & Hudson. Butler holds a Bachelor of Environmental Design from the University of Tasmania and a Master of Architecture from the University of Melbourne. She has been a peer juror, exhibition curator, guest university critic and speaker at various industry events and conferences.

Opposite:
C House (1998) in Brisbane by Donovan Hill.
Photography: David Chatfield.

Inside Becomes Outside: Queensland's Domestic Landscape

Silvia Micheli and Ashley Paine

La Scala (2021) in Bowen Hills, Brisbane, by Richards & Spence.
Photography: David Chatfield.

Pleasures of living outdoors

In contemporary Queensland, life is amply lived outdoors. This dominant social habit, made possible by a subtropical climate and comfortable level of urban security, has pervasively informed the realm of domestic architecture, which has become strongly associated with the idea of an outdoor lifestyle. While the house must still protect from heavy rains and hot, sunny days, access to outdoor spaces has become increasingly seamless: doors open wide and walls disappear to allow for an easy, spontaneous connection between inside and out. In this region, building, landscape and open sky are all part of the same architectural ensemble. Surprisingly, the close connection to the outdoors that is enjoyed and celebrated as a defining aspect of Queensland life today, hasn't always been possible in public space. For a long time, social rituals such as al fresco dining were curtailed by government regulation. It was only when the capital city of Brisbane hosted Expo 88 – an 'International Exhibition on Leisure' in 1988 – that eating outdoors was allowed. Before Expo, public life was largely set indoors – in clubs, church halls and homes. Despite the dramatic shift in social habits in the outdoors precipitated by Expo 88, the idea of the house as a public and semi-public venue has remained in Brisbane's architectural culture, informing design thinking.[1]

The residence La Scala, designed by Brisbane-based architects Ingrid Richards and Adrian Spence and completed in 2021, fully exemplifies this *modus vivendi* and the pleasures of living outdoors. Professional and life partners, the couple has built their home–office in inner-city Brisbane as a manifesto of the outdoor domestic experience. A swimming pool, positioned in the middle of the block, is its focal point and announces the emphasis on an open-air lifestyle. In fact, the pool terrace and adjoining lawn establish the datum of the *piano nobile* – the primary platform for living on the site – situated between and connecting the office at the front to the residential area at the rear. At the same time, the pool and lawn also form part of a continuous rooftop landscape that rises up and over the interiors in a series of large steps and terraces to frame the open sky. These over-scaled outdoor stairs – *la scala* – call for social gathering and draw attention to the house as a place for private entertaining as well as public occasions. They offer spaces to congregate casually in groups, to lie by the pool or simply to sit and watch the water, the sky or a passing parade of bodies. Indeed, the stairs turn the rooftop into a theatre and the pool into a stage, amplifying the sense of a collective in the private realm. Still, despite its scale and the possibility for different public forms of occupation, La Scala retains a high degree of domestic intimacy.

Richards & Spence's La Scala makes for a bold statement on lifestyle, drawing widely on historical precedents from around the world: its bare concrete surfaces and lush planting, for example, recall a certain kind of South American modernism; the building's ruin-like massing is reminiscent of ancient Roman landscapes; while the rooftop of monumental stairs makes a formal reference to the famed Villa Malaparte (1938) by Italian architect Adalberto Libera and owner Curzio Malaparte in Capri, majestically portrayed in Jean-Luc Godard's 1963 film *Contempt*. The latter building is clearly an important precursor, with its immense outdoor staircase and rooftop terrace that build upon and expand the natural cliff. Yet, conceived as part of the dramatic natural topography of the site, Villa Malaparte's stairs and terrace are physically and conceptually detached from everyday life indoors. By contrast, La Scala's stairs and pool terrace define an outdoor room that extends and complements the domestic realm.

C House (1998) in Brisbane by Donovan Hill.
Photography: David Chatfield.

Still, to fully understand the outdoor lifestyle so compellingly realised at La Scala, one must also look to precedents found closer to home, where this integrated approach to the outdoors in residential design is not just the prerogative of a few sophisticated owners and their architects. Rather, it has progressively become an intrinsic aspect of the local building culture. In fact, the idea of the 'outdoor room' has been circulating in Queensland architecture for nearly three decades, emerging in recent years as a defining – and highly desirable – component of much contemporary design, both domestic and civic. La Scala incorporates, intensifies and expands upon such design themes and architectural solutions that can be traced back to the specific architectural context of Brisbane since the early 1990s. With this in mind, we highlight a selection of key projects by the seminal Brisbane-based office Donovan Hill – projects that anticipate so many of the designs featured within these pages. Such projects offer some historical perspective on the evolution of ideas and approaches that shape Queensland domestic architecture today – works like La Scala that can be seen as engaging a productive dialogue with the residential work of Donovan Hill.[2] We explore how ideas such as the outdoor room have become an integral part of Queensland's recent constructive tradition and what avenues they have opened for contemporary residential architecture.

Testing the outdoor room in Donovan Hill's C House

One of the earliest – and most emphatic – demonstrations of the outdoor room is found in the C House (1991–98) designed by Donovan Hill. Although it was one of the office's first commissions, it took some eight years to complete, with fastidious attention given to the drawing and resolution of its details.[3] At the same time, the small practice grew in size and reputation, designing and building numerous other domestic and civic projects in parallel. In this way, the C House was a testing ground for many of the office's formative strategic design solutions — ideas that were to become paradigmatic in their subsequent projects. These ideas include the nascent concept of 'a significant – memorable – room (often outdoors)' as a principal strategy for organising domestic space and providing a focus for everyday life.[4] The label 'outdoor room' was adopted by the members of the Donovan Hill office to capture the particular nature of this covered, outdoor space conceived as such an integral, and intimate, part of the functional, spatial and programmatic operation of the building.

From the outset, the C House was conceived not so much as a house as an 'idealised landscape'.[5] In large part, this was made possible by the substantial use of concrete – with a smooth finish mostly in the enclosed spaces and with board-marking in the outdoor areas – allowing the architects to remodel the suburban hillside site with a series of stairs, platforms and indoor and outdoor rooms.[6] This use of mass concrete and the refashioning of the entire site quickly became a familiar characteristic of Donovan Hill's work, providing an alternative design approach to the traditional residential architecture of Brisbane – and Queensland more generally – where elevated timber houses (so-called 'Queenslanders') were built on stumps, floating indifferently above the natural ground. This shift in the use of materials and connection to the ground in Donovan Hill's work marked a turning point in Queensland architecture: a decisive break with the vernacular and with the previous generation of Queensland architects – including Rex Addison, Russell Hall, Gabriel Poole, and Lindsay and Kerry Clare – whose reputations were built upon the continuation and reinvention of the region's architectural identity, based on light-weight construction systems in tin and timber delicately put on the ground.[7] The C House thereby inverted the traditional Queensland model of an elevated house surrounded by gardens and lawn and, instead, established a strong relationship with the natural topography. In the C House, however, timber was not rejected, but deliberately used where human interaction was planned to occur. This is the case for the living room, bedrooms and dining nook, which are all lined in timber, but also of individual functional elements like handrails and soffits.

C House (1998) in Brisbane by Donovan Hill.
Photography: Jon Linkins.

Beyond the consistent use of the concrete as a new constructed terrain across the site, key to the reinforcement of the landscape metaphor is the reinvention and abstraction of domestic elements.[8] That's why in the C House windows become openings, doors become gates, walls turn into sliding screens and the lap pool into a stream, blurring the distinction between building and landscape. Fundamental to this design 'tactic' is the monumentally scaled outdoor room, the heart of the project. It is a double-height roofed space around which the interior domestic program is distributed centrifugally towards the periphery of the site. In the words of the architects, the house is 'a set of private rooms ... gathered around, under and above the "public" or "memorable" space of the site – a large outdoor room'.[9] This semi-open room, which also substitutes the traditional corridor, is fully integrated in the overall house thanks to the concept of the 'uninterrupted threshold'. This seamless transition inside out is achieved by the flushness of the various stone floor finishes in combination with the sliding screens and the continuous use of concrete.[10] The deliberate spatial and programmatic ambiguity of the outdoor room is further accentuated by the openness on two sides, and the incorporation of landscape elements, such as planters and a water rill, combined with typically interior elements, like the fireplace, light stands, woven timber soffit and detailed floor.[11] Skylights were included to top light the walls and accentuate the outdoor character of the room. Thanks to its intrinsic attribute of openness, the outdoor room was intended to be an architectural device to catch the natural light and breeze and distribute it to the internal rooms of the house – attending to their functional improvement. Given its interdependency with the other rooms of the house, to which access is granted by doors and sliding panels, the outdoor room has the intrinsic characteristic of constant change. The resulting flexibility of the space and its program fosters an idea of multiuse dwelling – a structure that can survive different scenarios over time.[12]

It is here in the C House that the prototype of the outdoor room was first tested as a space within the overall project that is cut out of the building to become a world in its own terms, with views of the city and the lush surrounding vegetation (see plan and section, page 29). Occupiable for most of the year in the benign climate of Queensland,[13] the outdoor room remained central to the practice's work since that time, with the architects themselves acknowledging that 'at both intimate and public scale the ordering, tectonic and memorable experiences associated with outdoor rooms have become a preoccupation' of the practice.[14] Indeed, the unveiling of the C House in the late 1990s set a new trajectory for architectural discourse and practice in Brisbane for decades to come, and a manner of practice that still reverberates today through projects like La Scala.[15] As such, the C House and La Scala can be seen as monumental bookends to what is arguably one of the most innovative periods of architectural production in Brisbane to date.

Of the many studios to engage with the ambiguous relationship between outdoor and indoor as a theme, the duo of Richards & Spence is arguably one of the most active, and certainly one of the most compelling. Together, Richards & Spence have made their presence felt in Brisbane and Queensland through a series of remarkable designs for high-end hotels, boutiques, restaurants and public works. Learning from Donovan Hill's city-making agenda, Richards & Spence turn otherwise conventional commercial projects into opportunities to re-imagine ways of living in a subtropical city, with an uncommon generosity in their treatment of the public realm. But the connection between the two offices goes beyond a shared ambition. Before founding their own office, Spence worked with Donovan Hill for several years, while Richards was intellectually close to director, Timothy Hill, for more than a decade. Richards has also acknowledged the deep formative influence of the C House on her as a young architect. Furthermore, both offices shared a fascination for Italian architect Carlo Scarpa, whose work was introduced in Brisbane architectural culture through a 1991 exhibition on Scarpa's renovation of Castelvecchio at Verona.[16]

Connections between the C House and La Scala are numerous, but the newer, latter project should in no way be reduced to an imitation of the former. Instead, it introjects the many key concepts and strategies deployed by Donovan Hill, including the idea of the outdoor room, and interprets them in its own terms. At La Scala too, domestic elements give way to more abstract elements. Concrete is chosen as the main material, but timber is substituted by slabs of travertine stones while, by contrast, giant monsteras, tentacular agaves and sculptural cactus animate the lush garden that overlays the whole property. In so doing, La Scala rethinks the relationship of the inside to the outside as an unapologetic celebration of outdoor lifestyle.

Strategies for a domestic landscape
The ideas developed by Donovan Hill in the C House were taken forward in numerous other residential projects completed by the office – not to mention many of their larger commercial projects as well. The most pervasive of these concepts, the outdoor room, may have obscured the fact that the integration of life into the outdoor realm employs other interrelated design solutions and spatial elements. What follows is a brief outline of some of these affiliated strategies deployed by Donovan Hill, examined through a selection of their most significant houses and how some contemporary practices have reinterpreted them.

Manipulated boundaries
For the outdoor room to fulfil its potential as the most significant space in a house, edges between the interior and exterior demand close attention. Not only must occupants be able to move seamlessly between conditions, but visual connections and continuity between inside and out also need to be ensured. In this respect, the HH House is an exemplary project. Begun in 1992 during the early design phase for C House, this low-budget and modestly scaled renovation was soon completed in 1993. Here, too, there is an outdoor room, this time added as an extension to the rear of a traditional timber house, and used as a kind of prosthetic architectural tool – a 'memorable space' that draws people through the old building and makes a physical transition between the house and garden, blurring their distinction. This strategy of dissolving edges and blending of spaces also extends to the entirety of the site. The outdoor room of the HH House works like a lens that edits out proximate neighbours while framing longer views over the backyard and landscape beyond. This is characteristic of Donovan Hill's practice wherein the apparent boundaries of a site are manipulated to draw larger landscapes into the property, connecting large and small scales, and engaging the imagination.[17] It is a way for the entirety of the site to be domesticated and inhabited.

In the hands of a new generation of Queensland architects, this blurring and manipulation of boundaries has been further developed, with James Russell Architect's work being particularly relevant. To a greater degree than almost any other practice – including Donovan Hill itself – Russell's architecture places the occupant in constant connection with the outside. Where Donovan Hill might have created openings to allow the bleeding of inside into out, Russell often does away with walls altogether.

Recomposed landscapes
Also in Brisbane, the D House, completed in 2000 in the inner-city suburb of New Farm, is one of the smallest residences designed by Donovan Hill, but is arguably one of the key houses in the city with national resonance. Despite, or perhaps because of its modest scale, the D House puts forward a new way of conceiving the domestic *locus*. Not only does the house adopt a distinct formal vocabulary in the dense urban fabric of mostly traditional character dwellings, but it also follows the lesson of the much larger C House in that it uses its domestic program to redefine the whole site.[18]

HH House (1993) in Highgate Hill, Brisbane, by Donovan Hill. Photography: Patrick Bingham Hall.

D House (2000) in New Farm, Brisbane, by Donovan Hill. Photography: Jon Linkins.

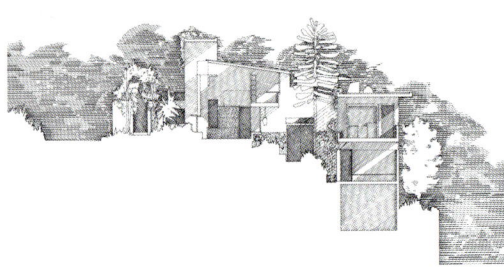

Z House section (2008) in Teneriffe, Brisbane, by Donovan Hill. Scale 1:500.

Z House (2008) in Teneriffe, Brisbane, by Donovan Hill. Photography: Jon Linkins.

With a building footprint that almost coincides with the entire property, the D House constructs its own artificial landscape. By situating the residence upon a raised platform behind a planted berm, the newly defined topography of the site has the effect of a slight but meaningful separation from the street. A large window and screen to the front elevation provide, respectively, a public connection and privacy control to the main living space, which is stretched along the street front boundary, and captured between a pair of courtyard gardens. Outside, a boundary wall is used to block views to and from the street in the middle ground, connecting instead the foreground scene onto the foliage of the immediate courtyard garden and a more distant outlook over the verdant suburb and the city – a reiteration and extension of the strategies tested out in the HH House. Likewise, thresholds between the living room and lateral courtyards are dissolved: floor surfaces extend inside and out, while panes of dividing glass are held in frameless suspension, braced only by the most minimal props that appear as weightless as rays of sunshine.[19]

The idea of a recomposed landscape is one that has also led to a remarkable degree of invention in the recent work of other Queensland architects. Notably, this includes John Ellway's Terrarium House, completed in 2017, where the front verandah has been turned into a vertical garden, which connects the floor at street level with the renovated undercroft of an original worker's cottage. This is a roofed, green space that acts as a buffer between the house and the street; a transitional area that evolves the more introverted character of Donovan Hill's private outdoor rooms and expands the possibility of their use.

The garden inside
Donovan Hill's Z House, completed in the suburb of Teneriffe in 2008, offered an opportunity to elaborate on the theme of the constructed landscape. Differently from the outdoor room of the C House, which forms an unprogrammed space at the centre of the plan, or the D and HH Houses with their extended visual landscapes, the centre of the Z House is occupied by a tropical garden – a *hortus conclusus* – that establishes a contained landscape in miniature. Hence, the delight of isolation in nature is not so much experienced externally, but as a room contained within the heart of the home – its central and open interior, around which the program is disposed. The house is situated on terraces carved into the hillside, made from walls that retain the land yet also form edges from which the rooms of the house emerge. The various rooms gain their character and quality from their relationship to this interior garden, much more so than from the functions they are designed for.[20] This use of a captured landscape is also similar to the strategy adopted for the D House: each make the most of their constrained inner-city sites, where neighbours are close and open space is limited.[21]

The central presence of the garden is also a principle that the practice of Vokes and Peters has adopted and progressed to preserve the tradition of the backyard in Brisbane, becoming a key part of the office's design agenda. The alteration and addition of Highgate Park House (2016–19), for example, shows the potential of the idea of living outside surrounded by nature. Here, the garden is defined by a porous cloister that establishes a continuity between the private site and the adjoining Highgate Hill Park, to the point that the garden acts as a bridge between the larger park and the street.

'The One and the Few': growing up alongside Donovan Hill
As the projects selected and discussed in this essay demonstrate, over twenty years of practice and more than twenty residential buildings, Donovan Hill's design ideas and architectural work radically shaped the architectural culture and community in Brisbane and in the region. Not only did they introduce original ways to conceive the domestic landscape of the Australian subtropics, but they applied their ideas with a determined consistency that earned them respect in both national and international

Highgate Park House (2019) in Brisbane by Vokes and Peters.
Photography: Christopher Frederick Jones.

contexts, as well as numerous awards from the Australian Institute of Architects.[22] Remarkably, the office's later involvement in larger public projects through joint ventures allowed the relatively small practice to also exert considerable influence through their urban ideas for the city. In the mid-2000s, Donovan Hill was arguably at its peak, following the completion of the highly regarded project for the State Library of Queensland (2006).[23] This building pushes the idea of the outdoor room to new extremes, blowing it up to a public scale in one of the most iconic areas of the city – the cultural precinct of South Bank. For an architectural office to achieve such a dominant presence was exceptional in the history of Brisbane, and in Queensland more broadly.[24]

But, as English historian, Reyner Banham, asked in his 1957 essay 'The One and the Few' concerning Alvar Aalto's eminence in relation to the production of modern architecture in Finland: 'How justified then, and how justified now, is world architectural opinion in concentrating its esteem on one man?'[25] The conclusion was that the rise of 'the one' (Aalto) was supported by – and even required – the work of 'the few' (his contemporaries assisting and challenging him). Adopting Banham's point for our antipodean context, we argue that Queensland's new domestic landscape should not be read exclusively through the work of Donovan Hill. Certainly, the work of Donovan Hill has become intimately associated with the image of the city's architecture, in the very similar way as Jože Plečnik's work has been affiliated with the modern identity of Ljubljana; Mario Botta's with the Ticino; Peter Zumthor's with the area of the Swiss Grisons; and Aalto's with Helsinki and Finland more broadly. But this is not to suggest that Donovan Hill alone were responsible for rewriting the narrative of the city's architecture at that time. Rather, they were a catalyst for change and probably the only office to theorise and consistently deploy a set of design ideas in a substantial number of projects: blurred thresholds, curated views, extended landscapes, miniaturised cities, new use of materials and the remaking of entire sites to construct a complex, choreographed journey through a sequence of indoor and outdoor spaces. Moreover, through their public advocacy for better design, Donovan Hill's presence inspired other ambitious architects and raised expectations of what was possible for architecture in the state.

In a quite distinctive way, Donovan Hill provided much more than an influence on its contemporaries. The office operated strategically as a 'design hub' for young architects – especially those graduating from the School of Architecture at the University of Queensland – helping many of them transition into the profession.[26] Effectively, Donovan Hill represented an incubator between academia and practice to transition and launch the promising architects of the following generation. There is a long list of collaborators who worked (in different capacities and for different lengths of time) with Donovan Hill over its two decades of practice, whose careers have been significantly shaped by the studio culture they nurtured, where design ideas were discussed as well as more practical aspects of the projects. Many of these individuals not only assisted Donovan Hill to grow and thrive, but also became instrumental to the dissemination and evolution of design ideas and architectural solutions tested during Brisbane's Donovan Hill chapter.

While the closure of Donovan Hill occurred somewhat prematurely in 2012 – the office merging with the much larger practice of BVN – this date does not mark the end of the intense design transformation Donovan Hill had initiated in Brisbane and across the state.[27] The shutdown of the office triggered a professional diaspora and a subsequent foundation of new practices in and beyond Queensland.[28] Indeed, it is through this multiplicity of practices that Donovan Hill's legacy still contributes directly to the development of domestic architecture in Brisbane and beyond. But, despite the different design trajectories and scales of the studios established in the wake of Donovan Hill, many of them have inherited the mission of contributing to the shaping of their city and the region's future. Hence, the most important legacy left by Donovan Hill is their design ideas deployed in their built works: ideas that have entrenched themselves deeply into the architectural culture of Brisbane and Queensland and have been instrumental in reimagining life, and lifestyle, in the outdoors, to which 'the few' have given a diversified range of architectural responses.

The popularisation of outdoor living in Queensland architecture
Today, the integrated approach to the outdoors in residential design is not just the prerogative of a few sophisticated owners and their architects. Rather, it has progressively become a culturally intrinsic aspect of the local building tradition. The quality and visibility of Donovan Hill's work set the standard for an entire generation of architects, as well as those who followed in their wake. Given the success of their architectural ideas, their designs attracted many imitators, and the formal language of Donovan Hill can still be detected in the work of architects throughout Brisbane, albeit in increasingly diverse and diluted ways. Likewise, their vocabulary of architectural terms and ideas were widely adopted by others. As Cameron Bruhn has observed, 'Within a decade of its completion, the tile patterns, timber detailing and quirked geometries of the D House (and other Donovan Hill buildings) had entered the architectural zeitgeist of south-east Queensland (and further afield), and the idea of the partly enclosed outdoor room had entered the parlance of local real estate agents.'[29] Since living outdoors has become a common habit in contemporary Queensland, the outdoor room – in all its variations – has indeed turned into a commercial trend, a popular feature in renovations and new design of both houses and apartments. The popularisation of the concept of outdoor living demonstrates one of the enduring legacies of Donovan Hill, achieving their initial ambition to set a new cultural framework for the city and its architecture.[30]

Donovan Hill has succeeded in injecting sophisticated design ideas into the popular consciousness: a process of 'democratisation' of architectural design that only a few architects – and their cities – can pride themselves in. But, if through the 1990s and early 2000s Donovan Hill reshaped the architectural terrain of Brisbane in their own singular image, the following pages of this book amply demonstrate that the domestic landscape today consists of a much more diverse field of practices. What those recent works have added is a series of new takes on the Queensland house – the right to continue the adjustment of local traditions beyond its confines. This is not to say that the projects presented here forego the habits of vernacular construction, the power of the well-framed opening, the sense of the deep shaded edge and the house-to-garden relationship that are conjured by Queensland living. On the contrary, they show a level of investment in the local that builds upon the design inventories of Donovan Hill – debuted at the C House – in ways that compel us to rethink what 'the vernacular' might now entail. That La Scala, for all its concrete terraces, stairs and gardens can still bring to the mind that fleeting memory of living in the Queensland subtropics shows how far the tradition has come – and where it still might go.

Silvia Micheli
Silvia Micheli is a senior lecturer in architecture at The University of Queensland. Her research investigates global architecture and cross-cultural exchanges in the 20th and 21st centuries. Among her publications, she co-edited the book *Italy/Australia: Postmodern Architecture in Translation* (2018) and co-authored *Storia dell'Architettura Italiana 1985–2015* (2013). Micheli studied architecture at the Politecnico di Milano and earned her doctorate at Università Iuav (Venice).

Ashley Paine
Ashley Paine is co-founder of PHAB Architects and a senior lecturer in architecture at the University of Queensland, where he teaches architectural design, history and research. He has contributed to journals including *Architecture Australia* and *Future Anterior*, and coedited the book *Valuing Architecture: Heritage and the Economics of Culture* (2021). Paine studied at The University of Queensland, where he earned his doctorate in 2015.

Notes

1. This essay is an outcome of the research conducted within a course jointly coordinated by Silvia Micheli and Ashley Paine at The University of Queensland, School of Architecture, in 2020. During the course, the coordinators organised a lecture series (Radio Brisbane), which gathered fourteen academics, critics, clients, and practitioners, who provided information about the history of Donovan Hill and the architectural culture generated around it. The authors wish to thank all the participants (in alphabetical order, Brit Andresen, Peter Besley, Cameron Bruhn, Katelin Butler, Geraldine Cleary, Jodie Cummins, Brian Donovan, Damian Eckersley, Timothy Hill, Michael Hogg, Michael Keniger, Antony Moulis, Ingrid Richards and Adrian Spence) for their generosity in providing background knowledge and archival material.

2. The practice was officially founded in 1992.

3. The design process of the C House is thoroughly documented in Michael Hogg, *The Idealised Landscape: The C-House, by Donovan Hill Architects*, undergraduate dissertation, Department of Architecture, The University of Queensland, Supervisor: Brit Andresen, 17 February 2000.

4. Brian Donovan & Timothy Hill, 'Donovan Hill: Inner-suburban residence, Brisbane', *UME* 1, 1996, pp. 10–17. Written by Donovan and Hill to accompany a 1996 publication of the HH House and known to Donovan Hill's collaborators as 'the poem', this article became a common reference for the office to share and discuss key design principles, including those concerning the construction of outdoor domestic spaces.

5. Michael Hogg, *The Idealised Landscape: The C-House, by Donovan Hill Architects*, undergraduate dissertation, Department of Architecture, University of Queensland, Supervisor: Brit Andresen, 17 February 2000, p. 2.

6. Clare Melhuish, *Modern House 2*, Phaidon Press, London, New York, 2004, p. 165.

7. See, *Australian Architects 5: Rex Addison, Lindsay Clare & Russell Hall*, Michael Keniger, Mark Roehrs, Judy Vulker eds., Canberra, Royal Australian Institute of Architects, 1990.

8. Michael Hogg, *The Idealised Landscape*, cit., p. 2.

9. Partners Hill, <partnershill.com/c-house>.

10. Peter Tonkin, 'The Domestic Ideal', *Architecture Australia* 88, no. 3, May/June 1999, pp. 30–41.

11. Michael Hogg, *The Idealised Landscape*, cit., p. 32.

12. Multiuse dwelling was Hill's topic of his Bachelors thesis at The University of Queensland.

13. Statement of the architects, in Tonkin, 'The Domestic Ideal'.

14. Donovan Hill quoted in Clare Melhuish, *Modern House 2*, Phaidon Press, London, New York, 2004, p. 150.

15. Talk by Ingrid Richards and Adrian Spence, 'Radio Brisbane' series, The University of Queensland, 14 October 2020.

16. Antony Moulis and Elizabeth Musgrave, 'Exhibiting Scarpa: Transcription of the Detail Narrative in Queensland', in *Italy/Australia: Postmodern Architecture in Translation*, Silvia Micheli and John Macarthur eds., URO, Melbourne, pp. 76–89.

17. 'Donovan Hill: Inner-Suburban Residence, Brisbane, Queensland, Australia', *UME* 1, 1996, pp. 10–17.

18. Talk by Damian Eckersley, 'Radio Brisbane' series, The University of Queensland, 12 August 2020.

19. 'Donovan Hill: D House, Brisbane, Queensland, Australia', *UME* 15, 2002, pp. 10–19.

20. *Donovan Hill: 1992–2010*, Edited by Donovan Hill, Donovan Hill, Brisbane, 2010.

21. Silvia Micheli, Antony Moulis, 'A Unity of Experience', *Architectural Review Australia* 124, 2011, pp. 78–85.

22. Charles Rowe observed that 'the practice became the most nationally awarded firm in Australia', Charles Rowe, 'A Changed Landscape: Brisbane after Donovan Hill.' *Australian Design Review*, 7 April 2014, <australiandesignreview.com/architecture/a-changed-landscape-brisbane-after-donovan-hill/>.

23. The project for the State Library of Queensland was designed by Donovan Hill with Peddle Thorp Architects.

24. Prior to Donovan Hill, architects in Brisbane had worked largely in a state of relative isolation. Only towards the end of the 1970s and 1980s did a more solid group start gravitating around UQ, but their work at this time remained very heterogenous with few observable connections. See, Michael Keniger, 'Queensland's New Breed', *Architecture Australia*, May/June 1990, pp. 40–42.

25. Reyner Banham, 'The One and The Few: The Rise of Modern Architecture in Finland', *The Architectural Review*, April 1957, pp. 243–248.

26. Before Donovan Hill, the initiative to bridge the gap between academia and practice in a city such as Brisbane, where these two realms were disconnected, was initiated by the 'Project Office' founded by Professor Peter O'Gorman in 1988 at the University of Queensland. Brian Donovan, founding partner of Donovan Hill, was part of the experience. While the 'Project Office' lasted for a short time and remained limited to a few significant projects, Donovan Hill, whose office was embedded in the city, had the capacity to effectively train a significant number of architects who would extend the experience started back at UQ into their own business. See talk by Brian Donovan, 'Radio Brisbane' series, The University of Queensland, 21 October 2020.

27. BVN began as a Brisbane-based office in 1926 and grew through various expansions, mergers and acquisitions into the international practice it is today. Brian Donovan, alongside numerous other key Donovan Hill staff, continues to contribute to that office, while Timothy Hill now works under the name Partners Hill. See Charles Rowe's account of the office's closure and legacy in: Charles Rowe, 'A Changed Landscape'.

28. The list of these new practices, as well as the list of collaborators of Donovan Hill, is extensive and constitutes a complex genealogy yet to be explored.

29. Cameron Bruhn, *MMXX: Two Decades of Architecture in Australia*, Melbourne, Thames & Hudson Australia, 2020, p. 13.

30. Donovan Hill's buildings, while remaining concentrated in Queensland, have received wide national and international media coverage for their original contribution to the making of Australian architecture.

C House

Donovan Hill, 1998
Photo essay by David Chatfield

After six years of construction and a set of architect's drawings that numbered almost 1000 A3 sheets (the majority hand drawn), Donovan Hill's seminal C House in suburban Brisbane was first revealed in 1998. Even before it was completed the house was profoundly and ambitiously evolving the conception of domestic life in the subtropical metropolis and it had 'sophisticated pilgrims swooning about its conceptual complexity and fine construction'.[1] And swoon they did – students of architecture parked in the bitumen carpark of a nearby church to catch a glimpse of the hillside villa, and the renowned Sri Lankan architect Geoffrey Bawa was thoroughly impressed on a visit during construction in 1996.

The architectural rigour and intellect of the project generated plentiful excitement in the Australian architectural scene at the turn of the century (and this was soon replicated much further afield). It also marked the national emergence of the eponymous practice it gestated – Timothy Hill and Brian Donovan had both graduated from The University of Queensland in the late 1980s. The C House and the urbane Neville Bonner Building, a government office block on the riverside in the Brisbane CBD, designed by Donovan Hill, Davenport Campbell, and Powell Dods Thorpe, were completed in the same year and published alongside one another in *Architecture Australia*. This impactful critical debut announced the capacity and venturousness of Donovan Hill, a firm adept in residential, public and commercial work and distinguished by their understanding of the local condition and studious attention to international precedents from across the canon of architecture.

The C House is equal parts influential and enigmatic, and these qualities position this photo essay by David Chatfield as an establishing and explanatory part of this volume. The building is a private sanctuary for its owners, and they have studiously maintained it over more than 20 years. There are very few images of the C House on the internet, just a handful captured in the year it was completed, and it was never cycled through the architectural awards and publicity tumble. In these new images the building, its enveloping landscape and the patterns and artefacts of everyday life merge beautifully and we see the building as it was first imagined by Brian Donovan and Timothy Hill and their visionary client almost 30 years ago.

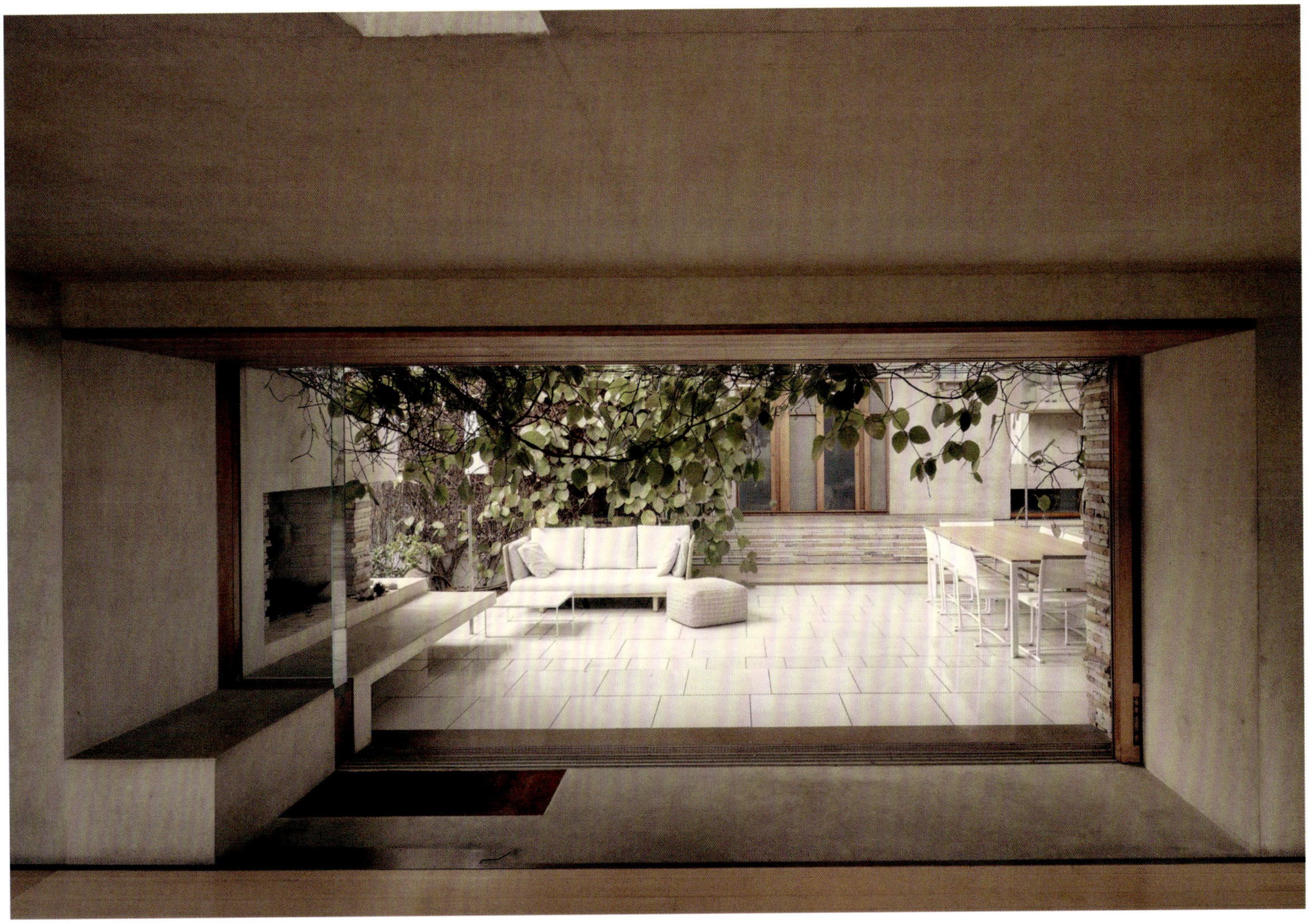

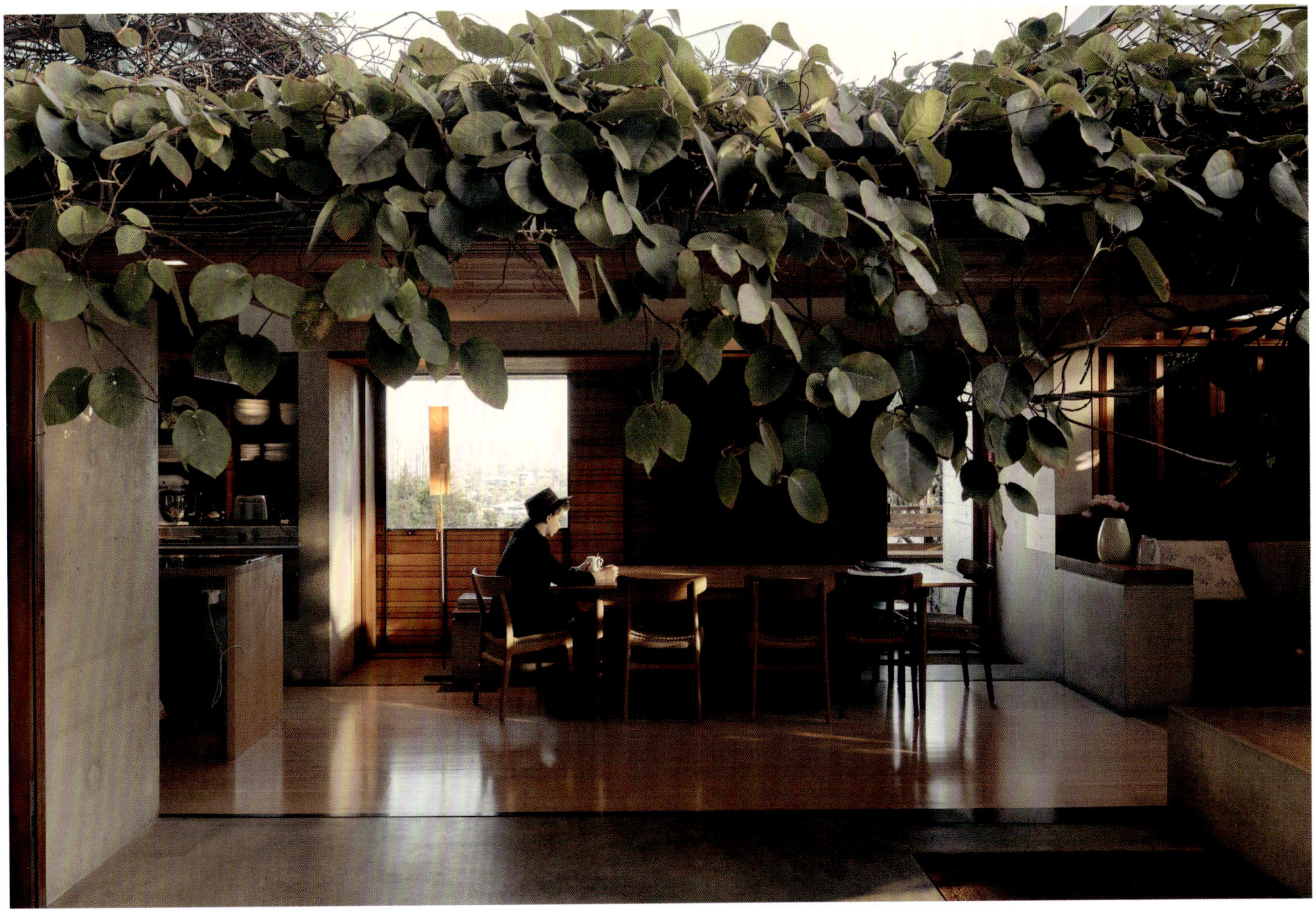

26

David Chatfield

David Chatfield is a photographer from Queensland who works across architectural, fine art and travel-based projects. His work with the built environment seeks to extend beyond pure representational documentation to convey the intangible elements of the spatial and social experience.

Note

1 Peter Tonkin, 'The Domestic Ideal', *Architecture Australia* 88, no. 3, May/June 1999, pp.30–41.

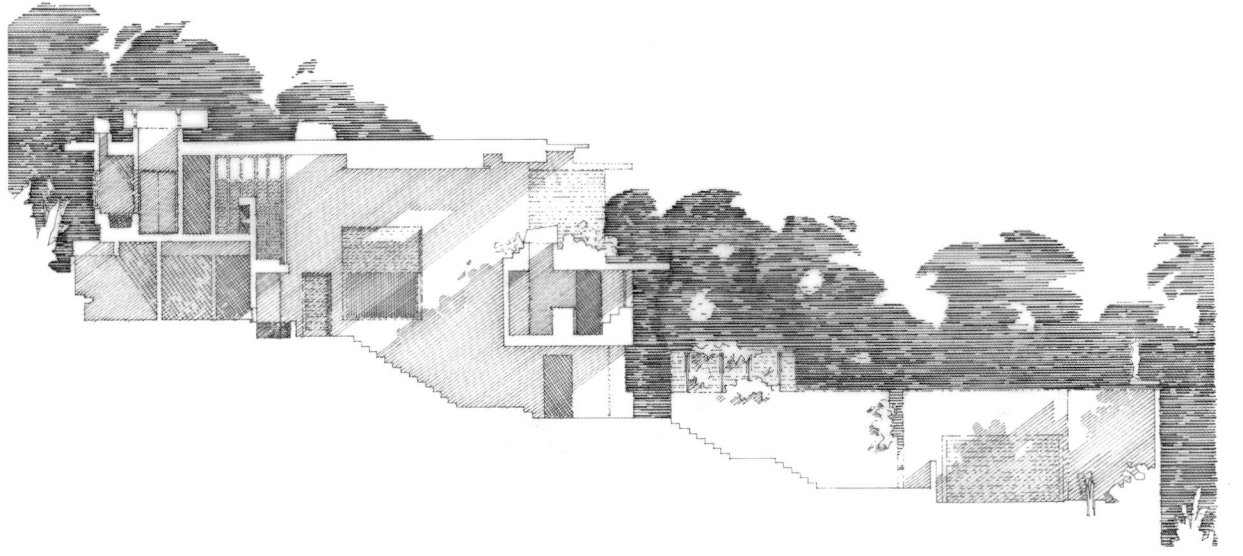

Section

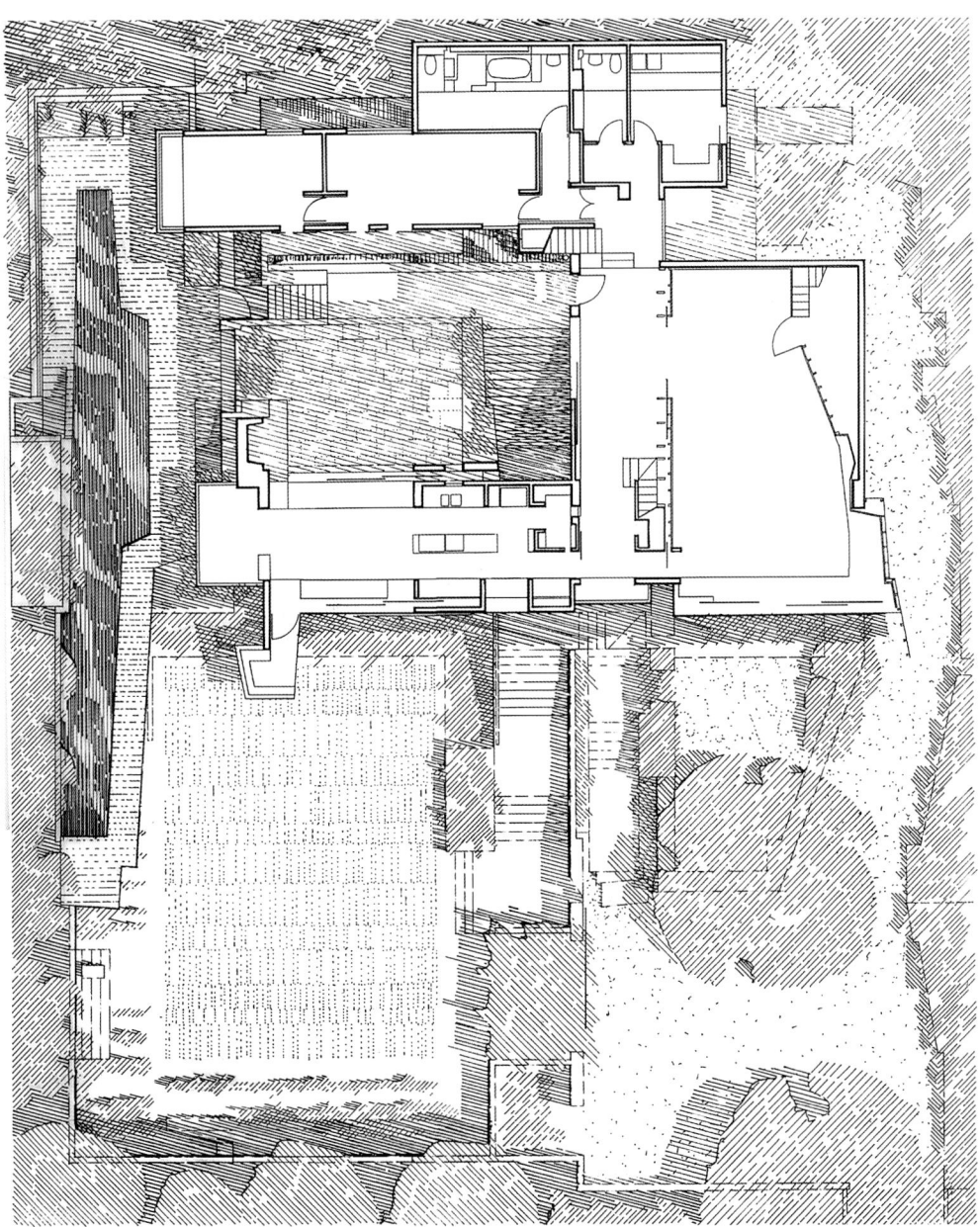

Plan

1:250

0   5m

Architect – Donovan Hill

Project team – Brian Donovan, Timothy Hill, Fedor Medek, Michael Hogg

Structural and civil engineers – Mattefy Perl Nagy

Landscape – Donovan Hill with Butler & Webb

Carpentry – Jim Evans

Joinery – Phil Green

Stonemason – Simon Brown

Concrete – Mr Rossi

Houses From a School of Ideas

Brit Andresen and Michael Keniger

Above:
Teacher's Union Building in Spring Hill (1983) by Michael Barnett.
Image courtesy of Michael Barnett.

In this essay we share a selection of our personal recollections of architectural teaching and praxis in house design within the landscapes of coastal South East Queensland.

We have drawn on our experiences of a land that was at first relatively unknown to us. Our first impressions on arriving in Queensland reveal not only our different backgrounds but also our very different introductions to the place. Brit Andresen's account of arriving overland via a sensuous rainforest landscape contrasting with Michael Keniger's reaction to arriving from the intensity of his home city, London, into the raw, laid-back and latent urbanism of the region's capital city, Brisbane.

Taking the form of eight written sketches spanning four decades, our essay illuminates aspects of the architecture of memorable houses and their circumstances within this subtropical territory. The sketches are positioned as freestanding landmarks in a terrain loosely linked by pathways discernible by locals and fellow travellers sharing our experiences, places and occasions. Readers unfamiliar with the setting may be able to discern traces of one or other of the sketches resounding in the houses selected for detailed presentation and review.

Our aim has been to enliven the understanding of the nature and concept of the gentle northerly aspect and to illustrate the development of selected ideas that have served to underpin and inform a shared architectural sensibility evident in the contemporary houses profiled as the core of this book. The sketches also convey the necessity of an active relationship between experience-based architectural education and practice.

Invited to contribute an account of our role from the late 1970s to the late 1990s, now recognised as a vibrant period in the development of architectural design in Queensland, we have drawn upon our contributions to teaching, scholarship and exemplary built works and those of our colleagues. The specificity of the brief and our career-long attachment to the University of Queensland (UQ) has required our efforts to be selective rather than encyclopaedic. Our account is inevitably flavoured by the activities and achievements of those associated with UQ, yet there are many accomplished colleagues, graduates and others whom we have not been able to include within the span of the essay.

Sketch One: First impressions
Appointed academics to the UQ architecture school in the late 1970s, we came bristling with the ideas, architectural investigations and teaching experiences that we enjoyed as practitioner–teachers at the Architectural Association in London and the School of Architecture at Cambridge University. As newcomers and outsiders, there was much to discover as we were introduced to the circumstances, practices and expectations that framed architecture and architectural education in Australia and at the UQ school in particular at that time.

The sensuality of South East Queensland's landscapes, the benign climate, the clarity and intensity of the light, the relaxed, easy pace of life and the sense of an imminent shift in the pace and scale of development all held sway in shaping our initial impressions. Particularly striking in Brisbane were the wooden houses as separate dwellings, each different from the next and yet all seemingly derived from the same underlying planning principles and materials – literally of timber and tin (corrugated iron sheeting). To find these timber houses in the inner areas of the state's capital city was remarkable, as was the almost complete lack of masonry or brick terrace houses, so unlike London from where Michael Keniger arrived in 1978.

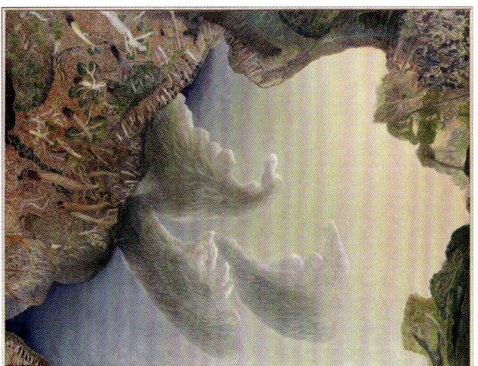

Above:
Creation Landscape: Water and Land (1991) by William Robinson. Oil on canvas, 183 x 732 cm. Private collection, UK, courtesy of Nevill Keating Pictures.

Although uncommon in an urban setting, these relatively frail timber structures possessed an order and sense of fit in contrast to the varied typologies of the more recent housing types. Further, the access to building new, stand-alone houses seemed to be much more prevalent and less bound by aesthetic planning and design principles than London.

Sketch Two: Houses fitted to the land
Travelling from Sydney by car on the inland route to Brisbane in the heat of February 1977 was to be lulled by wide landscapes of sameness that unfold for hours and hours on straight roads – that is, until woken by the drama of wilderness at Cunninghams Gap.

Nature's portal to the north is shrouded in dark subtropical forests ringing with bellbirds and cracking whipbirds. Eyes and ears attune in concert as hairpin bends on steep descent drop and drop towards the light of the plains below.

The pastures and fields in Fassifern Valley stretch out ahead and it's some time before the first house comes into view in a clearing among long grass, with its black shadows angling under the verandah eaves, in among the stumps and stretching checkerboard across a flimsy screen of timber slats. Unpainted, empty, the little timber house with a tin roof may be uncertainly perched on the land but sits tight in the memory.

Arriving in Brisbane to find the river with its hillsides of wooden houses was a revelation: we had somehow landed in a most beautiful suburban city.

Less than two hundred years earlier English explorers Oxley, Cunningham and Lockyer came for their first visit. Their 1820s surveys, together with their field books and other historical data, testify to the extensive forests growing along the river and the creeks that supported birdlife and other animals such as koala, possum and kangaroo. This rich forest ecology also underpinned the economic, technological, cultural and spiritual life of the First Nations peoples. A paradise; first stolen and then lost.

We came to learn that the timber getters and sawmillers arrived in the early 19th century and the lands around Brisbane River and the regions beyond were progressively cleared and logged for colonial expansion, including the agriculture and construction industries.

The timber houses built between the late 19th and mid-20th centuries formed a family of houses – a domestic building type developed in Australia's north and commonly referred to as the Queenslander. Some timber merchants turned to the prefabrication of kit homes designed by architects, such as those first offered to the public by Campbell Redicut Homes in 1903 through catalogues illustrating the options for the size and type of house and the range of ancillary decorative elements.

The Queenslander house type raised on timber stumps allowed a light-footed fit with hilly ground and responded to the hot, humid summer climate of tropical and subtropical regions. They became the common stock of houses across Queensland and were accepted as an Australian vernacular.

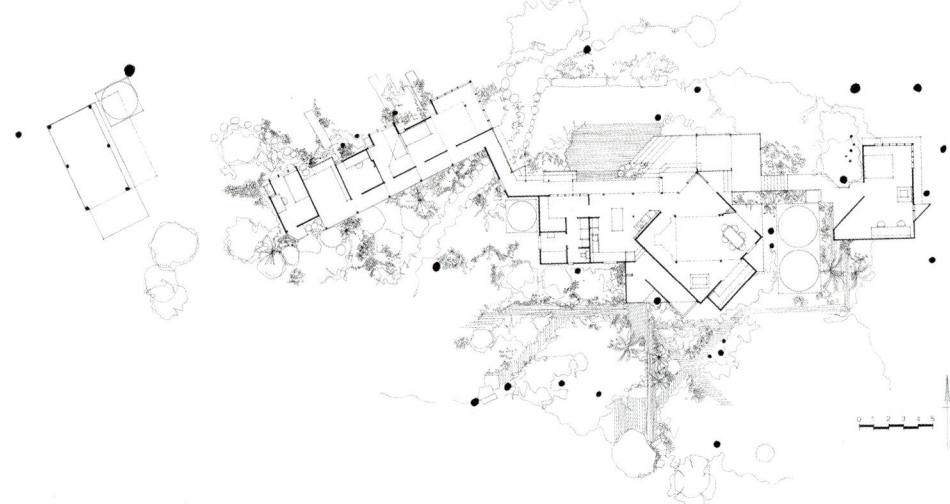

Postwar expansion of the outer suburbs by project-home builders in the 1960s and 1970s favoured houses constructed with slab-on-ground, brick-veneer walls and a tiled roof – all promised at low cost with low maintenance – and the Queenslander fell somewhat out of favour.

While the suburbs were increasingly populated by project homes and slab-on-ground kit houses that were typically destructive or indifferent to the form of the land, architects were custom-designing houses for individual clients, or for themselves, in ways that fitted with the land. Bruce Goodsir's Caterpillar House, 1974–76, at Mount Nebo is of particular note. Built on a large hillside site, this timber house of articulated parts achieves a close fit with the nap of the land, its watershed and its stand of trees within the greater bushland. The potential for experiencing the landscape is fulfilled and amplified by the forms of the buildings, their fenestration and the ways of moving about. The open-air access of the bedroom wing steps with the contours as they fall from the top of the slope to the valley below while closely linking each individual room with its own garden foothold. The design for this, and his other houses, also reveals Goodsir's affection for the spatial qualities of thresholds, bay-window seats and places for daydreaming and intimacy.

Sketch Three: Houses, theirs and ours
Our initial impressions of Brisbane and its architecture were of an abiding provisional character that, though hardly discussed, was evidenced by the numerous empty sites at the very heart of the city. Apart from a few notable examples, there seemed to have been a reluctance in the postwar years to invent and articulate innovative ways of generating an urban architecture that resonated with the character of the subtropical city.

In contrast, in among the spread of the surrounding low density suburbs there were houses that were exploratory and adventurous in their relationship to place, climate and culture. A network of younger architects was active in the 1970s and their work reflected critical lessons from the traditional Queenslander houses often further influenced by selected accomplished works of prominent interstate and overseas architects. Two Queensland houses from the early 1970s highlight how a place-related architecture might advance to establish and reinforce new design strategies. We also explore one of our own projects from that time that brought together ideas and design approaches from abroad, with recognition of the significance of place and climate in Brisbane.

Top:
Caterpillar House site plan (1974–76) in Mount Nebo by Bruce Goodsir. Scale 1:500.

Bottom:
Caterpillar House (1974–76) in Mount Nebo by Bruce Goodsir. Photography: Bruce Goodsir.

 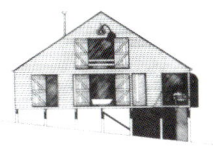

North east elevation   South west elevation

Top:
Dobie House (1972) in Buderim by Gabriel Poole.
Photography: Alkis Astras.

Middle:
The Addison House, Stage One elevations (1974–75) in Brisbane by Rex Addison. Scale 1:500.

Bottom:
Wirra Street House (1979–82) in Chapel Hill, Brisbane, by Andresen O'Gorman with Michael Keniger. Photography: Michael Keniger.

Dobie House, 1972, by Gabriel Poole, was somewhat shocking in that this modest structure projected an embrace of Miesian minimalism. A small, two-bedroom house, sited on an upper slope of Buderim Mountain north of Brisbane, Dobie House captured extensive views over the coastal landscape to the ocean in the distance. Two conditions governed its design: the need to provide a secure footing on the relatively unstable, sloping site; and the harnessing of cross ventilation to moderate the climate. Eschewing local conventions, Poole employed a steel structure, with the house effectively suspended from four deeply driven slender steel columns braced by tensile rods. Flat-roofed and with minimal eaves, its centre was signalled by the prismatic form of the large skylight that illuminated and ventilated the spaces at its core. The house and its use of a light steel frame with sheet materials resonated more with the Case Study Houses of California than the disciplined aesthetics of Miesian pavilions. Despite its small size, this house employed many of the design strategies evident in Poole's later works, including the Tent House and his own home at Lake Weyba where Poole continued to invent and reinvent adventurous structural and environmental systems.

The Addison House, Brisbane – Stage One, 1974–75, by Rex Addison, stands back and down from the adjacent roadway at the head of a steep, treed gully. The house has been skilfully positioned to maximise the possibilities of the awkward site and its setting. In its initial form, the house appeared as a simple, weatherboarded hut or hall with a flat, triangular face climbing high, increasing its presence in the streetscape. Addison was familiar with Robert Venturi's house for his mother in Philadelphia and with Frank Lloyd Wright's Oak Park house in Illinois, each with a formal, flat-fronted facade increasing scale and amplifying their presence in their respective settings. There is an acknowledgement of those works in the pared back, bald frontal plane of the Addison House. Its overall form was generated by slicing across the geometry of a traditional Queenslander and stretching the plane of the corrugated iron roof down to match the gradient of the fall of the site. The plane of the roof is cut and trimmed to provide shade and shelter as needed and to open up to the view and breeze where possible. In its initial form the house possessed a principal floor level with an open mezzanine level above and a small bedroom below; one volume, literally a timber tent. Thermal comfort largely depended on the house being open to the elements and, as with the Dobie House, benefiting from cross ventilation.

Despite the differences in their formal resolution these two modest houses offered innovative responses for subtropical climates. They each relied on being open to and at one with the immediate environment and their setting while revealing influences from architectural ideas and precedents from beyond Queensland.

In contrast, the Wirra Street House, 1979–82, that we designed brought together ideas and design approaches from abroad that were combined and deployed in response to the local tradition, with a recognition of the significance of place and climate in Brisbane. Accessed from below, the site rises steeply from a cul-de-sac typical of the rapidly spreading suburban development of Brisbane's western edge.

A governing idea was to draw views of the wider landscape across constructed hillside terraces into the house compound that is comprised of separate pavilions and garden courts. Two stairways ascend from the entry court, linking principal rooms and courtyards at each level.

The layout of indoor and outdoor rooms allows the occupation of the house to be configured and reconfigured to suit different patterns of seasonal occupation and to match the client's brief, which envisaged change over time.

At the uppermost level the principal 'great room', with its steeper separate roof that acknowledges the pyramidal roofs of traditional Queenslanders, opens onto the northern courtyard.

All other rooms sit under two skillion roofs aligned with the hillslope, and the linking spaces and porches are drawn in and sheltered by screens of timber battens and planting. By stretching the landscape into the courtyards as outdoor rooms, the design offers enhanced views, light, breezes and privacy to each of the principal

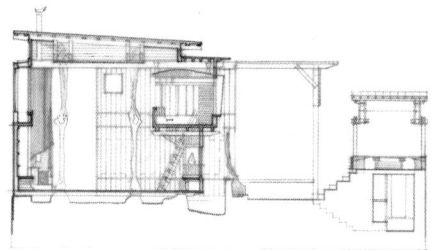

Section looking east

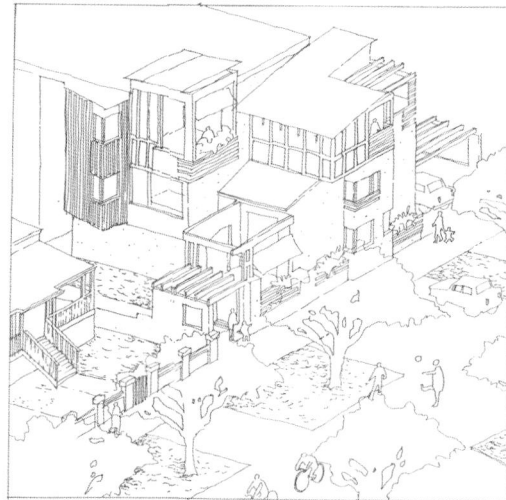

Top:
The Embrace competition entry (1993) by Sheona Thompson and Alice Hampson, Also Architecture Studio.

Bottom:
Additive transformation competition entry (1992) by Antony Moulis.

indoor rooms. This design strategy of designing for places to occupy across the site, with indoor and outdoor rooms, was to be explored in many of our later projects.

Sketch Four: Houses in the studio

For students, designing a house appears, at first, a simple task; after all there are many houses and at least one house is familiar territory. In teaching terms it is the very complexity of the house that lends itself to introducing both the poetic and the pragmatic realms of architecture and to developing exercises for beginning students in search of a viable design process.

The basics of ordering rooms for a single-family house on a suburban lot led UQ's Peter O'Gorman to develop the Magic Mats Game. Based on the dimensions of a standard tatami mat (1 m x 2 m), this house planning exercise involved juggling the demands of a limited number of pragmatic and often competing factors to achieve an accommodating floorplan including circulation, privacy, relations between activities, and solar orientation. As each tatami mat came with a dollar value, the aim of the game was to win by producing a plan not only demonstrating a best-practice planning solution but also at the lowest cost.

The underpinning intention of this Magic Mats Game was to begin a process of thinking in design where each factor among the myriad competing demands is reckoned with, moderated in relation to other factors and integrated in a synthesised design. Subsequently, the two-dimensional Magic Mats Game was extended to include the third dimension with the introduction of timber post-and-beam construction and then a later version, the Developers' Game, was introduced for senior students designing large urban housing projects.

We developed these process-focused games to promote agility in working strategically with metrics in designing a house and we equally developed exercises for the study of architecture's qualitative dimensions and their significant relationship with gardens, landscapes and their wider settings. Projects for thinking through ideas related to experiences, such as the dimensions of time and memory, were offered in the Constructing Architectural Space course where students explored the rooms of existing structures, working through texts, hand-drawing, collage and photography to define qualities that could be expressed in their final house design.

Texts with a focus on the lived experience of architecture were introduced, including Gaston Bachelard's *The Poetics of Space*, Jun'ichirō Tanizaki's *In Praise of Shadows*, Ann Cline's *A Hut of One's Own: Life Outside the Circle of Architecture* and David Malouf's essay 'A first place: The mapping of a world' with its close observations of the wooden house and the otherworldly, undercroft space of 'deepening dark'. Working with landscapes was also informed by texts and analyses such as *The Poetics of Gardens* by William Mitchell, William Turnbull and Charles Moore. Design lectures too included examples of spatial play in architecture with reference to houses such as John Soane's in London, Charles Moore's in Los Angeles and those found in John Summerson's *Heavenly Mansions*.

Even after five years in the studio, graduates find working towards an architectural design, where pragmatic and poetic aspects are unified in balance, is often an elusive venture given the myriad competing demands that come with an architectural commission. As an alternative, graduates have discovered that 'open ideas competitions' for architects can provide the conditions and opportunities to further test their design ideas.

For example, graduates Sheona Thomson and Alice Hampson of Also Architecture Studio entered *Japan Architect*'s 1993 house competition. Their award-winning design for a house titled The Embrace is a poetic nesting of shelters, from the outer, loosely bound enclosure to areas of innermost shelter, all gathered to fit on a tiny site.

Similarly, graduate Antony Moulis entered a 1992 ideas competition for mixed-use housing that demonstrated a strategy to resolve many competing factors. In a reworking of his final year project, he proposed an additive transformation of a suburb to achieve

both greater mix and density over time. To support this concept Moulis reimagined the space of the street as a place for enhanced urban life and where the six-metre zone between private and public realms can be progressively infilled with diverse activities and landscapes. This strategy continues to offer a viable urban design option for Brisbane City Council.

Sketch Five: Two towers

The late 1970s and 1980s at the UQ school were particularly active in advancing critical teaching methods and in strengthening a focus on fundamental ideas that underlie the nature of dwelling and guide the shaping of a coherent relationship with place and setting.

Despite the coherence of the program at the time, there were gaps in many students' knowledge and experience of the wider world or of Queensland other than the cities and towns along its coastal fringe. Our long-standing study of Queensland country towns by successive third year groups commenced in 1979. Over a ten-year period, close to one hundred towns across Queensland were visited by students working in pairs, who surveyed and documented their nominated town in terms of its main street, principal public buildings and notable features including dwellings.

Broadening the knowledge and experience of architecture further, we undertook a series of study tours that challenged the familiar patterns of the suburban house. Field trips to Papua New Guinea centred on joint projects with the School of Architecture in Lae included travel to Mount Hagen and Mendi in the remote highlands. Other study destinations in the region included Java and the School of Traditional Architecture in Bali.

A crucial initiative in this period, that advanced the standing of the UQ school and enlivened its teaching program, was to appoint prominent international architects as visiting staff to co-teach with core staff. Pancho Guedes (South Africa), Ingrid Morris (UK), Chris Macdonald (Canada), Jeanne Sillett (UK), and later, Tom Heneghan (Japan), Andrew Holmes (UK), Paul Shepheard (UK) and Lisa Findley (USA) all contributed critical thinking to the design program at different levels of the course.

Among the most engaging was Sir Peter Cook (UK) of Archigram fame, who was appointed as a visiting professor in 1983. Cook is known to enjoy provincial places – and people – and brought an acuity to his analysis of the architecture of Brisbane's city heart, good and bad. Working side by side with students in the fifth-year studio, he created a scheme of his own, illustrated with a major drawing of fan bridges and towers that, together, stitched the projected Expo precinct on the south bank of the Brisbane River with the 'modern' downtown bank opposite. Struck by the delicacy and distinctiveness of the 19th and 20th century 'bungalows', the residential tower

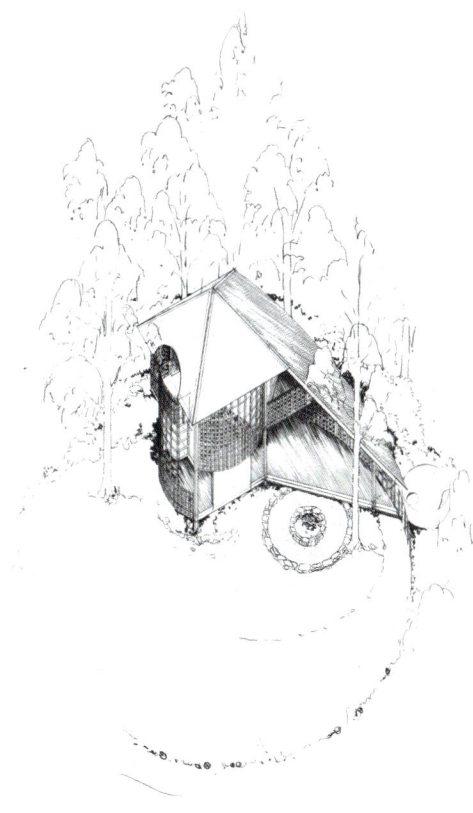

Top:
Peter Cook: Tower Projects 1983–1984.
John Oxley Library, State Library of Queensland. Record no. 21108124880002061.

Bottom:
Mount Nebo tower house axonometric (1983) by Peter O'Gorman.

HOUSES FROM A SCHOOL OF IDEAS

Top:
C House (1998) in Brisbane by Donovan Hill.
Photography: Patrick Bingham Hall.

Bottom:
Left Over Space House (2015) in Paddington, Brisbane, by CultivAR Architects.
Photography: Christopher Frederick Jones.

in the scheme was designed as a 'rack upon which can be hung a series of updated and extended bungalows – with colour, walkouts, verandahs, trellises and layered screens ... features taken on from the old bungalows'.[1]

The bravura of Cook's residential city tower resonated with a modest, three-storey tower house built among tall trees at Mount Nebo beyond Brisbane's urban fringe. Designed by Peter O'Gorman in 1983, the house has a diminutive footprint minimising its encroachment on the pristine bushland and centred on its 4.8 m x 4.8 m spatial and structural core. Each level of the house engages with a different experience of the surrounding forest and of the light and outlook. The core recalls the compact, enclosed heart of the traditional Queenslander houses stripped of their fringing verandahs. Here the core is ringed by a curved lattice screen that embraces the internal spaces of the house; its external decks, entry and the stairs connecting the several levels.

The pyramid roof stretches out and down and is trimmed to follow and shelter the space captured by the curve of the screen. All these elements and the many qualities derived from the nature of the setting and the shifting patterns of light and shade illustrate many of the qualities that are knowingly suggested within Cook's tower, yet here result not from an outsider's insight and discovery but from O'Gorman's ingrained understanding of the inherent possibilities opened up by an innovative and purposeful response to the inherent qualities of place.

Sketch Six: Houses shaped over time

The buoyant 1980s closed with a recession stretching into the early 1990s. The reduction in demand for architectural services brought amalgamations and reshaping of practices. One positive outcome was that a cohort of recently graduated architects, undaunted by the difficulties of the time, established fledgling practices, each energised by a design ethos related to place and circumstance.

One such was Donovan Hill Architects formed by Brian Donovan and Timothy Hill, who were brought together by common interests and the potential of several nascent residential projects. Of these, the C House, 1998, offered an extraordinary opportunity to explore a breadth of design strategies that came to be employed across many of their later works.

The grounding intention for the design of the C House was that it was to take shape from a relatively modest initial stage and to expand as the clients' family grew and as future needs emerged. An early sketch model projected a strong ordering idea governing a clear design strategy. It proposed a stepped and sculpted concrete armature stretching across the width of the site onto which a relatively modest grouping of timber planes and frames was to be overlaid onto and inlayed into the armature to shape the spaces of the early stages of the house. The intention being that this interlocked sequence of planes and frames, of nests, pavilions and focal spaces would grow along and across the whole of the armature over time as the needs of the family grew and developed.

With these ordering ideas in place, the construction of the house took form over a period of some six years. The intricacy and high quality finish of the initial stages of the underlying concrete base of the house gave time for a variety of conditions linking it to its setting to be experienced, evaluated and enhanced in situ. This allowed a range of refined design intentions to be explored as the work progressed.

The many interactions involved in the design and construction of the house became the catalyst for a suite of emerging elements and design strategies to be deployed in other schemes over the life of the practice. The principles established by the open, but sheltered, outdoor room at the heart of the C House reappeared in the major public spaces within the Queensland State Library and the Translational Research Institute (TRI) both of which drew upon Donovan Hill's design intentions together with those of their collaborating practices, Peddle Thorpe for the library and Wilson Architects for the TRI.

Top:
Fifth Avenue House (1992) in St Lucia, Brisbane, by Bud Brannigan Architects. Photography: Michael Nicholson.

Bottom:
Campbell House (1989) in Graceville, Brisbane, by Don Watson. Photography: Richard Stringer.

Also born of investigative design over an extended timeframe is the Left Over Space House, 2013, by Rebekah and Casey Vallance of CultivAR Architecture. The project commenced shortly after their graduation from UQ and following its completion a decade later this, their first house, was awarded World House of the Year at the World Architecture Festival in Singapore under the name of the Cox Rayner practice where they were working at the time.

The site for the project was challenging in sloping down steeply from a narrow frontage to the main street to the south, with heritage controls over adjacent buildings to the east and west which in each case encroached on the Vallance's property. The available area of the site was further constrained by easements to either side of the property and across the lowest level of the site to the north.

These constraints were imaginatively responded to in jointly guiding the intricate design resolution of the house in its setting. The Vallances were physically involved in all stages of the building of the house – and constructed a detailed 1:50 model to help convey to collaborators how its spatial and physical elements would come together. The design process was guided by testing solutions and proposals on site with some options being rejected and others enriched by a greater understanding and control of material and by the relationship of physical elements and ordering spaces. The house is distinguished by a finely arranged procession of interlocked volumes and spaces that offer many invitations to pause and enjoy the sense of the house and its relationship with its setting.

'Within the open framework of the linear plan, the architects have extended ideas of containment and release to offer a range of scales. Small shelters have been constructed for retreat and intimacy – the library's book-lined bed-box and various alcoves, corners and window and door surrounds – and each has been detailed to enhance daily rituals and experiences of moving about the house. Harnessing the dynamics of light and unfolding views has also inspired the detailed design of transitional spaces such as staircases, thresholds, walkways, and landings that incorporate discreet places for artworks, "light shrouds", and furniture pieces to enrich these connecting social spaces within the house.'[2]

Sketch Seven: Houses on show

Many architecture schools overseas have been led by practitioner–teachers. Professor–practitioner Charles Moore, for example, led the school at UCLA, while at the Cambridge School professors Lesley Martin and later Colin St John Wilson successfully combined teaching and research with their atelier-style practices. Arriving in Brisbane in the late 1970s from the Cambridge and London schools where it was assumed that lecturers would build as well as teach, we were surprised to find only a few practitioner–teachers at UQ and these colleagues were generally designing houses.

The house as a building type has long been a testbed for exploring conceptual design ideas that are made more vivid as demonstrated through constructed built works and when experienced in their context. Peter O'Gorman, for example, was constructing affordable houses made of small-section hardwood lengths assembled as composite posts and beams – a timber building system that was to be further developed and to reappear in his later house projects and design lectures. Additional architecture practitioner–teachers were appointed academics at UQ including Don Watson, Max Horner, Bud Brannigan, Peter Skinner, John Hockings and Ian Clayton.

This valuable interactive relationship was put under strain because by the 1990s there was a growing separation between the architectural school and practice. Driven by national policy, the universities were placing greater emphasis on higher degrees as a condition of appointment and on conventional research indicators. As Andrew Saint said in his reflections about the Cambridge School of Architecture, 'The biggest loss has been the withering of the practitioner–teacher tradition among permanent appointments.'[3]

HOUSES FROM A SCHOOL OF IDEAS

Top:
Mooloomba House (1995) on Minjerribah
(North Stradbroke Island) by Andresen O'Gorman.
Photography: Anthony Browell.

Middle:
Mooloomba future city drawing (1996)
by Andresen O'Gorman.

Bottom:
Cantala Avenue House (2019) in Miami,
Gold Coast, by ME.
Photography: Christopher Frederick Jones.

Top right:
Granny Flat (2014) in Burleigh Heads, Gold Coast,
by Clare Design.
Photography: Peter Hyatt.

Coinciding with this university-wide shift was the growing interest in the architectural work of the practitioner–teachers and their graduates at the UQ school whose work in the 1980s and 1990s was becoming widely illustrated in books, journals and exhibitions both interstate and internationally giving impetus to the launching of three major exhibitions in Brisbane.

House Styles was a collection of works from the period 1984–94 by ten UQ graduates and staff that was exhibited in the Australian Embassy in Paris and elsewhere. In his review of the show the late Professor Paul Reid wrote: 'At first thought, the idea of flimsy Queensland houses displayed inside Seidler's sculptured concrete, set in Paris, is an extraordinary juxtaposition of images. It succeeds because each layer has such distinct aims and achieves them so well. The exhibition comprises 10 double A0 sheets of text and images from 10 firms or individuals, hanging freely in the space below Seidler's radiating T beams. This room is the result of Seidler's mature, sophisticated and uncompromising statement of abstract form. It tells Parisians to take Australians seriously. The young Queensland architects dance on Seidler's stage. They take their work, but not themselves, seriously. The texts and images are complex; focusing on the craft and technology of timber, the handling of light, the environment of the bush; emphasising personal impressions.'

In 1996 the XIX Congress of the International Union of Architects UIA was held in Barcelona. In response to an invitation from the organiser to contribute to the theme 'Present and Futures: Architecture in Cities' we presented two papers illuminated by the exhibition *From Edge to Centre: Future Housing for the Sub-tropical City*. As a response to future densities forecast for Brisbane, seventeen contributing practices and graduates were invited to propose hypothetical multiple housing derived from one of their single-family houses. The exhibition was displayed in Barcelona and later at the Australian Embassy in Paris.

Included in the exhibition was Andresen O'Gorman's (AOG) Mooloomba House – their beach house on Minjerribah. Its design 'explores the proposition that; to defer to the existing landscape, to allude to a mythical landscape and to create a constructed landscape can together intensify the place of the house in its wider setting'.[4]

The composition of its principal elements of major and minor courtyards, framing cloistered walkways and the two principal rooms interweave a constructed landscape of spatial and structural elements around and within the given landscape.

This vital design intent was extended and repeated to define the AOG proposition for a future city where the repetitive presence of the framing and sheltering elements of the future city weave their way through larger sustaining and mediating landscapes (existing, mythical alluded and constructed) to evoke a gentler, future urban format.

The third exhibition, *Place Makers: Contemporary Queensland Architects 2008*, was the first major exhibition of Queensland's contemporary architecture in the state's gallery. Among the fifty-five projects from the period 1986 to 2006 presented in the exhibition there were thirty-two houses; the majority of these by UQ practitioner–teachers and graduates completed in the decade 1996 to 2006.

Sketch Eight: Practice sustaining culture
Our survey of incidents and highlights concerning the nature and quality of architecture through the design of houses in Queensland is intended to illuminate how the well-directed teaching of architecture can underpin and advance ideas in practice – and how lessons from practice can strengthen teaching. These brief sketches sit within the frame provided by the suite of houses selected for the overall book and together they reveal a breadth of design approaches to houses that directly relate to Queensland's environmental and cultural context.

Despite all that has been achieved, we are concerned that changes to higher education in Australia since the mid-1990s have increasingly constrained the teaching of architecture and will continue to do so into the foreseeable future. We are more optimistic about the practice of architecture partly because of its resilience and partly

because of the evident sensibility shared by notable Queensland practices.

Of the many practices that exemplify a future-focused commitment to place-based design and related design research, we have selected just a few to illustrate a breadth of purpose, achievement and impact essentially as they relate to city and coast.

The Brisbane practice of Vokes and Peters brings a dedication to the design process that results in an architectural civility where each proposal is strongly wedded to its site and setting. Their designs for notable houses capture and advance the fundamental principles and pleasures of dwelling derived from the Queenslander house type. Their considered focus on advancing these qualities serves to enrich and sustain the development of a place-based architectural culture within an urban framework.

The city of the Gold Coast is thought of by many as Australia's Miami. Its image is one of rampant high-rise development serving the tourist market. Less well known are the low-rise suburbs that follow the ocean frontage from the core of the city to the border with New South Wales. Matt Eagle, practitioner–teacher at Bond University, argues that this part of the city has the ingredients to establish a strong sense of place for the communities there that have generational longevity. His practice focuses on devising and utilising a sensibility of form, colour, construction and planning that is sensitive to the local context and that strengthens the architectural culture of the Gold Coast.

Among the detached bungalows of these low-rise suburbs are emerging projects that aim to respond to the Australia-wide push for increased densities and the supply of more varied and affordable housing. On the Gold Coast these include the multi-generational mixed-use compound in Palm Beach by Clare Design and, in Southport, the Anne Street Garden Villas – a social housing project – by Anna O'Gorman Architects.

While the individual client is likely to continue to commission the architect for a bespoke home, the suburbs of the future will only retain their desired environmental qualities if multi-residential housing adheres to tighter dimensional limits, less onsite car parking, more outdoor rooms as gardens, with big shade trees along street verges.

Looking ahead, the challenges facing university programs in architecture are best met by strengthening the interaction with critical practice. A strong, mutually supportive interrelationship will ensure the advancement of a culture, of the making of fine buildings and places that respond to Queensland's specific climate and further invigorate the openness of structure and form that may be enjoyed in the gentle northerly.

Notes

1. Don Watson (ed), *Peter Cook Tower Projects 1983–1984*, Ray Hughes Gallery, Brisbane, 1984, p. 14.

2. Brit Andresen, 'Left Over Space House', *ArchitectureAU*, 17 November 2014, <architectureau.com/articles/left-over-space-house/>.

3. Andrew Saint, 'The Cambridge School of Architecture: a Brief History', Cambridge School of Architecture Compendium Exhibition catalogue, 2006.

4. Brit Andresen, 'Mooloomba House', *Fryer Folios*, vol. 7 no. 1, July 2012, The University of Queensland Library, Brisbane.

Brit Andresen

Brit Andresen is a Norwegian architect, professor and independent scholar. She has taught at the University of Cambridge, held positions at UCLA, the Architectural Association School of Architecture in London and the University of Queensland, and currently teaches at the annual Glenn Murcutt International Architecture Master Class in Sydney. Her teaching and research include building design with landscape, architecture and urban change, and relationships between ideas and practice. Andresen was awarded the Gold Medal by the Royal Australian Institute of Architects in 2002.

Michael Keniger

Michael Keniger is Honorary Professor of Architecture at Bond University, Queensland. Following graduation from the Architectural Association School of Architecture and a period of practice and teaching in London, Keniger accepted a position at the University of Queensland, going on to ultimately serve as a member of its senior executive. Throughout his career he has advocated the value of high-quality architectural design in shaping and enriching the public realm. Keniger was awarded the Australian Institute of Architects 2017 National President's Prize for an outstanding career.

A life lived outdoors

In sun-drenched contrast to colder climes, the development of a climate-responsive residential architecture for Queensland eschews the traditional, enclosed and rarefied sense of the interior in favour of a more relaxed, porous space that embraces the benign climate and informal lifestyle. The verandah of the traditional Queenslander house is often its best room, both in terms of the intensity of the architectural detail and as the setting for the reception of guests. This condition is the prototype for a contemporary architectural approach where the prime room in the house is an enclosed or partly enclosed outdoor space. In these new build and renovation projects the architectural approach prioritises this liminal environment, creating the ideal setting for a life lived outdoors.

Chelmer House

Chelmer, Brisbane
Bligh Graham Architects

Completed – 2012
Project type – Alteration and addition
Total site area – 1088 m²
Internal area – 196 m²
External area – 100 m²
Number of residents – 5
Number of bedrooms – 5
Number of bathrooms – 3

Chelmer House is built on the land of the
Turrbal and Yuggera peoples

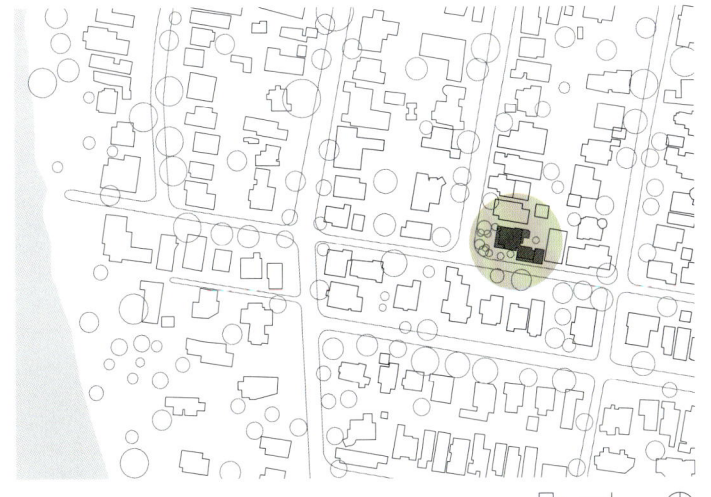

Location plan 1:5000

CHELMER HOUSE

The architectural setting

A house arranged around an occupied, open courtyard is an ideal arrangement for northern Australia, delivering a connection to the landscape and a climate responsiveness that the traditional, raised, timber and tin houses lack. This housing type is rare, but in the story of residential architecture in Queensland there are moments of delight and experimentation.

In the mid-century this form of housing was popular in Melbourne and Sydney, exemplified in the work of Melbourne architect Robin Boyd and the Sydney School architect Donald Gazzard, who exported this thinking to the tropics with work on the central coast of Queensland in the early 1980s (see House for the Central Coast of Queensland, page 292). In Brisbane there are several innovative houses from the mid-century that record the modernist re-engagement with this historic housing type. These include the 1966 Mocatta House by Robin Gibson (see page 293), where an internal courtyard is edged by a screened verandah, and the 1967 Malouf Residence by Bligh Jessup Bretnall (see page 293), where two L-shaped wings frame a square courtyard.

In the project of renovating a Queenslander house the creation of a direct connection with the garden is a priority and in the Chelmer House renovation by Bligh Graham Architects this was a key aspect of the clients' brief. The courtyard house is a hallmark of the work of this practice and the generation of architects it belongs to, shaping both thoughtful renovations and new homes in a practice that further refines modernist ideals through the use of vernacular traditions.

Previous:
At Chelmer House, the original circa 1890s home has been sensitively updated to suit a subtropical way of life.

Opposite:
Where the 'hovering' Queenslander and the courtyard meet, a terraced garden brings the ground up to deck.

Above:
Embracing an open courtyard, the home re-engages with a mid-century architecture that responds to the tropics.

CHELMER HOUSE

The lived experience

Brisbane is known as a hilly city, but the leafy riverside suburb of Chelmer is relatively flat in contrast. The wide streets are lined with the thick trunks of camphor laurel trees and a plethora of preserved old colonial Queenslander houses. Alan and Angela Maguire's original circa 1890 home is part of this picturesque scene and has since been sensitively updated by Bligh Graham Architects to suit the subtropical way of life.

Unlike many Queenslanders, Alan and Angela's home was only slightly raised from the ground plane and this informed the design approach of anchoring the addition to the gentle topography of the site. A new living and kitchen space is grafted onto the rear of the existing house and extends out to a deck that hovers just above the luscious, terraced garden. On the southern boundary of the site, a new bedroom/rumpus wing flanks the garden and defines the outdoor space as the focal point of the home. Since the Maguire family moved into the renovated home over ten years ago, the greenery has grown up high against the northern glazing and makes the interior spaces feel like they are sunken into the garden itself. Being surrounded by planting has a cooling effect in the hot and humid Brisbane summers, as the northern breeze flows through the garden into the home. Like many other houses in Brisbane, the best spot to perch for a cup of tea, or a glass of wine, at the Chelmer House depends on the time of the day or the season, as Angela comments, 'Our garden is part of day-to-day life. It's a living space – we sit in the garden on picnic rugs or chairs to read, relax and eat, we perch on the bluestone steps or lounge on the verandah. It has changed the way we live.'

Opposite:
The new living area sits under the old verandah roof, with trusses exposed to increase the ceiling height.

Above:
New interiors are washed with a soft light that contrasts with the darker rooms of the existing house.

Above:
Greenery has grown up against the northern glazing, creating a cooling effect for the hot, humid summers.

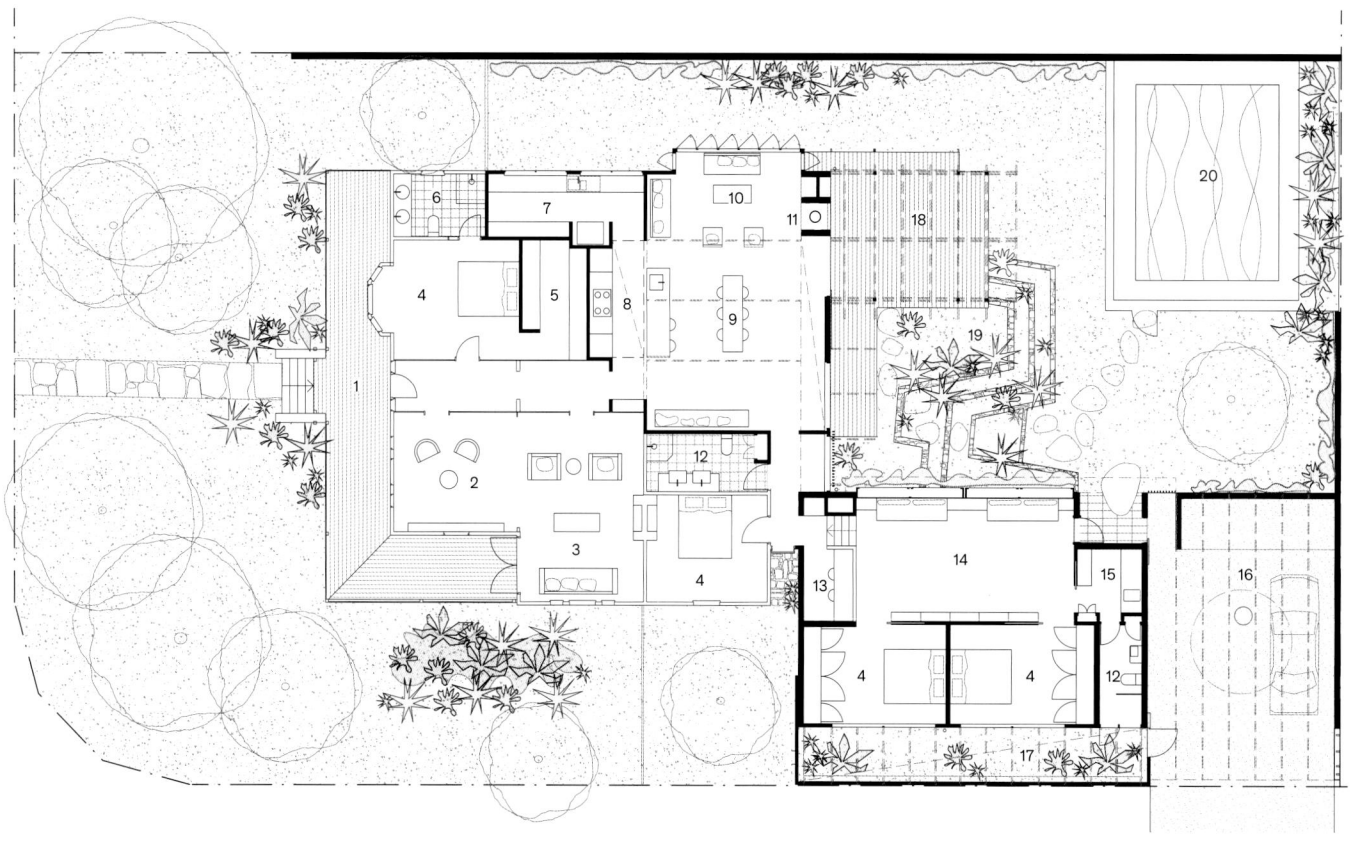

Plan

1	Verandah	11	Fireplace
2	Library	12	Bathroom
3	Lounge	13	Study
4	Bedroom	14	Rumpus
5	Wardrobe	15	Laundry
6	Ensuite	16	Carport
7	Scullery	17	Courtyard
8	Kitchen	18	Deck
9	Dining	19	Terraced garden
10	Sitting	20	Pool

1:250
0 5m

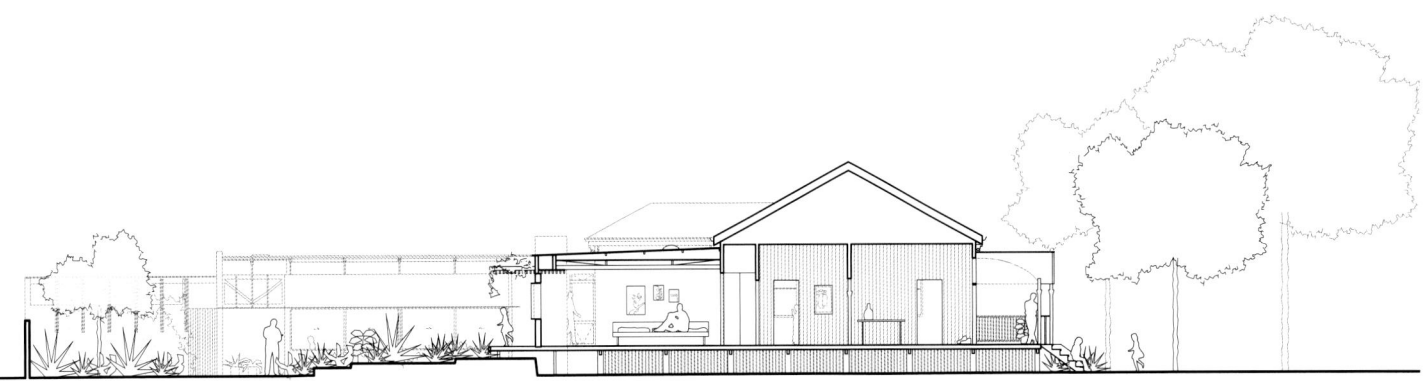

Longitudinal section

Cross section

1:250
0   5m

Architect — Bligh Graham Architects
Project team — Chris Bligh, Sonia Graham, Douglas Lo, Camden Cummings
Landscape architect — Steven Clegg Design
Builder — GMG Refurbishments
Structural engineer — Bligh Tanner
Photographer — Scott Burrows

Oxlade Drive House

New Farm, Brisbane
James Russell Architect

Completed — 2013
Project type — New build
Total site area — 519 m²
Internal area — 200 m²
External area — 147 m²
Number of residents — 5 + 2 (extended family)
Number of bedrooms — 5
Number of bathrooms — 3

Oxlade Drive House is built on the land of the Turrbal and Yuggera peoples

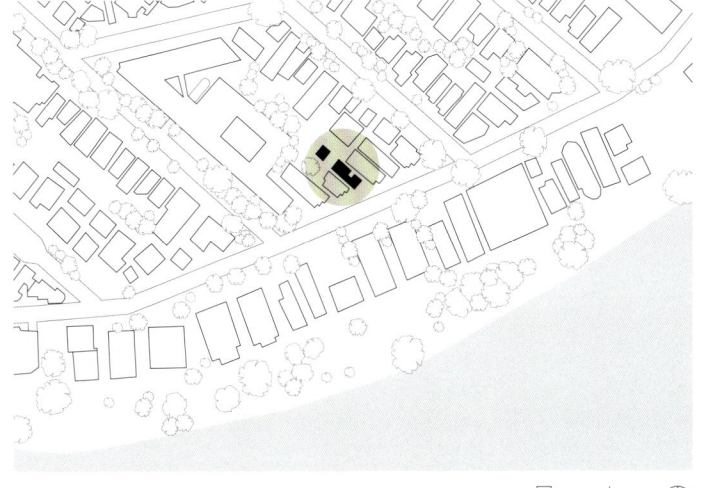

Location plan 1:5000 0 10 50m

OXLADE DRIVE HOUSE

The architectural setting

The stripped-back, fibro sheet houses of the postwar suburbs are the outcome of the population boom and severe housing shortage that Brisbane experienced in the 1940s and 1950s. This austerity segued to the suburban optimism of the 1960s and the emergence of the brick-veneer, tile-roof, slab-on-ground houses of the local and national project builders. There were a handful of instances of architects participating in the development of this now-ubiquitous building type, notably the Sydney-based architect Ken Woolley, who worked with local architect Patrick Moroney on the design and construction of Pettit+Sevitt project homes in Brisbane and the Gold Coast (see Pettit+Sevitt two-level Split Level House 2H, page 294).

As the populace looked to this new suburban dream on the fringes of the capital cities and the car-dependent, shopping centre culture it generated, leading architects across Australia began thinking about the process of urban renewal in the 1960s. This saw the deployment of a sensitive infill architecture, exemplified by the re-emergence of Paddington in Sydney, Carlton in Melbourne, and Spring Hill and New Farm in Brisbane (see Railton House and Office, page 294).

The project of urban rehabilitation and the opportunities of typological experimentation continue to occupy the minds of leading architects and this project underpins the approach of James Russell Architect. The Oxlade Drive House in New Farm presents as a unique, hybrid building; a house that captures the unique qualities of the place, delivered with an industrial-scale and replicable construction thinking that offers a practical critique of the past 50 years of suburban housing development in Australia.

Previous:
Oxlade Drive House comprises a series of living spaces punctuated by shade cloth-wrapped courtyards.

Opposite:
The home's timber cladding and gable roof respond to the material and profile of an existing neighbour.

Above left:
The front courtyard extends the kitchen and dining space, and includes a productive garden.

Above right:
Upstairs, three bedrooms are arranged side by side, accessed via robes off the corridor.

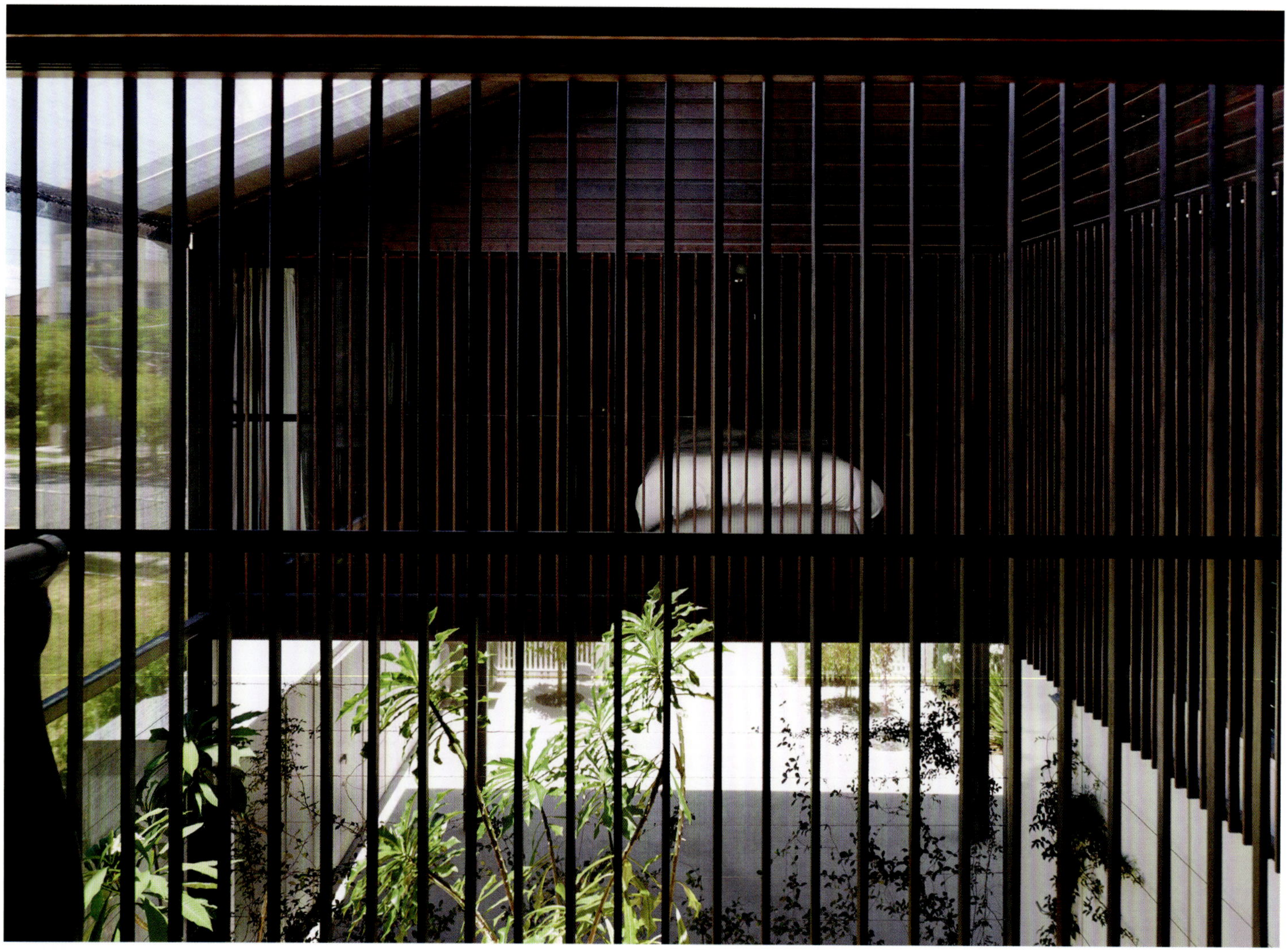

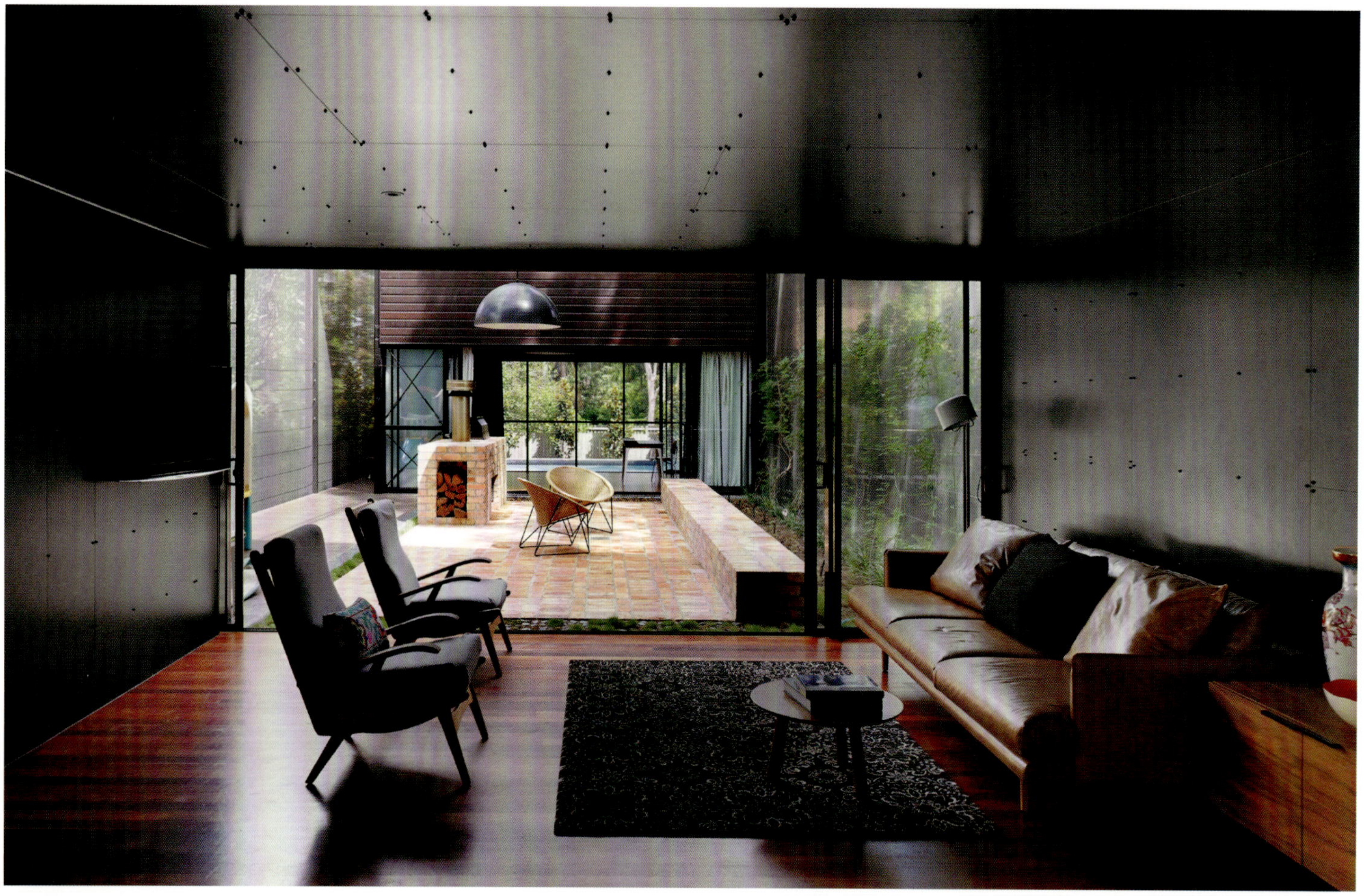

The lived experience

When owners Louise and Matt Fitzgerald approached architect James Russell to design their new home in Brisbane's New Farm, they briefed him to create a space that was connected to the outdoors and permanently open to breezes but also protected from the hotter weather and associated insects. James's pragmatic solution of punctuating the series of habitable spaces with courtyards addresses this desire for a continuous connection to the outside. However, lateral thinking was required in order to protect these spaces from the harsh sun and persistent insects, while maintaining the desired seamless connection to the outdoors. James's clever, yet unconventional idea of entirely wrapping the two courtyards in black shade cloth has been fully embraced by the family of five and allows free movement between indoors and outdoors at all times of day and in all seasons.

These cloth-bound courtyards are both the lungs and the heart of the home. They each have different functions in daily family life as Louise explains, 'The front courtyard is an extension of our kitchen and dining space – so it's a productive garden and an eating space. It is beautiful in the morning sun. The central courtyard is more about gathering and lounging, and in the afternoon we enjoy sitting around the outdoor fireplace'. Sunlight is tempered through the tight weave of the UV-protective fabric and when it rains the shade cloth filters the water droplets into mist. Neighbouring trees add another layer of filtering to the sunshine and aid in cooling the garden sanctuary. Despite its inner suburban locale in New Farm, a memorable and immersive experience is created within these outdoor rooms.

Opposite top:
Slatted screens allow for strong visual connections between spaces, upstairs and downstairs.

Opposite bottom:
Interior living areas are wrapped in black melamine and connect directly with the courtyards.

Above left:
The sheer layer of black shade cloth that wraps the courtyards allows the house to breathe.

Above right:
The courtyard spaces serve as outdoor rooms protected from insects and the warm climate.

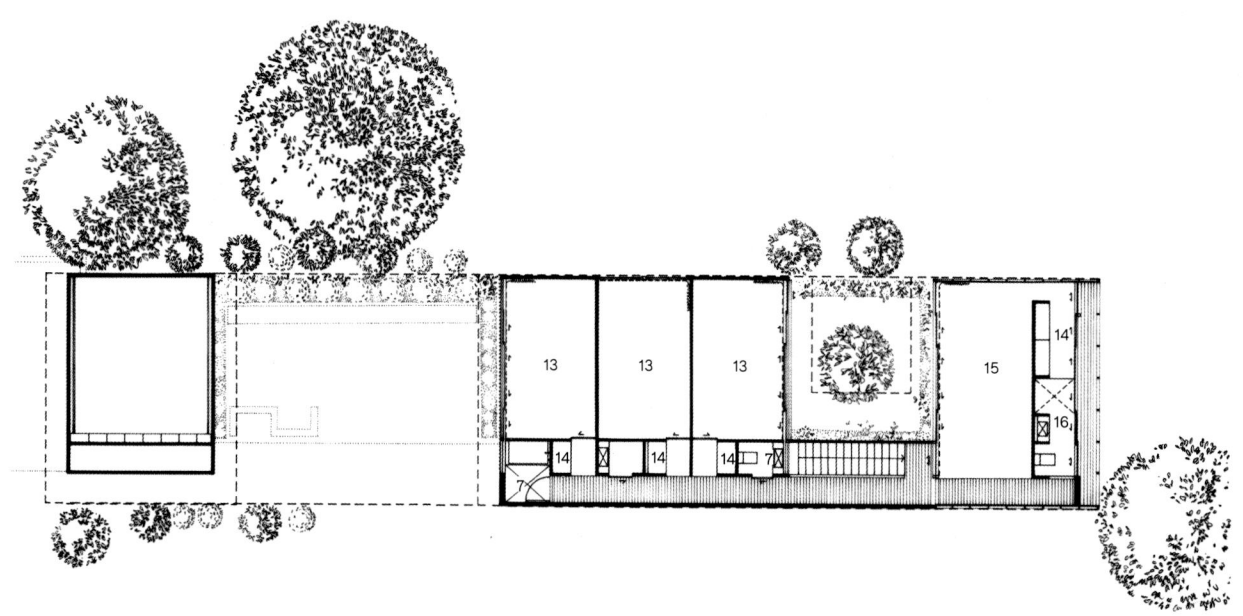

Upper level

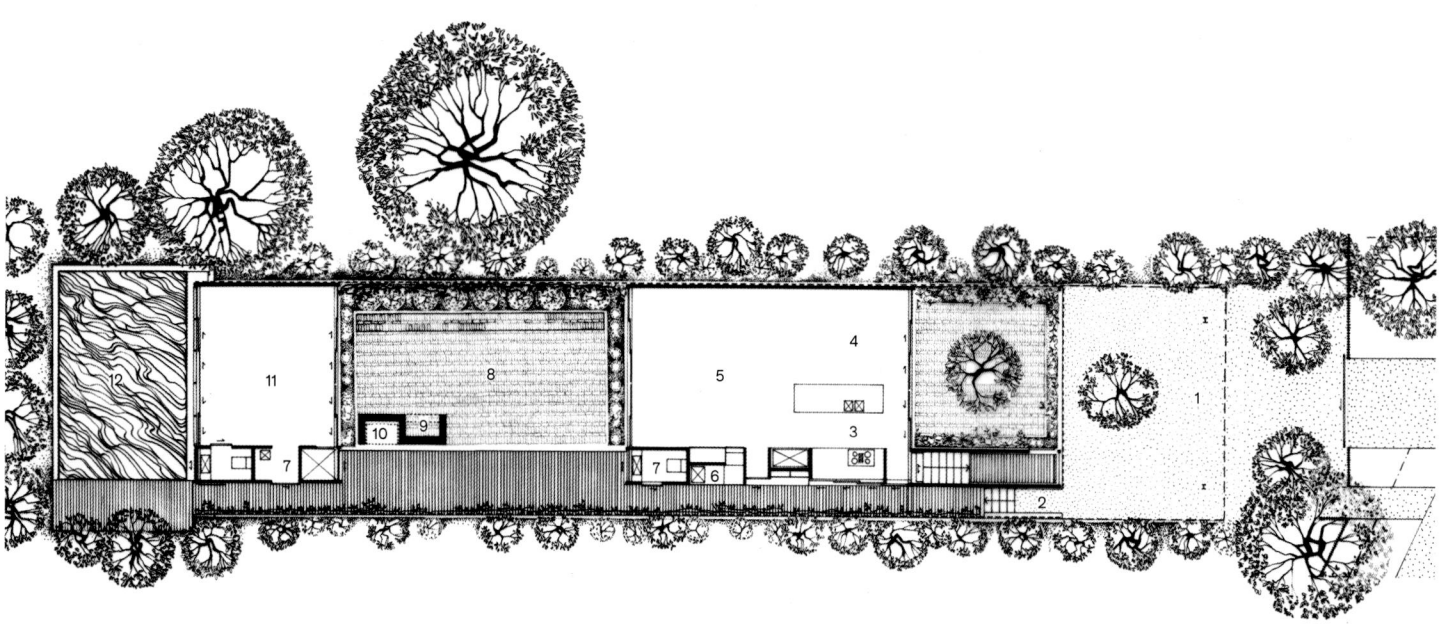

Lower level

1	Carport	9	Fireplace
2	Entry	10	Barbecue
3	Kitchen	11	Office/guestroom
4	Dining	12	Pool
5	Lounge	13	Sleeping
6	Laundry	14	Robe
7	Bathroom	15	Main bedroom
8	Courtyard	16	Ensuite

1:250

OXLADE DRIVE HOUSE

Sectional perspective

1:250

0 ⎯ 5m

Architect — James Russell Architect
Project team — James Russell, Andrew Schindler, John Ellway
Builder — Ben Kendall
Engineer — Westera Partners
Photographer — Toby Scott

Rosalie House

Paddington, Brisbane
Owen Architecture

Completed – 2015
Project type – New build
Total site area – 1630 m²
Internal area – 324 m²
External area – 113 m²
Number of residents – 6
Number of bedrooms – 5
Number of bathrooms – 2

Rosalie House is built on the land of the
Turrbal and Yuggera peoples

Location plan 1:5000 0 10 50m

Previous:
The materiality of Rosalie House references the interwar brick and tile home that once stood on the site.

Top:
Located between the two primary gardens, the kitchen pavilion can be completely opened to the elements.

Bottom:
The main garden acts as a playing field, with the home wrapping around the boundary.

The architectural setting

The foundation narrative of built environment heritage protection in the inner-Brisbane suburbs that were developed before the 1940s is the preservation of the modest timber and tin buildings. The fabric and character of these picturesque suburbs has been shaped and enriched by diverse architectural episodes and many of these interleafing buildings have interstate and international architectural connections.

These moments include the sweet art deco houses and small apartment buildings, like those of Elina Mottram in Kangaroo Point and New Farm; the interwar Mediterranean revival–style villas, particularly the poised work of Mervyn Rylance (see Clayfield House, page 292); and the grand arts and crafts house of the early 1900s, exemplified in the innovative work of Robin Dods (see Kitawah, page 292). The Queensland chapter of the Australian Institute of Architects recognises Dods's contribution to architecture in the state through an eponymous award that celebrates the best new residential building of the year, and the Rosalie House by Owen Architecture was the recipient of this pinnacle of honour in 2016.

The architectural scale, materiality and detailing perfected by Dods at the turn of the century resonate in the contemporary Rosalie House. This exemplary, subtropical dwelling has a sophisticated aesthetic and a spatial dexterity that speaks to the values and diversity of Queensland's architectural heritage and is a beautiful reminder of the lineage of innovation over the past century.

Above:
The exemplary subtropical house is characterised by a sophisticated aesthetic and spatial dexterity.

The lived experience

Former professional rugby league footballer Darren Lockyer approached architect Paul Owen of Owen Architecture with dreams of a new family home on a 1600 m² battle-axe block behind a local shopping strip in the Brisbane suburb of Rosalie. An interwar brick and tile house once stood high on the block, with a lower flat terrace for a tennis court to the east. Drawing on a deep understanding of Brisbane's suburban condition, Paul designed a new house that references the old house, particularly in terms of its materiality, while also embracing the opportunities of a generously proportioned site.

The promise of ample space and landscape is at the heart of the suburban ideology. At Rosalie House, a series of living pavilions wrap around the perimeter of the site to provide a sense of containment for the garden, giving the sense of 'a house within a parkland'. Working with landscape architect Dan Young, the project team planted trumpet trees and crepe myrtles directly into the grassland to amplify the feeling of a park setting. The main lawn is transformed into a playing field for footy or cricket for Darren and Loren's four children, and extends to an open-air fireplace and swimming pool. The kitchen pavilion at the southern end of the lawn can be completely opened up to the north via sliding panels and acts as a shaded and breezy viewing platform for the field. A portico screen extends from the kitchen pavilion along the western edge of the lawn, providing an alternative place to perch within the parklands.

The Rosalie House and meadow stitches itself into its suburban terrain via selected views to surrounding ridges, trees and urban landmarks, while ensuring the privacy of this landscaped sanctuary is retained.

Opposite:
The children's playroom connects with a small garden, encouraging indoor–outdoor play.

Above:
A meadow with six crepe myrtle trees screens the bedrooms at the rear of the site.

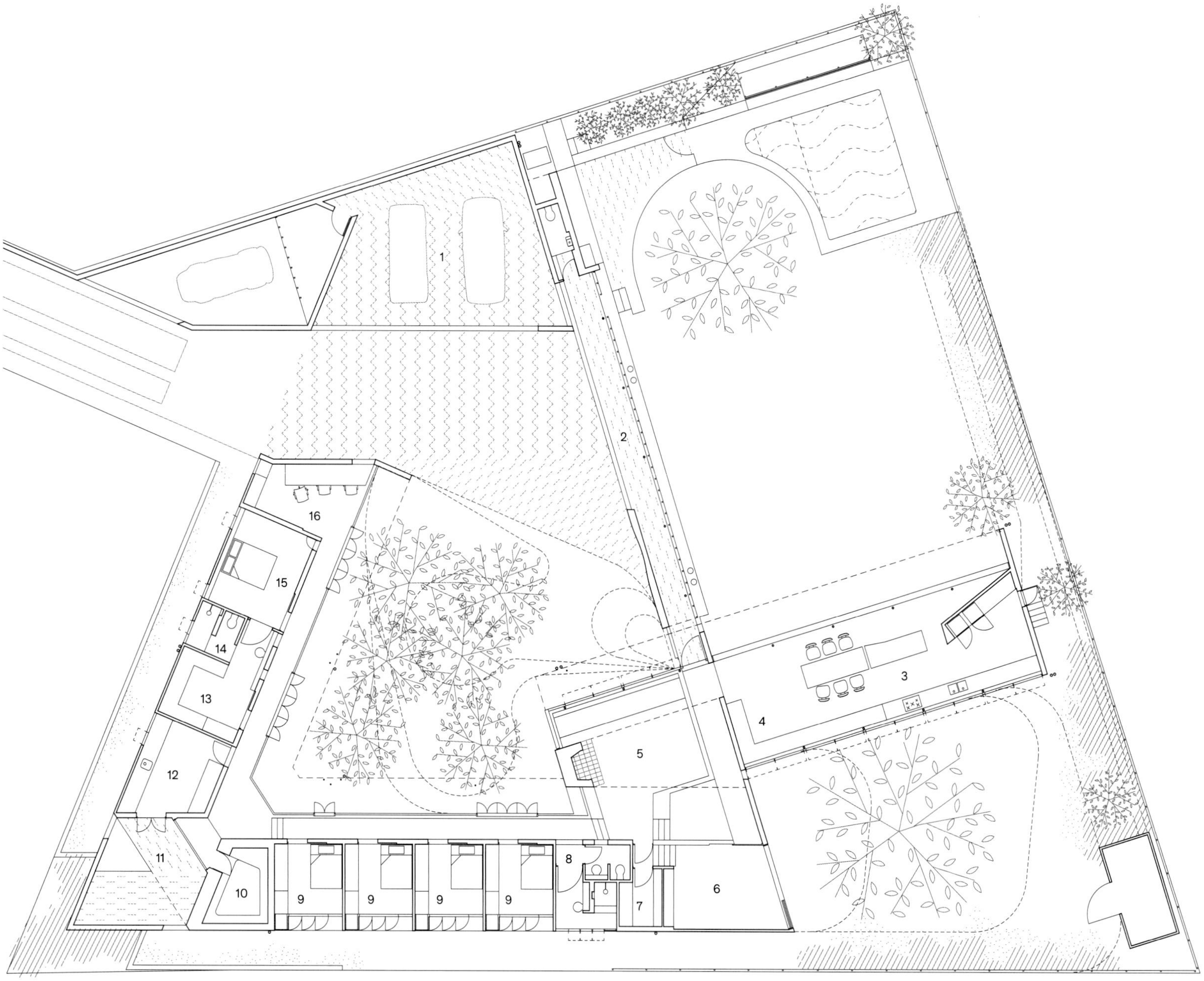

Plan

1:250

1	Garage	9	Bedroom
2	Entry	10	Cellar
3	Kitchen	11	Laundry court
4	Sitting	12	Laundry
5	Living	13	Robe
6	Playroom	14	Ensuite
7	Store	15	Main bedroom
8	Bathroom	16	Study

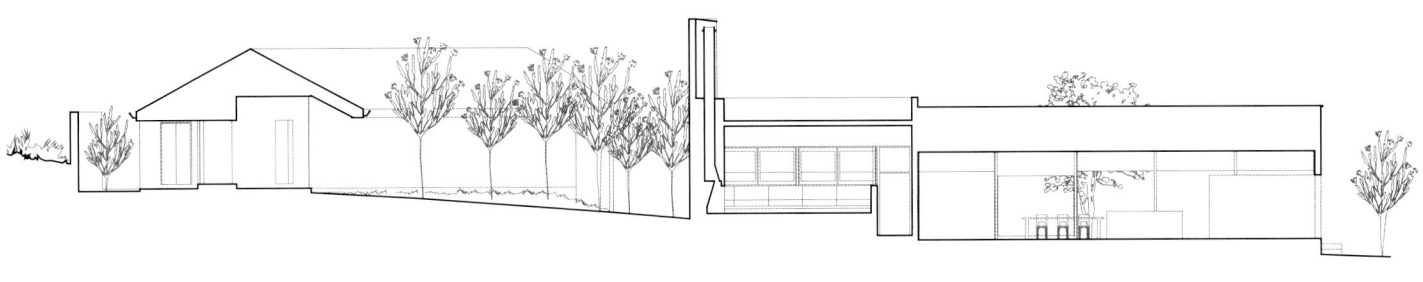
Longitudinal section

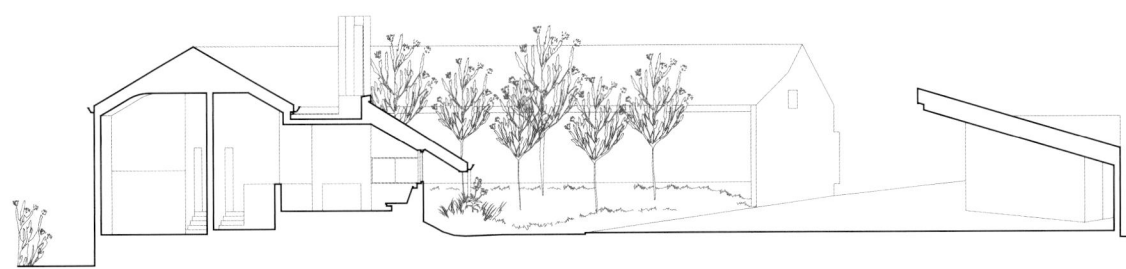
Cross section

1:250
0 5m

Architect — Owen Architecture
Project team — Paul Owen and Michael Lineburg
Builder — Robson Constructions
Structural engineer — Westera Partners
Landscape architect — Dan Young Landscape Architect
Photographer — Toby Scott

Cantala Avenue House

Miami, Gold Coast
ME

Completed – 2019
Project type – Alteration and addition
Total site area – 509 m²
Internal area – 209 m²
External area – 338 m²
Number of residents – 4–6
Number of bedrooms – 4
Number of bathrooms – 2

Cantala Avenue House is built on the land of the Kombumerri people

Location plan 1:5000 0 10 50m

CANTALA AVENUE HOUSE

The architectural setting

The enduring architectural image of the Gold Coast is that of the agglomeration of high-rise apartment buildings sited on the perfect, white-sand surf beach, and the city's coastal skyline features some of Australia's tallest residential buildings. With a population of almost 700,000 people the Gold Coast is the second-largest city in Queensland and the sixth-largest city in Australia. In parallel with the ambitious, global-scale tourism development that has shaped the Gold Coast since it emerged as a popular holiday destination in the 1950s is a lineage of innovative and informal beach houses, including mid-century works by noted Queensland architects Hayes and Scott, Geoffrey Pie (see Ravenscraig II, page 294), and Robin Gibson.

The Cantala Avenue House by ME is located on an unassuming residential street in Miami, a coastal-edge neighbourhood that straddles the defining line of the Gold Coast Highway as it runs from north to south. The precise alterations and additions thoroughly re-make the unremarkable 1970s split-level dwelling and the deft architectural moves are sympathetic to the unique culture and heritage of the Gold Coast. This refreshing and inquiring approach respects and elevates the value of the housing stock of the city's developer-driven suburban tracts and eschews the ubiquitous knockdown and rebuild approach that continues to undermine the authentic and nuanced character of this special place in the Queensland sun.

Previous:
Cantala Avenue House updates a ramshackle 1970s home to provide inviting family gathering spaces.

Opposite:
The relatively narrow core opens to both the front and back yards, expanding the interior.

Above:
At the front, a playful brickwork entry sequence invites engagement with the street and passers-by.

Top:
The backyard's skyward view is framed by the garden walls, giving privacy from neighbouring homes.

Bottom:
A brick ledge and fireplace mark the courtyard edge, while a 'ha-ha' ditch provides a boundary to the pool.

The lived experience

Owner and builder of Cantala Avenue House, Brett Ivey spent ten years developing and building homes on the Gold Coast prior to working with architect Matthew Eagle of ME. Matthew has been reinterpreting the traditional beach shack in a playful and refreshing series of homes in the region, and this appealed to Brett and his sensibilities. He approached Matthew with a desire for an alteration and addition to a ramshackle 1970s-era house that would accommodate his family of six.

Although relatively small in footprint, the inhabitable spaces of the house spill out into the adjacent outdoor spaces. With a central but narrow core that opens out to the front and back yards, there is an architectural pull from both edges of the home. 'We are drawn out to the front by the brick entry wall and seating, and the painted garden wall in the backyard does the same,' says Brett. In particular, the garden wall frames the backyard, editing out the neighbouring properties and promoting mindfulness and refuge. 'When you are in the pool and look up to the sky, framed by the garden wall, you have a sense that you could be anywhere.'

If the backyard is the private outdoor room to the home, the front brickwork entry sequence is the public outdoor room. Inviting engagement with the street, this space is for everyone – a place to gather with the neighbours for pizzas or a glass of wine while the kids jump over the walls or kick a ball in the street.

Above:
Garden voids strengthen the connection with nature and encourage moments of pause.

A LIFE LIVED OUTDOORS

72

Above:
The clean lines and simple materials of the low-pitched gable roof reflect a mid-century modern sensibility.

CANTALA AVENUE HOUSE

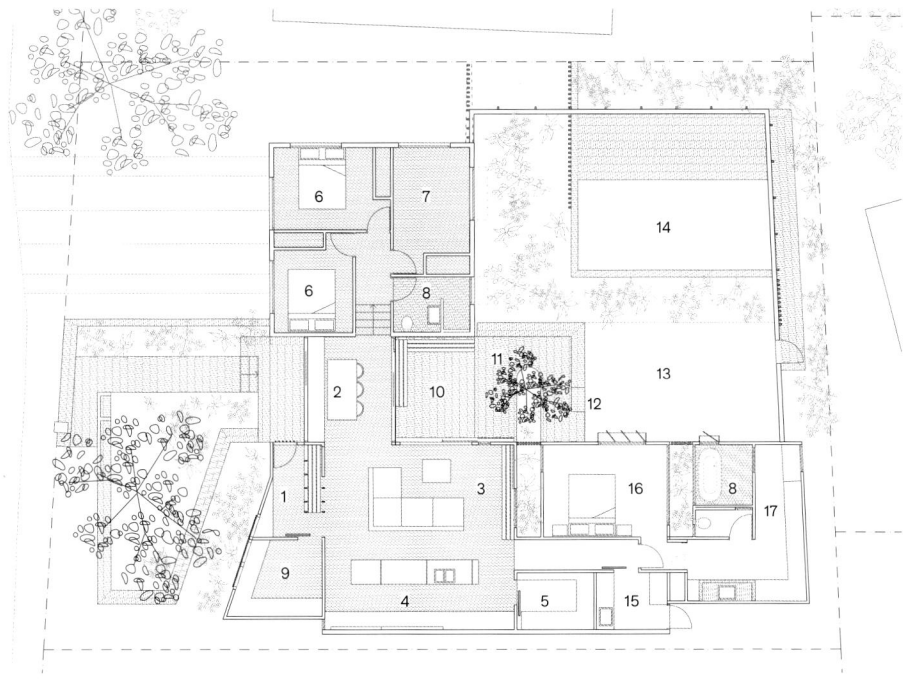

Plan

1 Entry
2 Dining
3 Living
4 Kitchen
5 Pantry
6 Bedroom
7 Kids' room
8 Bathroom
9 Study
10 Outdoor room
11 Courtyard
12 Fireplace
13 Lawn
14 Pool
15 Laundry
16 Main bedroom
17 Robe

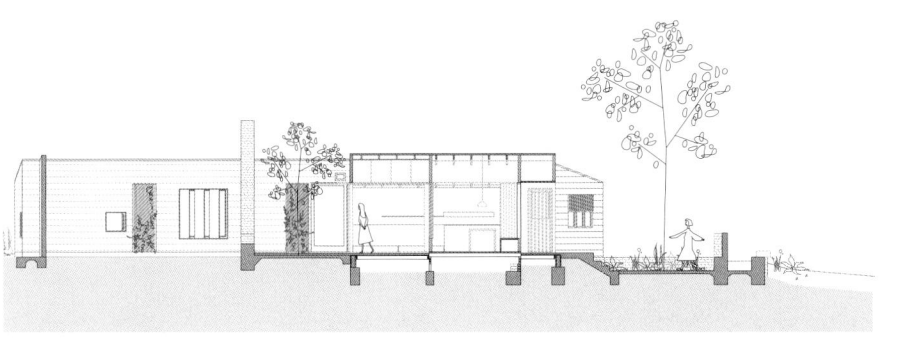

Longitudinal section

1:250
0   5m

Architect — ME
Project team — Matthew Eagle, Samara Hayes, Shane Collins
Builder — Ivey Built
Engineer — Rymark Engineers and Westera Partners
Survey — Alan Sullivan and Associates
Photographer — Christopher Frederick Jones

Beck Street

Paddington, Brisbane
Lineburg Wang

Completed – 2019
Project type – Alteration and addition
Total site area – 712 m²
Internal area – 316 m²
External area – 58 m²
Number of residents – 4
Number of bedrooms – 4
Number of bathrooms – 3

Beck Street is built on the land of the
Turrbal and Yuggera peoples

Location plan 1:5000 0 10 50m

The architectural setting

Brisbane has experienced catastrophic flooding six times over the past two centuries, the most recent being the 2022 event which peaked at a level of almost 4 metres and damaged thousands of houses. The city-defining Brisbane River has an unpredictable cycle of inundation and once the relatively high banks of the winding watercourse are breached the flat terrain of the suburbs along the river is rapidly submerged. During flooding, sections of the inner-western suburbs of Milton, Rosalie and Auchenflower went under, with the flood and storm waters tracing the path of what was once Western Creek, a tributary of a suppressed, ancient network of creeks and swamps.

The Beck Street house by Lineburg Wang is the renovation of a well-built, but unremarkable, mid-century house in this flood-prone locale and the architecture is thoughtfully responsive to these environmental and urban conditions. A firmly grounded, permeable brick base satisfies planning controls designed to anticipate future flood events and contains a series of robust, hose-out spaces that provide ample utility. The architectural rigour of this project seamlessly integrates old and new, reconciling the legislated and the aspirational to create a home that has a profound connection to place.

Previous:
Beck Street, located in a Brisbane flood zone, has a clever lower level that is permeable to floodwater.

Opposite:
Openings in the raked roof let in sunlight and frame views to the trees and sky.

Above:
The brick base contains a series of hose-out spaces and satisfies planning controls around flooding.

Top left:
A bedroom window seat provides an ideal place to soak up the sunshine and garden view.

Top right:
The planting selection complements the tones and textures of the home's materials palette.

Bottom:
The lightweight kitchen and dining extension hovers over the water flow path during flooding.

The lived experience

Queensland's tall blue skies, bright sunshine and verdant subtropical greenery is alluring to those who live in the cooler southern states of Australia. Owners Liz Evans and partner Cameron Brooks both grew up in Tasmania, but the appeal of warmer weather and an active outdoor lifestyle all year round took them north to Brisbane. When approaching an architect to design their home, the couple wanted to celebrate the Queensland way of life that they were so drawn to – a life genuinely lived outdoors.

One of the more unfortunate aspects of the Queensland weather is a susceptibility to erratic swings in weather such as strong La Niña weather patterns and tropical cyclones causing severe flooding. Beck Street House in Brisbane's Paddington, built for Liz and Cameron, is located in the Brisbane flood zone. This put the couple's brief of a seamless indoor–outdoor connection into conflict with its site's constraints but, undeterred, architect Michael Lineburg of Lineburg Wang chose to use this conflict as a driver for the conceptual design for the alteration and addition to the 1960s home.

A masonry undercroft is retained to the front of the site, now functioning as a semi-formal colonnade entry, and a lightweight kitchen and dining room extension hovers over the western water flow path, braced against the half-height terrain created by retaining walls. The primary outdoor gathering space is also nestled and elevated at the rear of the property, where the garden is directly connected to the extension and becomes an integral part of daily life as the family room. 'We pull all the doors back, throw out a couple of picnic blankets or bean bags on the lawn and get the pizza oven going,' shares Liz. 'You're always outside at our house.'

Above:
Nestled at the rear of the property, the main outdoor gathering space is directly connected to the extension.

Following:
Old and new elements are seamlessly integrated to create a profound connection to place.

A LIFE LIVED OUTDOORS

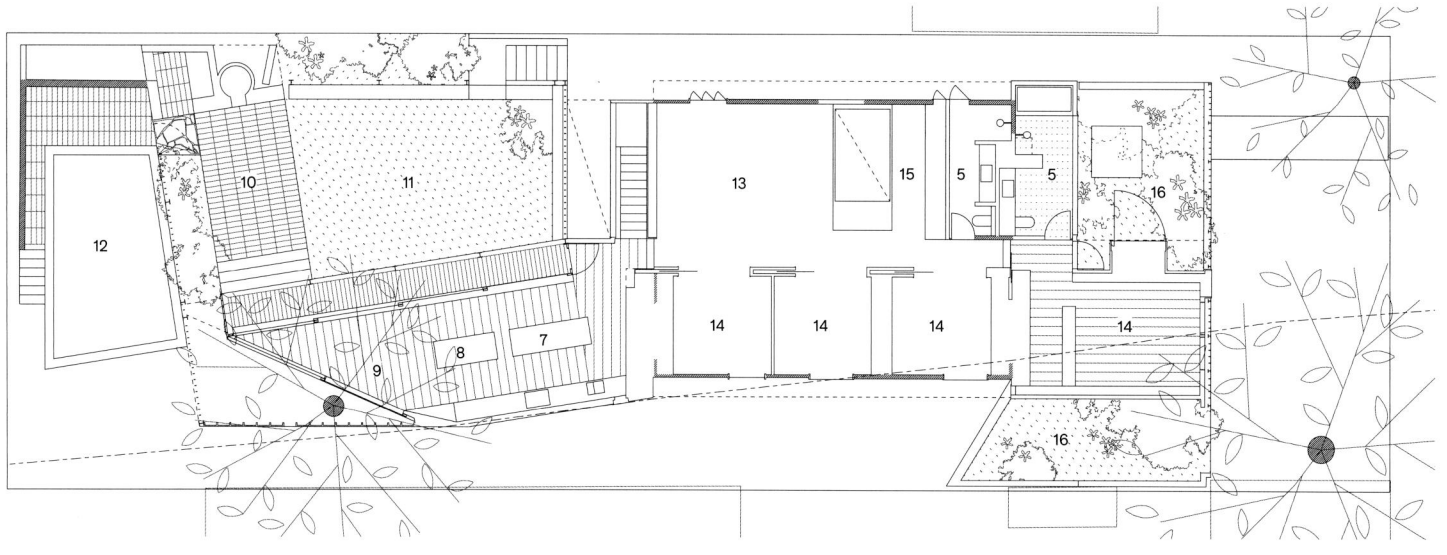

Upper level

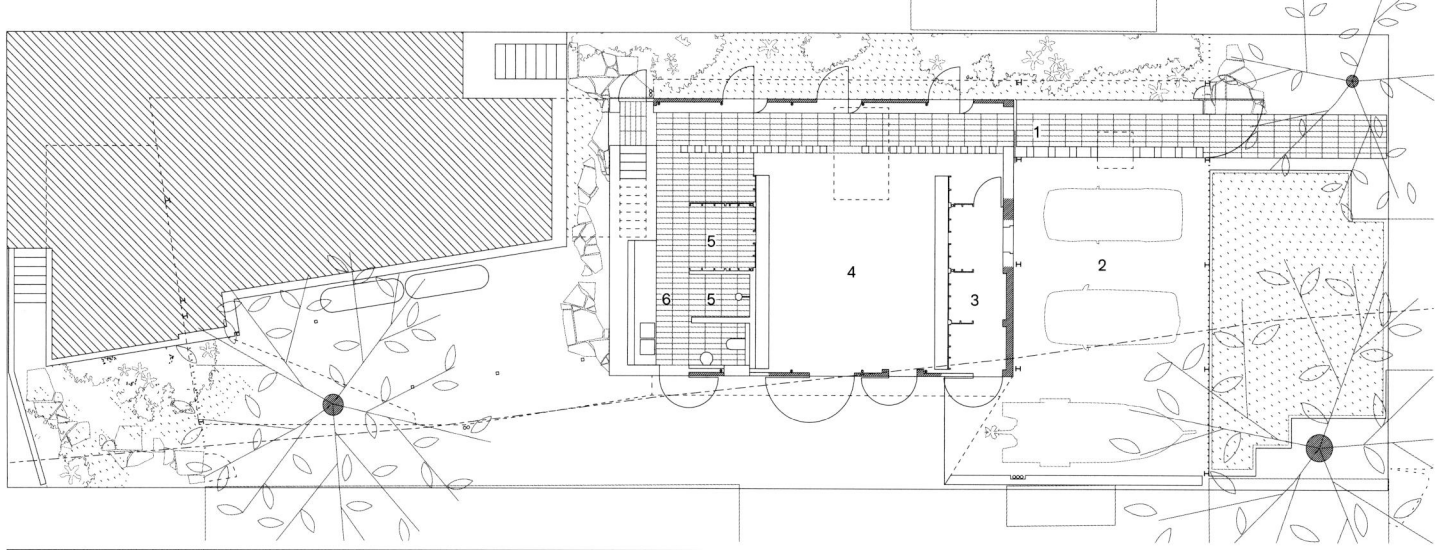

Lower level

1	Entry	9	Sitting
2	Carport	10	Arbour
3	Store	11	Courtyard
4	Flexible space	12	Pool
5	Bathroom	13	Living
6	Laundry	14	Bedroom
7	Kitchen	15	Family study
8	Dining	16	Rooftop garden

1:250

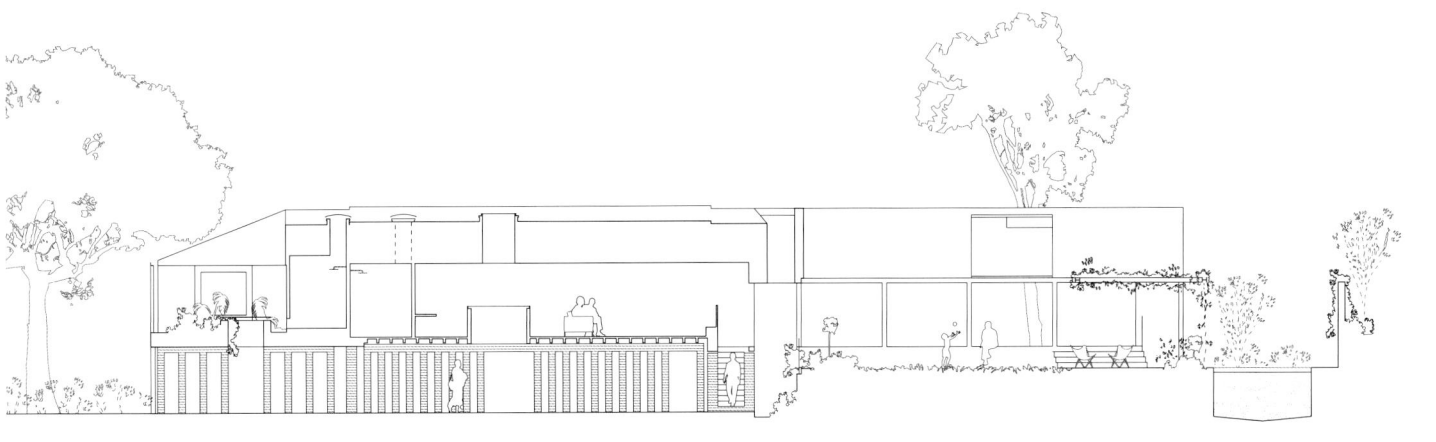

Longitudinal section

1:250
0 5m

Architect — Lineburg Wang
Project team — Michael Lineburg, Lynn Wang
Builder — Struss Constructions
Structural engineer — Optimum Structures
Civil consultant — Storm Water Consulting
Town planner — Property Projects Australia
Certifier — Cornerstone Building Certification
Photographer — Christopher Frederick Jones

Earl Parade

Manly, Brisbane
Cavill Architects

Completed – 2020
Project type – New build
Total site area – 506 m²
Internal area – 164 m²
External area – 40 m²
Number of residents – 4
Number of bedrooms – 4
Number of bathrooms – 3

Earl Parade is built on the land of the Quandamooka people

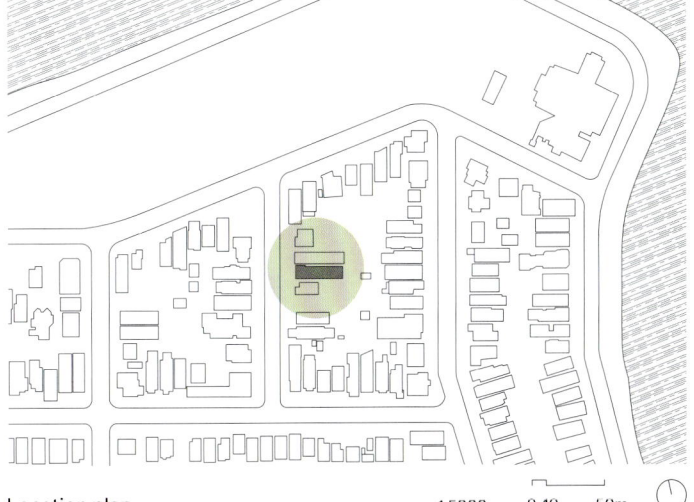

Location plan   1:5000   0 10   50m

The architectural setting

Manly Beach Estate was developed for house allotments in the late 19th century. This seaside Brisbane suburb is located on the picturesque, mangrove-lined edge of Moreton Bay. The relaxed character of the contemporary suburb retains much of the charm and scale of its fishing village past.

Cavill Architects' Earl Parade is located within proximity of the lively foreshore and boat harbour and the architectural language of this home is informed by the landscape setting and its architectural history. In a thoughtful nod to the simplicity of the fibro beach shacks of the mid-20th century, the outer shell of the building is a crisp, white, asymmetrical portal that is clad in flat wall sheeting dressed by simple cover battens. This practical architectural envelope is carved out and pierced to create the immersive, double-height garden room that runs right through the building, connecting its public and private facades, a project-defining architectural motif that has been thoughtfully deployed in residential, public and commercial projects by the generation of architects that Cavill Architects is contemporary with (see B&B Residence by Hogg and Lamb, page 292).

Earl Parade has a clarity and economy that elevates it from a one-off residential project to a replicable model for the development of smaller lot, compact housing across Brisbane.

Previous:
At Earl Parade, the architectural envelope has been carved out to create a double-height garden room.

Opposite:
The home was designed to be private, yet not let the family 'hide from one another.'

Above:
With generous volume and permeability, the garden room is the heart of the home.

The lived experience
When clients Tara and Paul Gardiner approached architect Sandy Cavill of Cavill Architects to design their new home in Brisbane's Manly, they had one young son and another on the way. They asked Sandy for a home with an openness that would enable genuine family interaction, yet was private to the outside world.

At the core of this family's sanctuary is a lush grove within the frame of an outdoor room. The edges of this central hub are permeable to the various interior spaces on the ground floor as well as the rooms above, promoting genuine interactivity between zones. 'We didn't want a house that we could hide from one another in,' Tara says. Cavill Architects' internal spatial arrangement disrupts the distinction between indoors and outdoors through composed moments of connection and inhabitation. The two-storey volume captures breezes and light via choreographed openings to the sky and backyard, and the garden spine spills into the backyard via wide timber steps.

The architects worked with Green Care Project and landscape architect Dan Young. Plant choices in the grove and backyard respond to the warm and humid climate. An orange trumpet creeper (*Pyrostegia venusta*) flowers during late autumn and winter and adds a warmth to the interior of the home and a young flowering gum (*Corymbia ficifolia*) in the backyard will eventually add a pop of colour in the summer months. In this house, it's not the kitchen that is the heart of the home, it's the gardens – internally and externally.

Opposite:
Making a civic contribution, the garden room facilitates interaction with the streetscape.

Above:
Inside, the tactile materials palette enhances a connection with the lush planting.

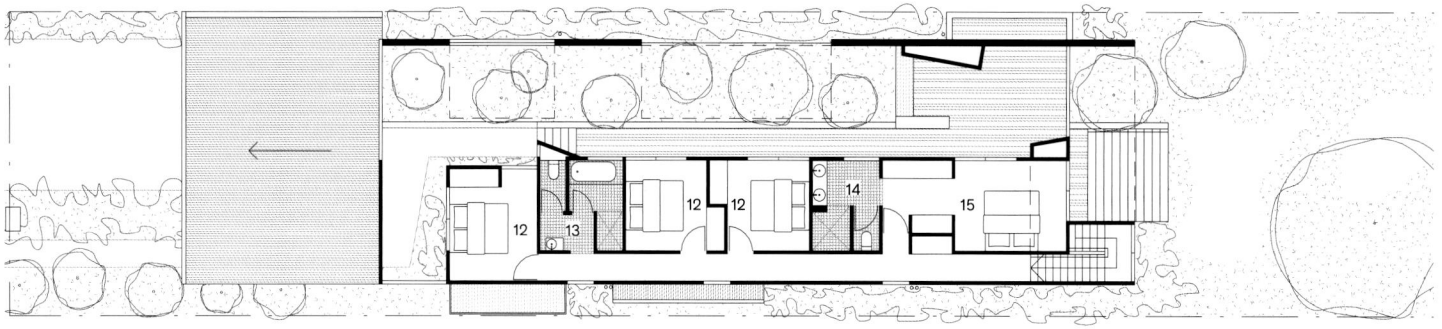

First floor

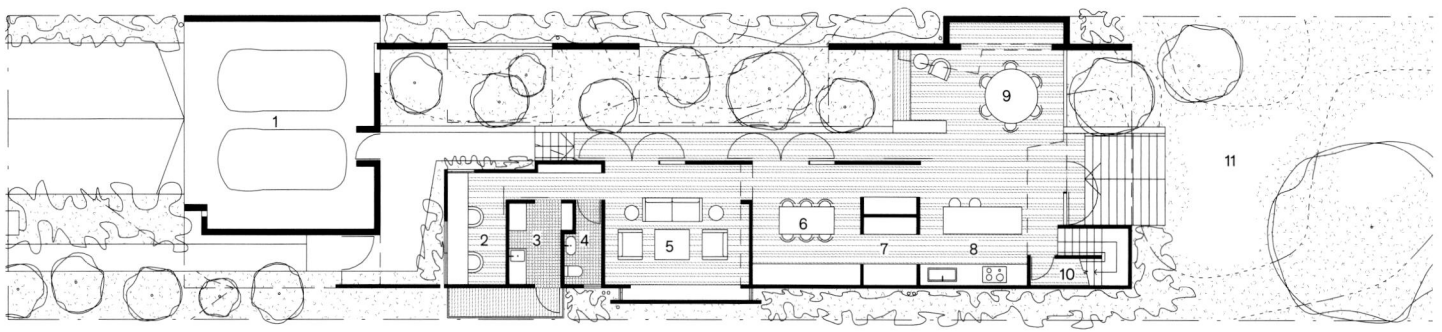

Ground floor

1	Carport		9	Outdoor room
2	Study		10	Store
3	Laundry		11	Garden
4	Powder room		12	Bedroom
5	Living		13	Bathroom
6	Dining		14	Ensuite
7	Pantry		15	Main bedroom
8	Kitchen			

1:250

0   5m

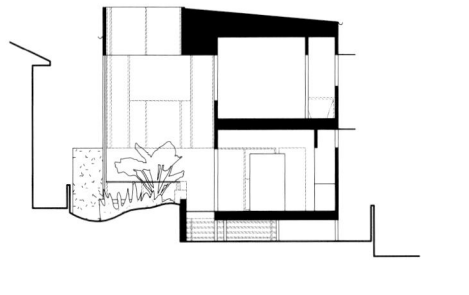

Cross section

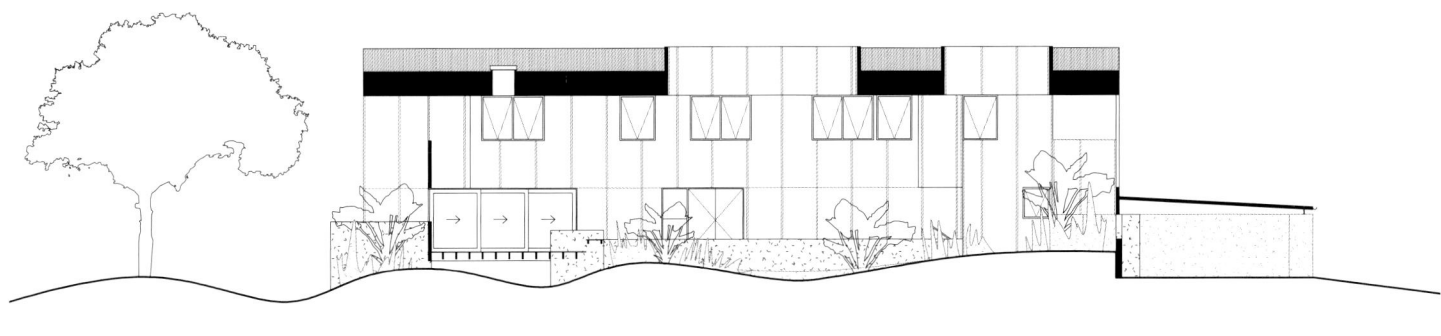

Longitudinal section

1:250
0   5m

Architect — Cavill Architects
Project team — Sandy Cavill, Andrew D'Occhio, Christopher Kotmel
Builder — Concord Built
Structural engineer — Optimum Structures
Landscape architect — Dan Young Landscape Architect
Landscape — Green Care Project
Photographer — Christopher Frederick Jones

La Scala

Bowen Hills, Brisbane
Richards & Spence

Completed – 2021
Project type – New build
Total site area – 604 m²
Internal area – 310 m²
External area – 604 m²
Number of residents – 2 (main dwelling)
Number of bedrooms – 2–3
Number of bathrooms – 3 + powder room + outdoor shower

La Scala is built on the land of the Turrbal and Yuggera peoples

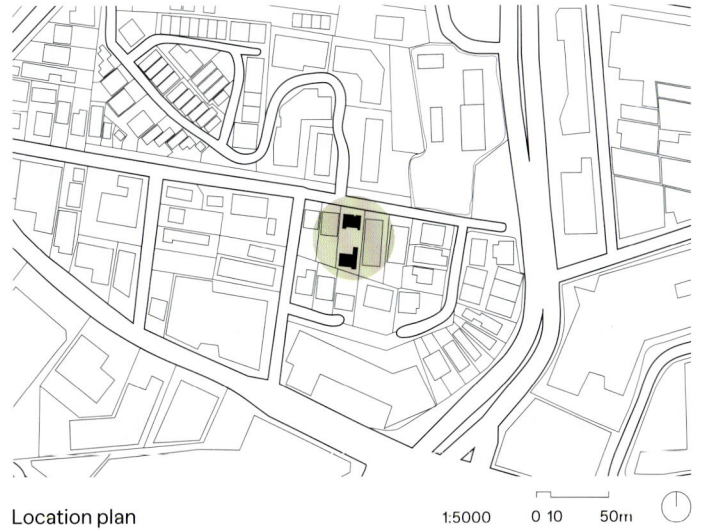

Location plan 1:5000 0 10 50m

Previous:
Conceived as a ruin, La Scala's white concrete blocks with horizontal coursing appropriate a stone wall.

Above:
The multi-occupancy structure portrays refined brutalism with a subtropical character.

The architectural setting

The focus on functionality and efficiency in the modernist architecture of the 20th century created new, use-specific building types, including the carpark, the office and the tall apartment tower. Many of these innovative structures have had a much shorter lifespan than the highly adaptable and resilient buildings of the 19th century.

The timber and tin Queenslander houses of the suburbs have been used as single dwellings, rudimentarily divided in times of economic downturn to create small, self-contained flats, and easily adapted to create offices or shops. In the former dockside areas like Teneriffe and Newstead, the handsome red brick warehouses – designed by leading architects of the early 20th century to facilitate the profitable trade in wool and gold – have had enduring relevance through conversion from their century-long use for commerce and industry to uplifting spaces for apartment living and urbane lifestyles.

At La Scala by Richards & Spence, in the enviable hillside setting of Bowen Hills, the lessons of modernism and the architectural values of the 19th century find equally firm repose. Located on the periphery of a mixed-use commercial zone, this striking villa is the calling-card for its architects' pursuit of a refined and gentle brutalism that has a unique subtropical character. The building is configured as a multi-occupancy structure, with handsome rooms that are largely unprogrammed, and this approach predicts a long life and anticipates future uses that respond to the changing character of the city.

Above:
Private spaces of the home offer
a sense of familiarity while echoing
elements of hotel design.

Above:
Rooms are largely unprogrammed,
anticipating changing uses and
allowing the building to have a long life.

The lived experience

When we invite guests into our home, we usually entertain them in our 'good room' – and in the case of La Scala by architects and owners Ingrid Richards and Adrian Spence, the 'good room' is clearly the garden. This is an urban oasis of lush exotic plants draped over a collection of stepped masonry walls, animated by the subtle shimmers of the pool as gentle breezes move through. With two discreet masonry buildings planned at the north and south of the site, a sense of interiority is given to the outdoor zone and disorientates the visitor's awareness of where they are in the world. 'In the pool, you can look up and not see any buildings at all,' notes Ingrid. 'You can float on your back in the pool and feel like you're somewhere else.'

Designed to be functional for two people or a party of seventy people, the home's organising element is always the garden. The kitchen is positioned for a simple transition between inside and outside, allowing the house to easily shift into party mode. 'Everyone knows how it operates now – all we need to do is throw rugs and cushions out on the lawn.' The opportunity of occupying the house in different ways over time is also embraced, as explained by Ingrid: 'We wanted to make a building that could evolve over time. A non-prescriptive building that could be a home, an office, a gallery or a restaurant.'

Embracing this outdoor room as an integral part of day-to-day life keeps Ingrid and Adrian (and their many guests) acutely in touch with the seasons. 'One week we have the fire on and the next week we swim. The focus shifts from fire to pool, but it's always on what we do in the outdoor space.'

Opposite:
With a pared-back palette of concrete and masonry, the interior can be adapted for a variety of uses.

Above left:
The robust yet refined concrete interior could serve as a home, an office or even a restaurant.

Above right:
Design details effortlessly reference the work of Italian architect Carlo Scarpa (1906–1978).

Following:
Two masonry buildings are arranged around the garden, or 'the good room,' the smaller one addressing the street.

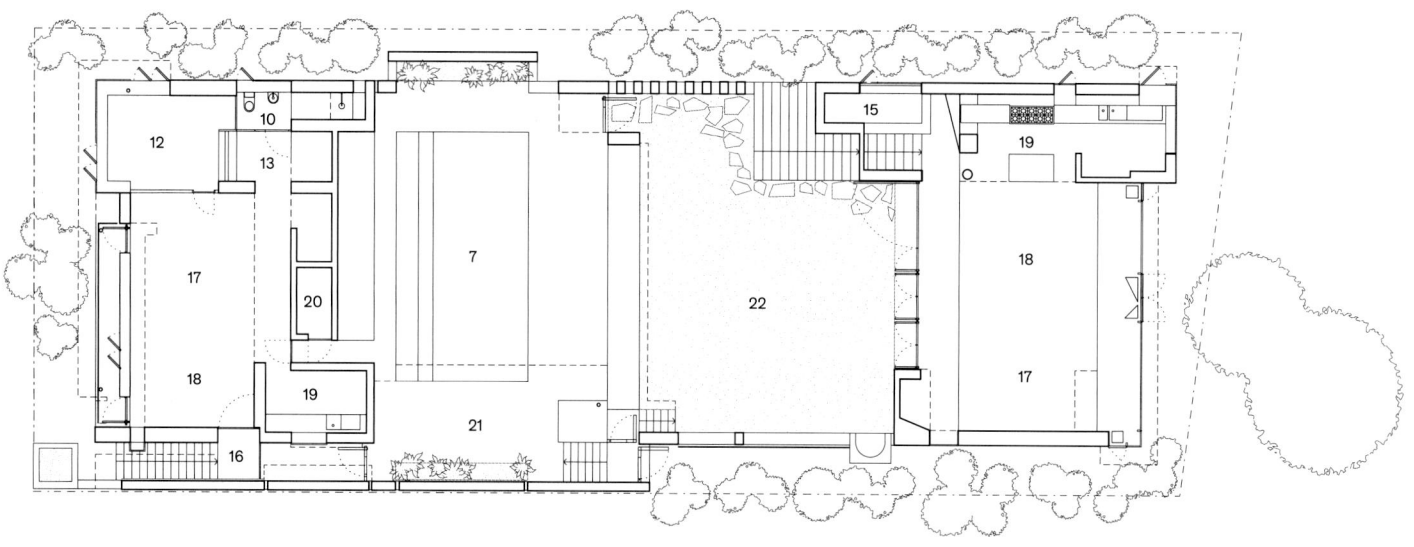

First floor

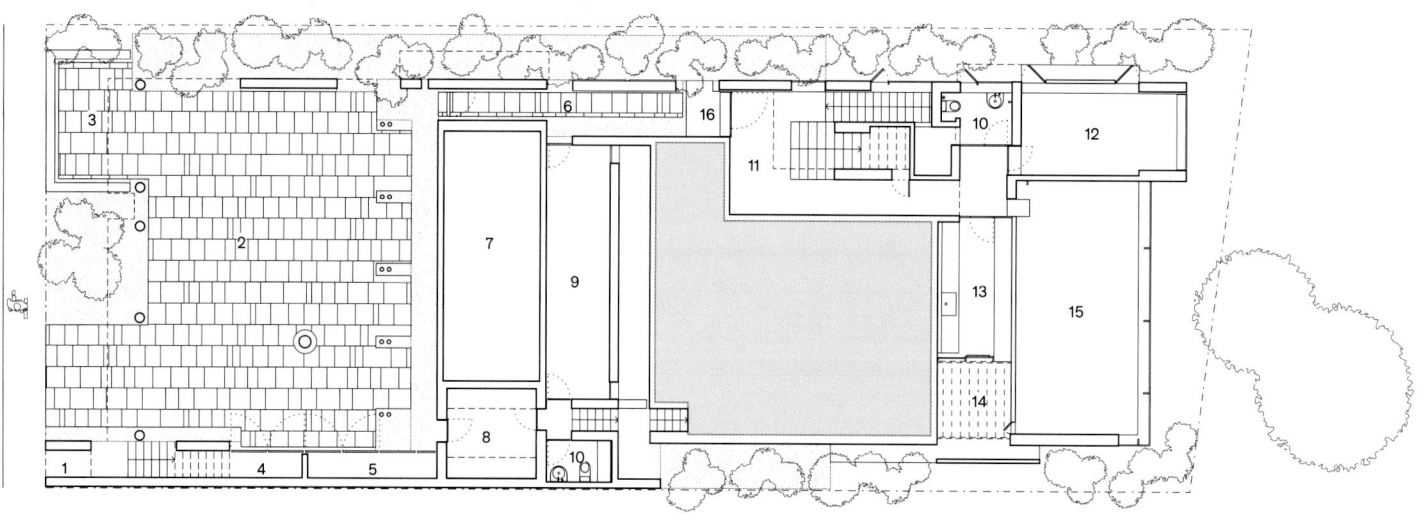

Ground floor

1	Gatehouse	12	Bedroom
2	Garage	13	Laundry
3	Terrace	14	Drying
4	Bin store	15	Void
5	Store	16	Entry
6	Covered link	17	Living
7	Pool	18	Dining
8	Steam room	19	Kitchen
9	Cellar	20	Pool Store
10	Bathroom	21	Outdoor room
11	Foyer	22	Lawn

1:250

0   5m

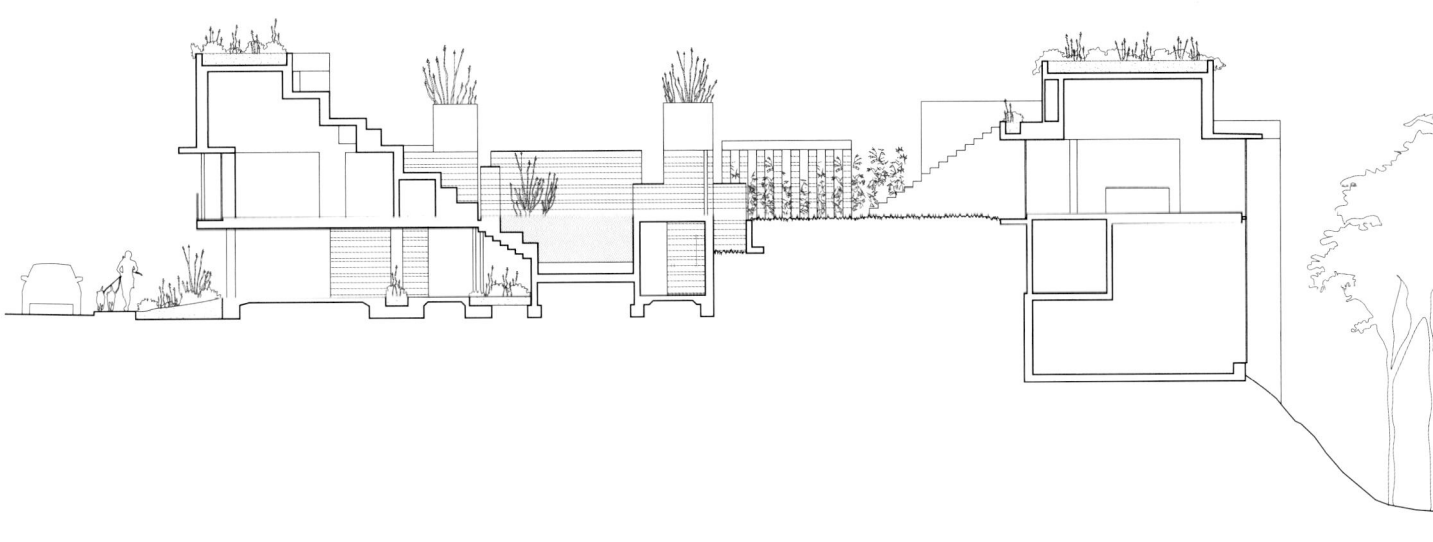

Longitudinal section

1:250
0   5m

Architect — Richards & Spence
Project team — Adrian Spence and Ingrid Richards
Structural engineer — Westera Partners
Photographer — David Chatfield

A home in the landscape

The landscapes of Queensland are diverse, from tropical islands to sandy beaches, flat river plains to elevated plateaus. The state's four climate zones – tropical, subtropical, hot arid and warm temperate – call for nuanced architectural design that maximises comfort all year round. In these projects the architect has set up a special relationship between the house and its landscape setting, blurring, celebrating and finessing the relationship between the built and natural worlds. The awe-inspiring scale and other-worldly presence of the landscape shapes the design response – scenic, distant views are captured in large expanses of glazing and carefully framed openings, and building forms warp and nestle into their site, with vegetation that envelops the house and animates the interior.

Cape Tribulation House

Cape Tribulation, Daintree National Park
m3architecture

Completed – 2013
Project type – New build
Total site area – 12,000 m²
Internal area – 181 m²
External area – 133 m²
Number of residents – 10 (formally) or 20 (informally)
Number of bedrooms – 3–4
Number of bathrooms – 2.5

Cape Tribulation House is built on the land of the Eastern Kuku Yalanji people

Location plan 1:5000 0 10 50m

The architectural setting

Queensland has almost 7000 kilometres of mainland coastline and along the Pacific Ocean coast there are a small number of north-facing, protected beaches that create an idyllic, seaside escape.

At Cape Tribulation, in Tropical North Queensland, the tangle of the ancient rainforest rolls right down to meet the white sand and shimmering blue water of one of these exquisite environments. This remote headland is a meeting point for the World Heritage Listed Daintree Rainforest and the Great Barrier Reef, and the discreet Cape Tribulation hamlet is encircled by the vast rainforest. This Wet Tropics ecosystem sustains many endemic animals, including the Daintree River ringtail possum, Bennett's tree-kangaroo and the endangered southern cassowary.

This pristine and engaging setting is the site for the architectural escapism of the climate-responsive Cape Tribulation House by Brisbane-based m3architecture. Clad in black plastic and mirrored glass, this immersive, off-the-grid house has been designed to disappear into the lush vegetation and has been positioned in a natural clearing to ensure that no mature trees were removed. The architectural rigour of the Cape Tribulation House and the poised choreography of the landscape experience creates the perfect backdrop for getting away from it all.

Previous:
A boardwalk leads from the beach to a series of pavilions that make up Cape Tribulation House.

Opposite:
Clad in black plastic and mirrored glass, the off-the-grid structure disappears into the landscape.

Above:
Rather than fighting the forest, the house was designed to occupy the site on the forest's terms.

The lived experience

Camping in remote locations allows for a complete immersion into the natural world. Carey Lyon and his family regularly escape Melbourne's concrete jungle (that they call home) to enjoy the rugged ecology of Queensland's Daintree Rainforest, the lands of the Eastern Kuku Yalanji. To secure this part of the world as a second home, the Lyon family purchased a plot of partly cleared freehold land where the rainforest meets the reef and invited m3architecture to design them a holiday home, now known as Cape Tribulation House.

The rainforest ecosystem is continuous across the arbitrary property boundaries and minimising the impact on the land was of primary concern. The footprint of the holiday house has been carefully positioned within existing clearings and a loose rope, elegantly draped between the trees, guides the holidaymaker along a gentle path up a boardwalk to the house, where the rope becomes an animating and practical architectural device. This meandering path continues to become the spine of the dwelling with the built form broken down into dark-coloured hovering pavilions grafted onto this ordering device. As Carey explains, 'The house occupies the forest on the forest's terms. The house isn't fighting the forest, it is finding equilibrium with the forest.'

More like a semi-permanent campsite than a house, the habitable spaces comprise two wings cranked either side of the path. The nexus of the two wings is the sheltered deck, which Carey describes as 'living central. You sit on this deck and you get the distinct rainforest smells, the noises of birdlife in the impressive tree canopies above and can watch the cassowaries wandering through the wait-a-while creeper vines (*Calamus australis*).' At Cape Tribulation House, the delights of camping meet the comforts of home.

Opposite:
The habitable spaces sit in two wings cranked either side of the path, with a sheltered deck between.

Above:
The bedroom's double-height volume addresses the vast scale of the forest.

Following:
The kitchen and lounge are lined in hoop pine plywood, while full-height glazing adds a luscious green backdrop.

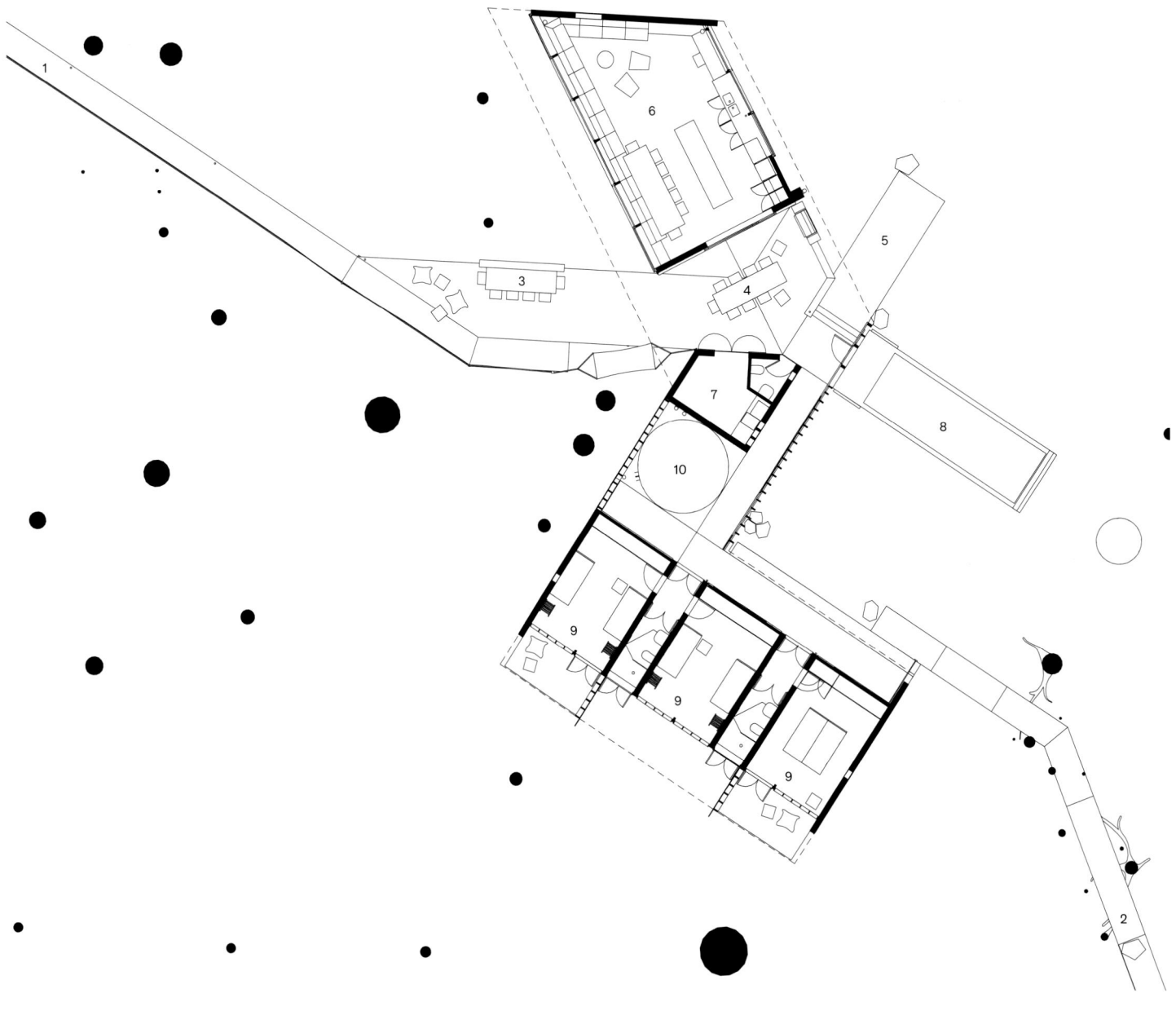

Plan

1:250
0 5m

1 Board walk to road
2 Board walk to beach
3 Canopy deck
4 Breezeway deck
5 Sun deck
6 Living
7 Utility
8 Pool
9 Bedroom
10 Water tank

CAPE TRIBULATION HOUSE

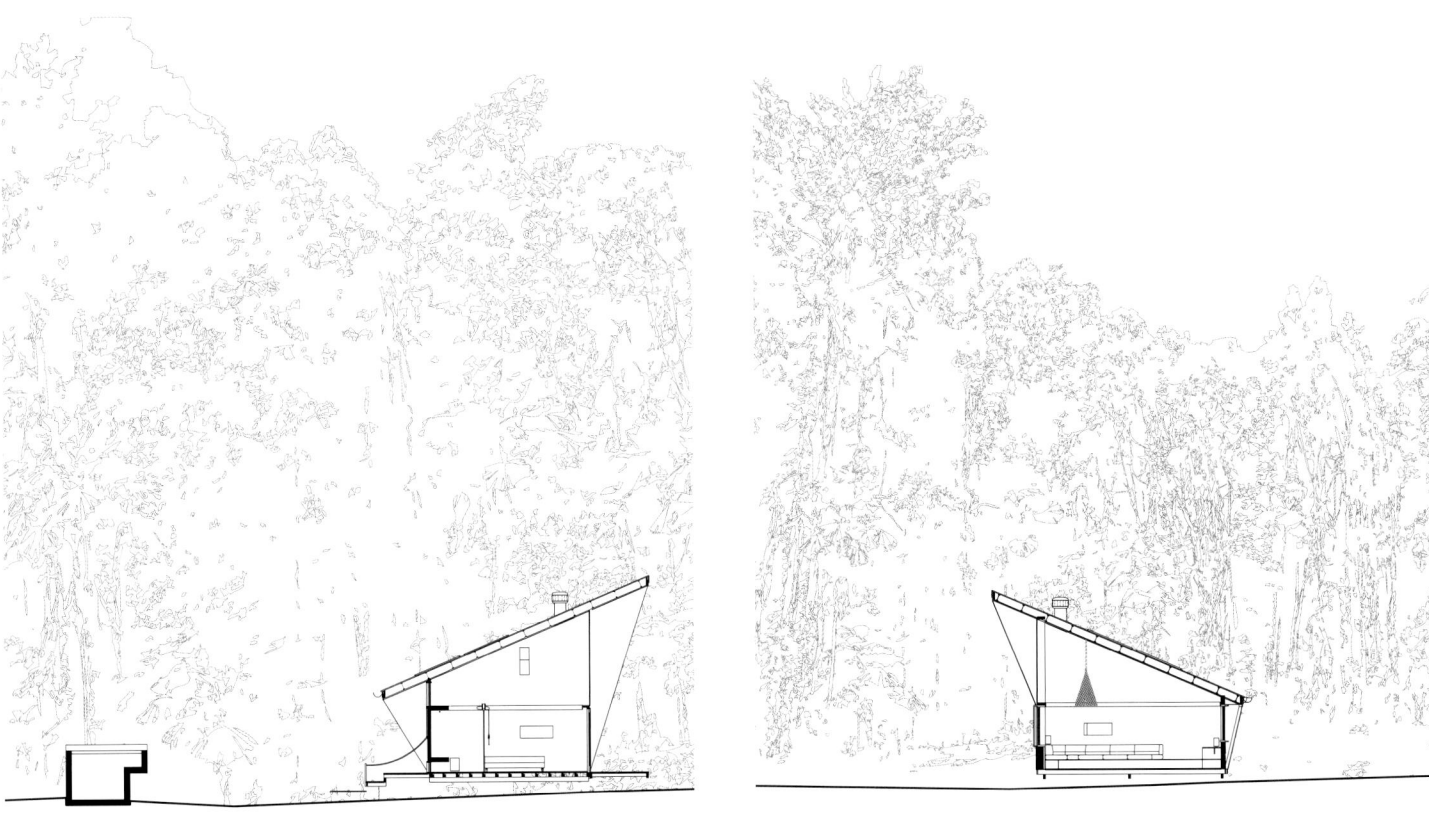

Cross sections

1:250
0   5m

Architect — m3architecture
Project team — Ben Vielle, Michael Banney, Amy L'Estrange
Builder — Keith Tesch Homes
Environmentally sustainable design (ESD) — Integreco
Structural engineer — Mills Engineers and Bligh Tanner
Certifier — GMA Certification Group
Photographer — Peter Bennetts

Jule House

St Lucia, Brisbane
Claire Humphreys and Kevin O'Brien Architects

Completed – 2014
Project type – New build
Total site area – 770 m²
Internal area – 256 m²
External area – 514 m²
Number of residents – 1 + guests
Number of bedrooms – 4
Number of bathrooms – 2

Jule House is built on the land of the Turrbal and Yuggera peoples

Location plan 1:5000

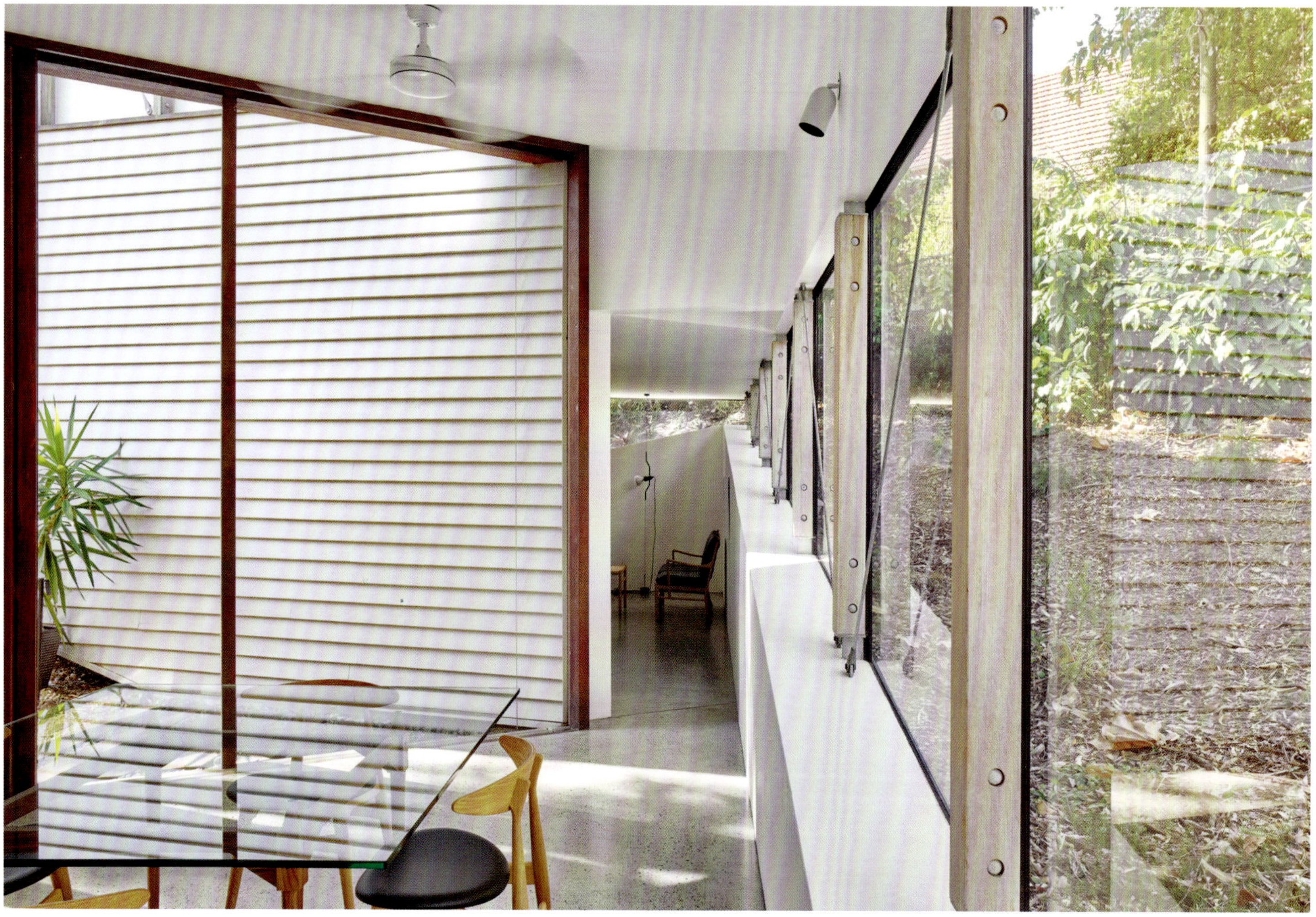

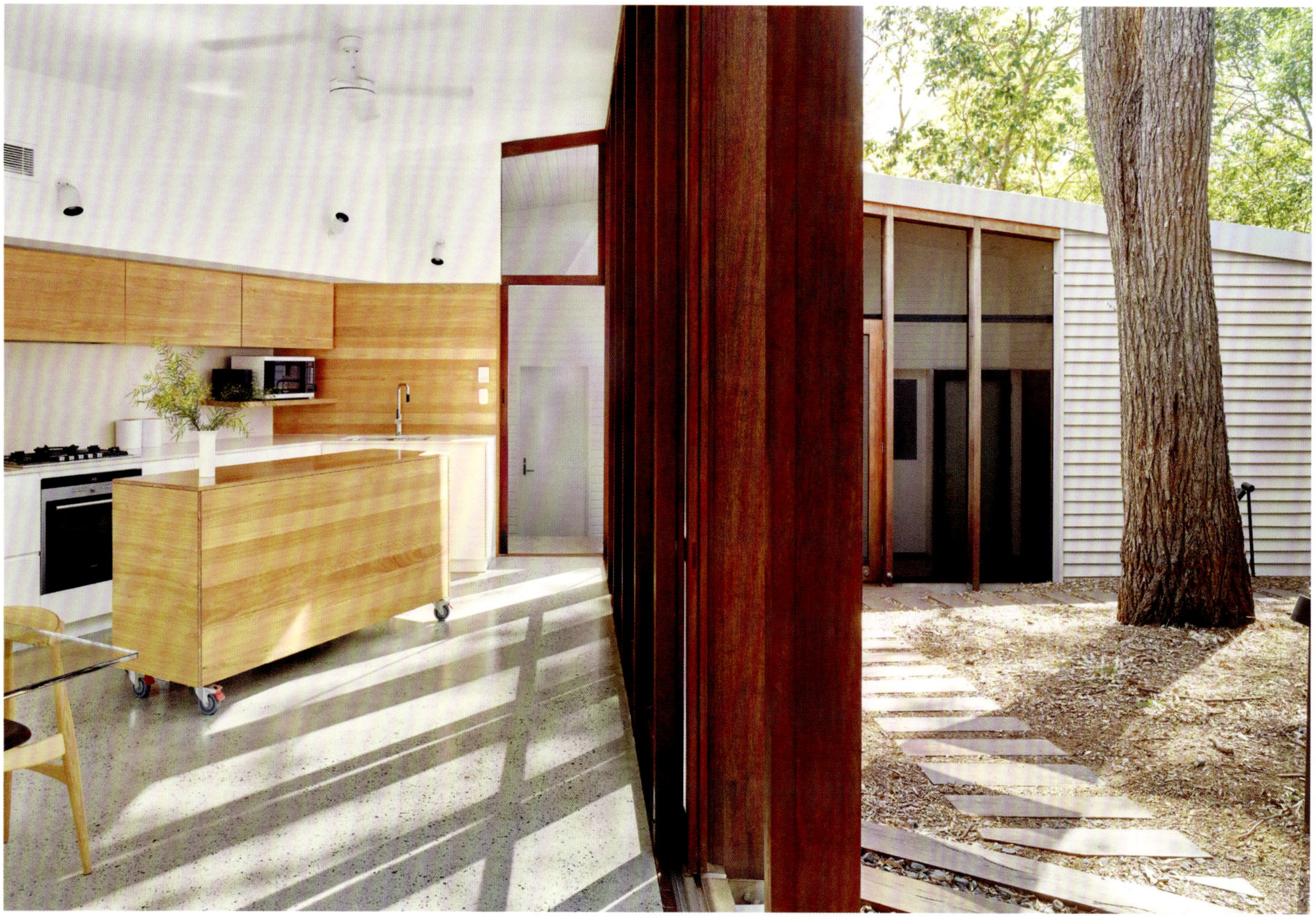

JULE HOUSE

The architectural setting

The leafy suburb of St Lucia is located on a peninsula within a meandering bend of the Brisbane River, seven kilometres south-west of the city centre. The University of Queensland's picturesque campus, which spreads out to the east, welcomed its first students in 1946 and the residences built for the university's emerging academic community in the postwar period are among the city's most venturous modernist homes.

This energetic body of work gained national attention at the time and an article published in *Architecture* magazine in 1950 by Robin Boyd and Peter Newell describes an exciting period of advancement for architecture in Queensland, exemplified through houses built by emerging architects (for themselves and their clients), including works by Hayes and Scott (see EJ Hayes House, page 293) and the work of emigre practitioners, notably Karl Langer (see Langer House, page 293).

Jule House by Claire Humphreys and Kevin O'Brien Architects adds a contemporary layer to the story of innovative residential architecture on the St Lucia peninsula. Located on a challenging, heavily treed, battle-axe subdivision, the house is an ingenious response to the site and the client brief.

Previous
Located on challenging terrain, Jule House is an innovative response to the site and brief.

Opposite top:
A light-filled sitting area is located at the transition between levels, open to landscape views.

Opposite bottom:
The plan folds around a central courtyard in response to existing trees and neighbours.

Above:
Partially cut into the site, the home folds and tilts to engage with the vegetation.

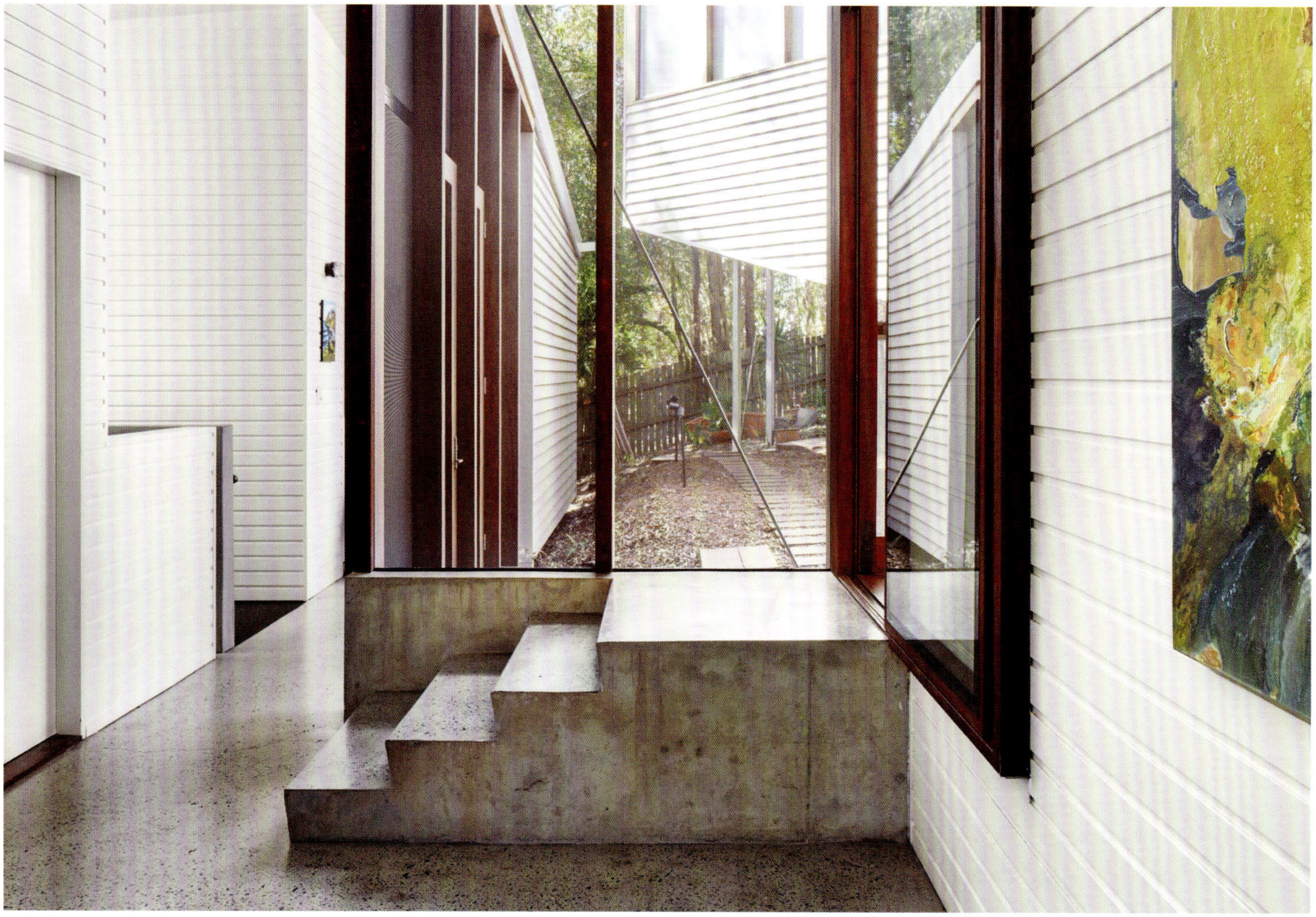

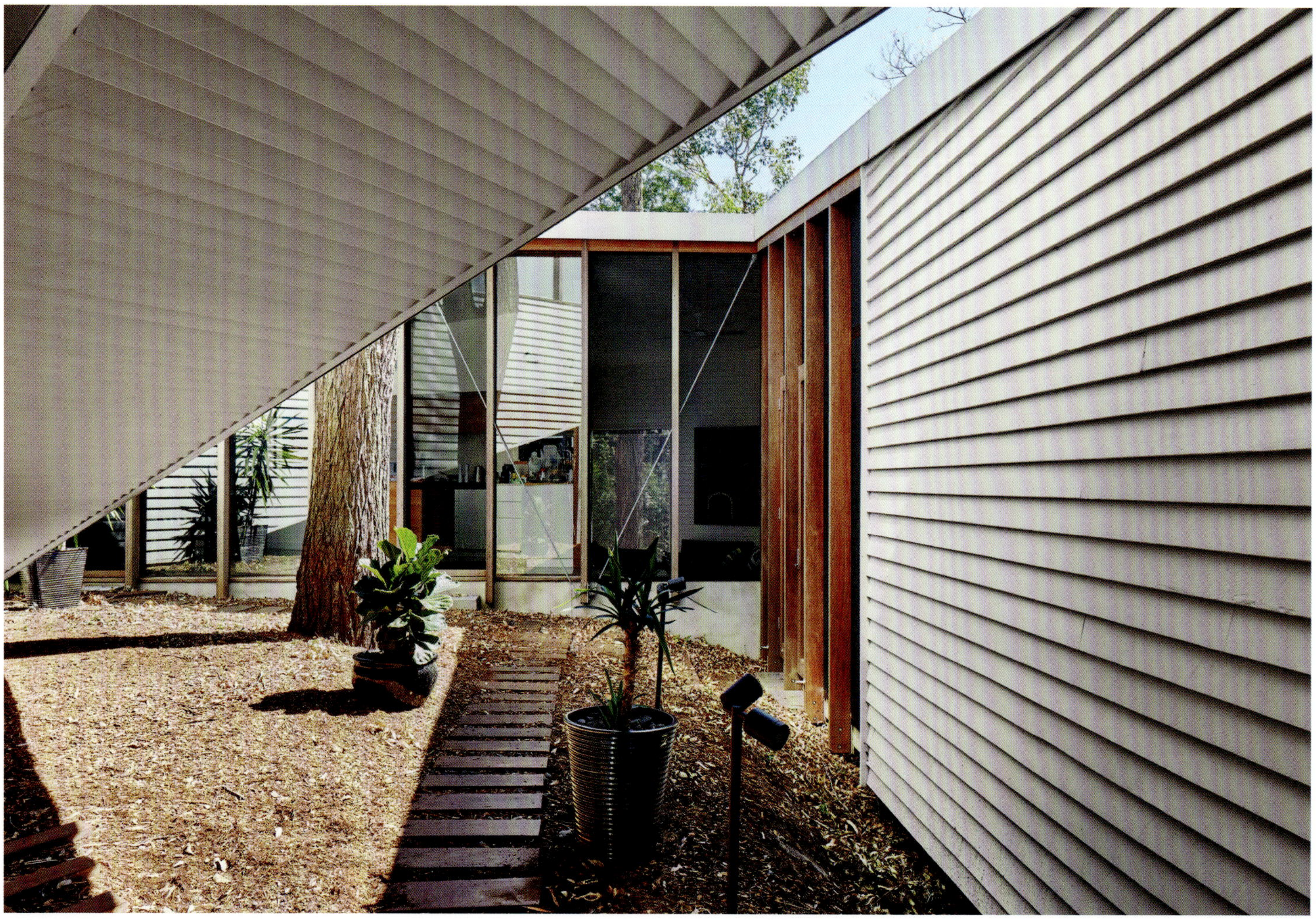

The lived experience

The site for Jule House was home to eight significant trees and a plotted overland flow waterway, creating a challenging set of site parameters for young architectural graduate (at the time) Claire Humphreys and her mentoring architect, Kevin O'Brien. As Claire's mother and owner of Jule House, Julia Shaw said, 'Our lives were run by an arborist for a long time.' As challenging as the site was, Claire had a deep appreciation for its nuances after growing up in the house next door, designed by architect Jon Voller in the 1980s. Affectionately known by Claire and Julia's family as 'the tree house', this house was a useful reference for how to manage the landscape.

A considered response to the landscape is what defines Jule House. Partially cut into the site, the plan and section are crisply bent, folded and tilted, creating interior, exterior and liminal spaces that engage deeply with the retained and tended vegetation, and carefully curate the relationship between the dwelling and the eight neighbouring houses. With walls set into the ground, a different perspective of the landscape is garnered through high-level windows angled along the sloping terrain. Via the unusually shaped courtyard formed by the spiralled plan, the house opens up to a framed view of a green gully swathe to the north-east. A single iron bark tree occupies the courtyard space and its aloneness gives it a monumental presence. The home itself allows for an immersion in the vastness of the bushy suburban landscape, with continual ambiguity between indoors and outdoors.

Opposite top:
Securely screened external circulation enhances the connection with the subtropical climate.

Opposite bottom:
The rise of the stair is expressed externally, while the weatherboard emphasises a connection to the ground.

Above:
Glazing is strategically placed to maintain privacy from neighbouring dwellings.

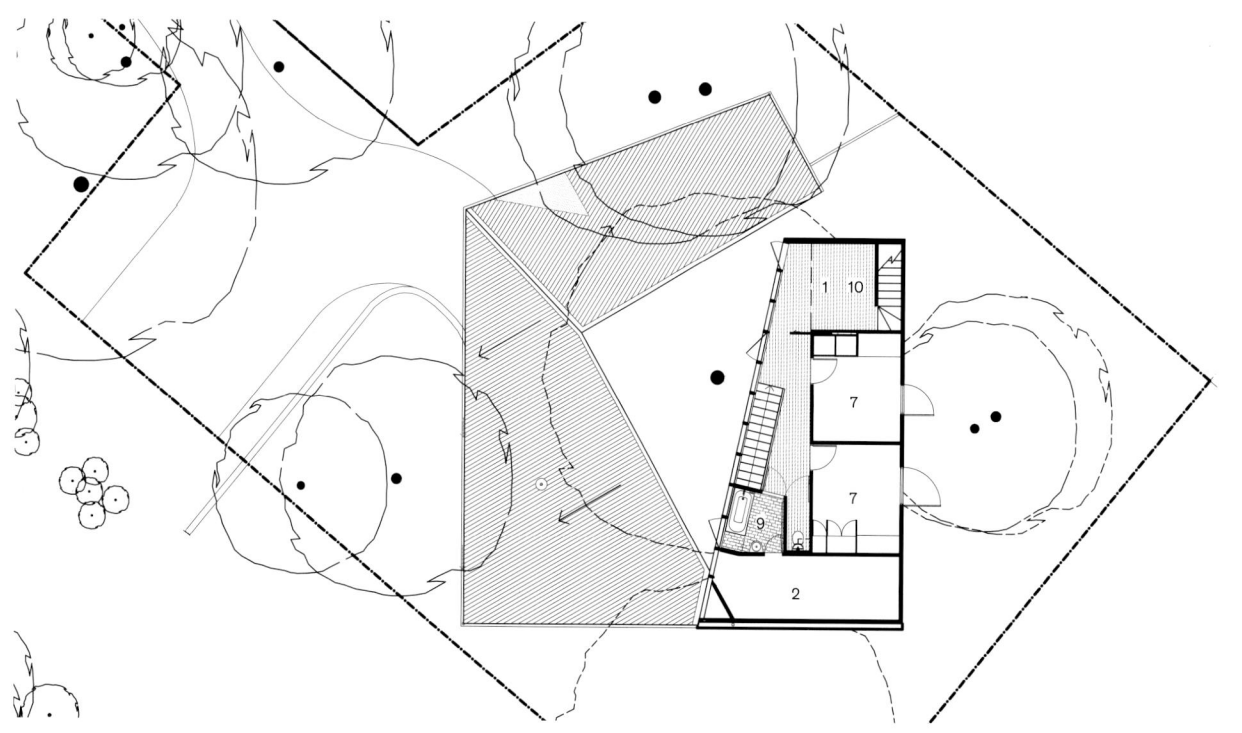

First floor

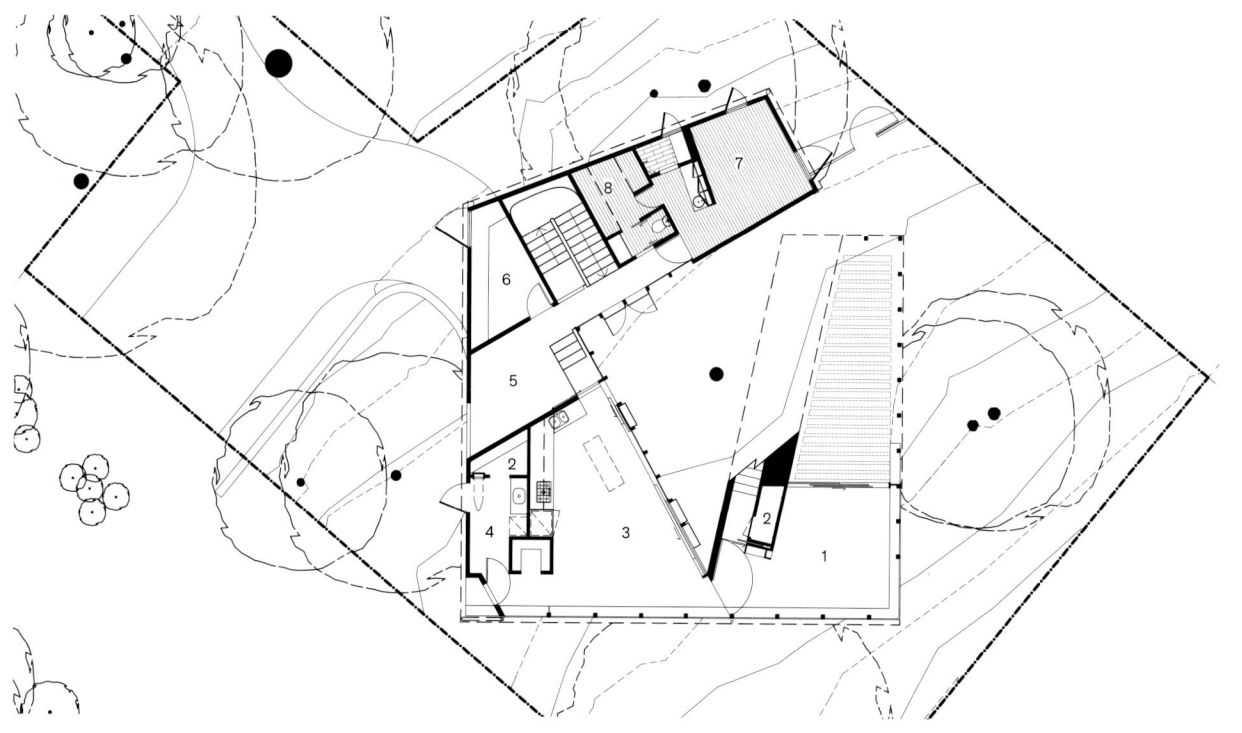

Ground floor

1:250 0 5m

1	Living	6	Study
2	Storage	7	Bedroom
3	Kitchen/dining	8	Robe
4	Utility room	9	Bathroom
5	Deck	10	Loft bedroom above

JULE HOUSE

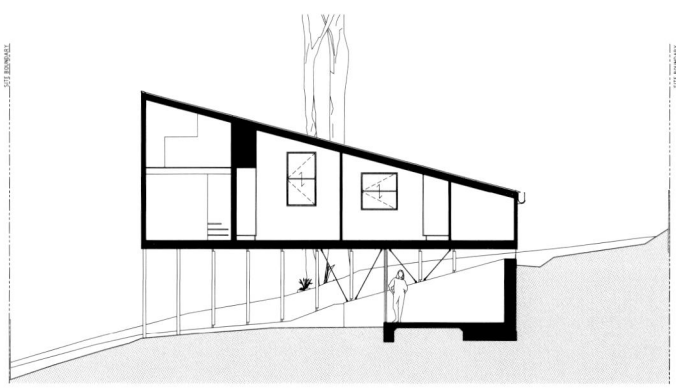

Cross section

West elevation

South elevation

1:250

0   5m

Architect — Claire Humphreys and Kevin O'Brien Architects
Project team — Claire Humphreys and Kevin O'Brien
Builder — Greg Thornton Constructions
Engineer — Terrell Consulting Engineers
Arborist — Heritage Tree Care
Hydraulic engineer — Interior Engineering
Photographer — Toby Scott

Planchonella House

Edge Hill, Cairns
Jesse Bennett Studio

Completed – 2014
Project type – New build
Total site area – 4818 m²
Internal area – 245 m²
External area – 35 m²
Number of residents – 2
Number of bedrooms – 3
Number of bathrooms – 2

Planchonella House is built on the land of the Yirrganydji people

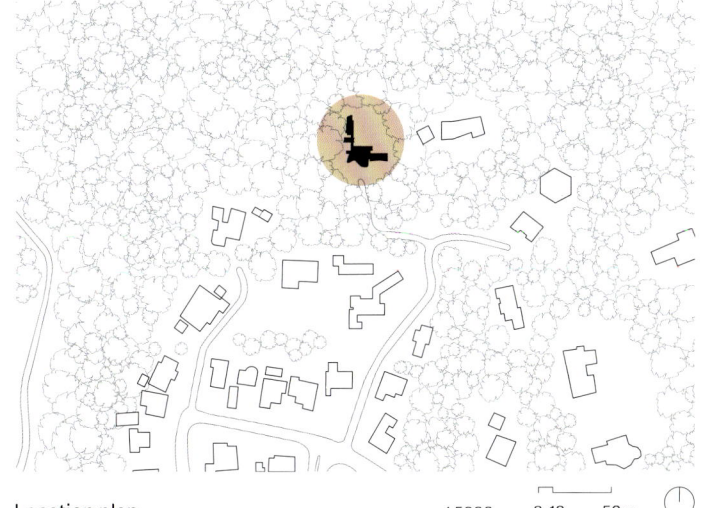

Location plan   1:5000 0 10 50m

The architectural setting

The Australian Institute of Architects launched the National Architecture Awards in 1981 and the program's highest award for residential architecture is named in memory of the mid-century Melbourne architect and critic Robin Boyd.

In the first two decades of the awards program eight Queensland architects received this prestigious gong. More than half of these houses are located on the Sunshine Coast and this exemplary cluster are predominately homes designed by the architects for themselves, including the ground-breaking Tent House by Gabriel Poole (see page 294) and the Pie Residence by Geoffrey Pie (see page 294). The urbane D House by Donovan Hill (see page 292) was the first Robin Boyd winner from Queensland in the new century and in 2015 Jesse Bennett Studio's Planchonella House in the tropical north of the state was recognised.

Bennett is the youngest architect, to date, to be awarded this honour. This enigmatic, climate-responsive villa is deeply immersed in the lush landscape hinterland of Edge Hill, a suburb of Cairns and the location of the city's Botanic Gardens. This is a distinguished work of residential architecture and an enthralling statement about the future direction of its author's collaborative practice.

Previous:
Planchonella House is a climate-responsive villa immersed in a luscious rainforest.

Opposite:
Two curving concrete slabs create the form of the house, with full-height glazing in between.

Above:
A low timber bench against the kitchen servery offers the perfect place to perch and relax.

The lived experience

Architect Jesse Bennett moved from Brisbane to Cairns in Queensland's tropical north with his wife Anne-Marie Campagnolo in 2010. While the couple were in the region visiting Anne-Marie's family, the allure of the majestic tropical rainforest intrigued Jesse. Having grown up on a farm three hours' drive from Cairns, Anne-Marie was more familiar with the extremity of the climate and landscape in this part of the world – but was similarly inspired by the prospect of building a home that genuinely embraces its unique tropical setting.

During Jesse and Anne-Marie's family visits to Tropical North Queensland, Jesse was struck by the way many of the farmers would gather in the timber sheds for a beer or a cup of tea. Shaded and breezy, these structures are akin to cool undercroft spaces. Jesse designed the couple's new home, Planchonella House, taking cues from these simple sheds. Double the area of the floor plate it hovers above, the roof amply protects the internal and external spaces from the harshness of the sun. Breezes pass down the mountain through the wet foliage and are cooled, even in the thick humidity of the summer months, before passing through the home, from back to front.

The harshness of the wet tropical weather dictates the climatic response, but it's the embrace of the forest's immensity that creates the home's calming ambience. 'You open the kitchen window and the energy of the forest is in your house,' says Anne-Marie. Floor-to-ceiling glazed walls give way to unobstructed views to the surrounding landscape from every room, allowing the proven benefits of biophilia to permeate the home. It's a miniature world of delight and escapism.

Opposite:
A high level of craft is evident, with most joinery elements handmade by the architect/owner.

Above left:
Rather than usual flyscreens, curtains can be drawn across windows to protect against insects.

Above right:
The bathtub is at the edge of the structure, creating the feeling of bathing high up in the trees.

Following:
Every room features floor-to-ceiling glazing, allowing for unobstructed views to the rainforest.

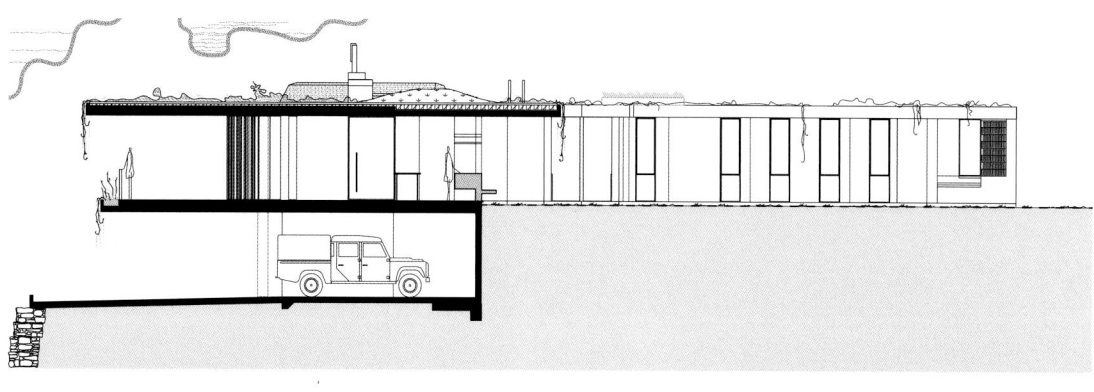
Longitudinal section

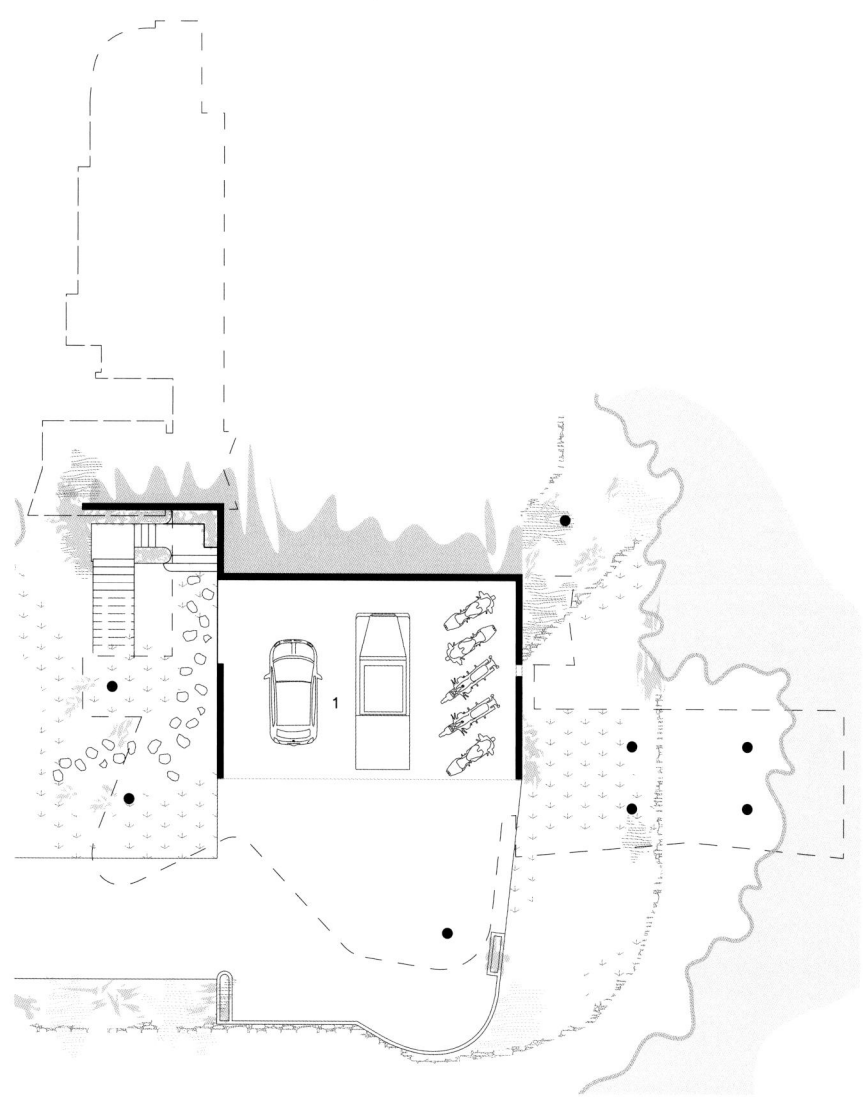
Ground floor

1:250
0 — 5m

1	Carport	8	Bedroom
2	Entry	9	Ensuite
3	Lounge	10	Dressing
4	Dining	11	Study/bedroom
5	Kitchen	12	Bathroom
6	Pantry	13	Laundry
7	Deck	14	Courtyard

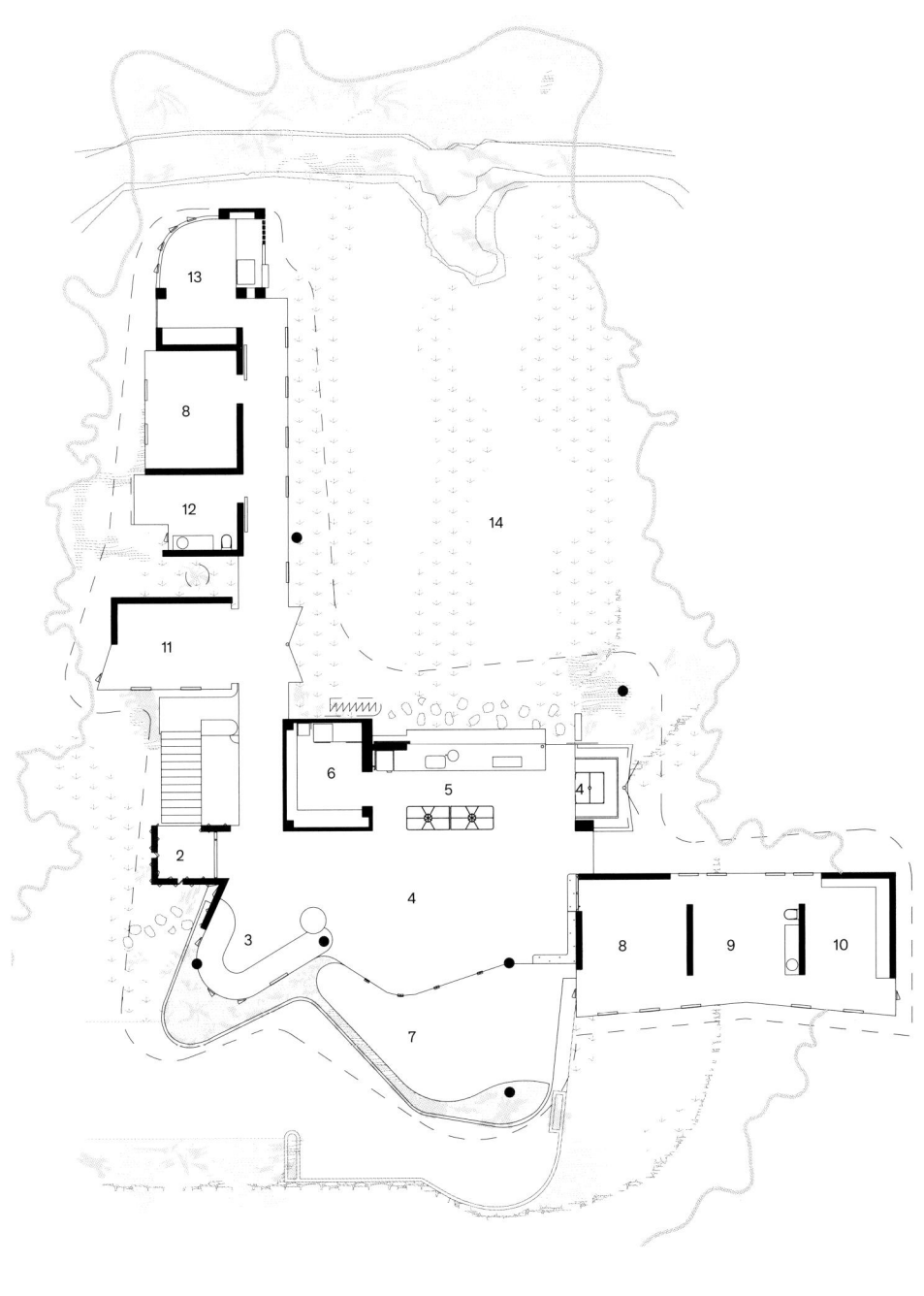

First floor

1:250
0   5m

Architect — Jesse Bennett Studio
Project team — Jesse Bennett and Anne-Marie Campagnolo
Engineer — Kel Bruce Engineers
Interiors — Anne-Marie Campagnolo
Photographer — Sean Fennessy

Moonshine

Minjerribah (North Stradbroke Island)
Brit Andresen Architect

Completed – 2018
Project type – New build
Total site area – 600 m²
Internal area – 125 m²
External area – 120 m²
Number of residents – 6–8
Number of bedrooms – 2–3
Number of bathrooms – 2

Moonshine is built on the land of the Quandamooka people

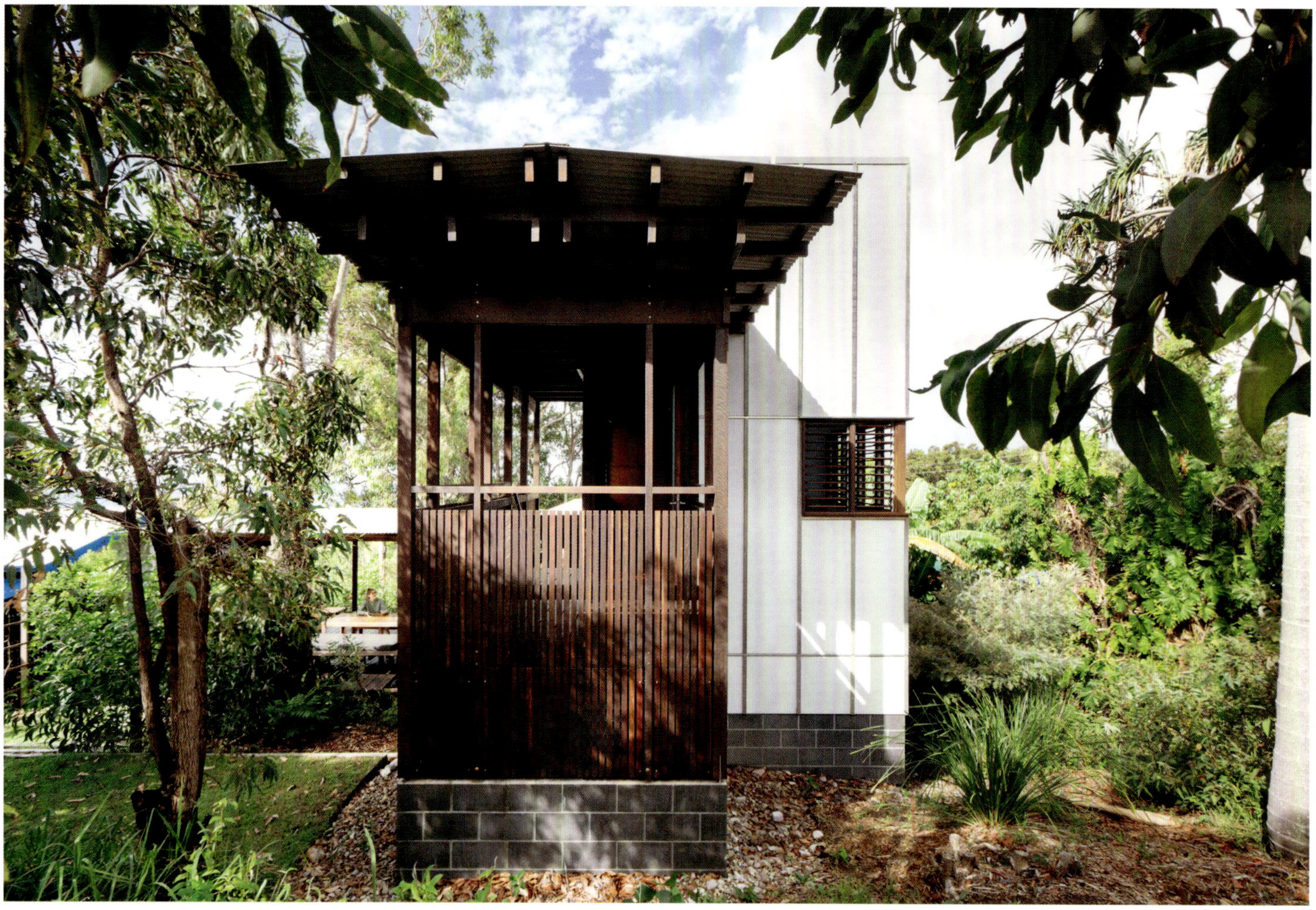

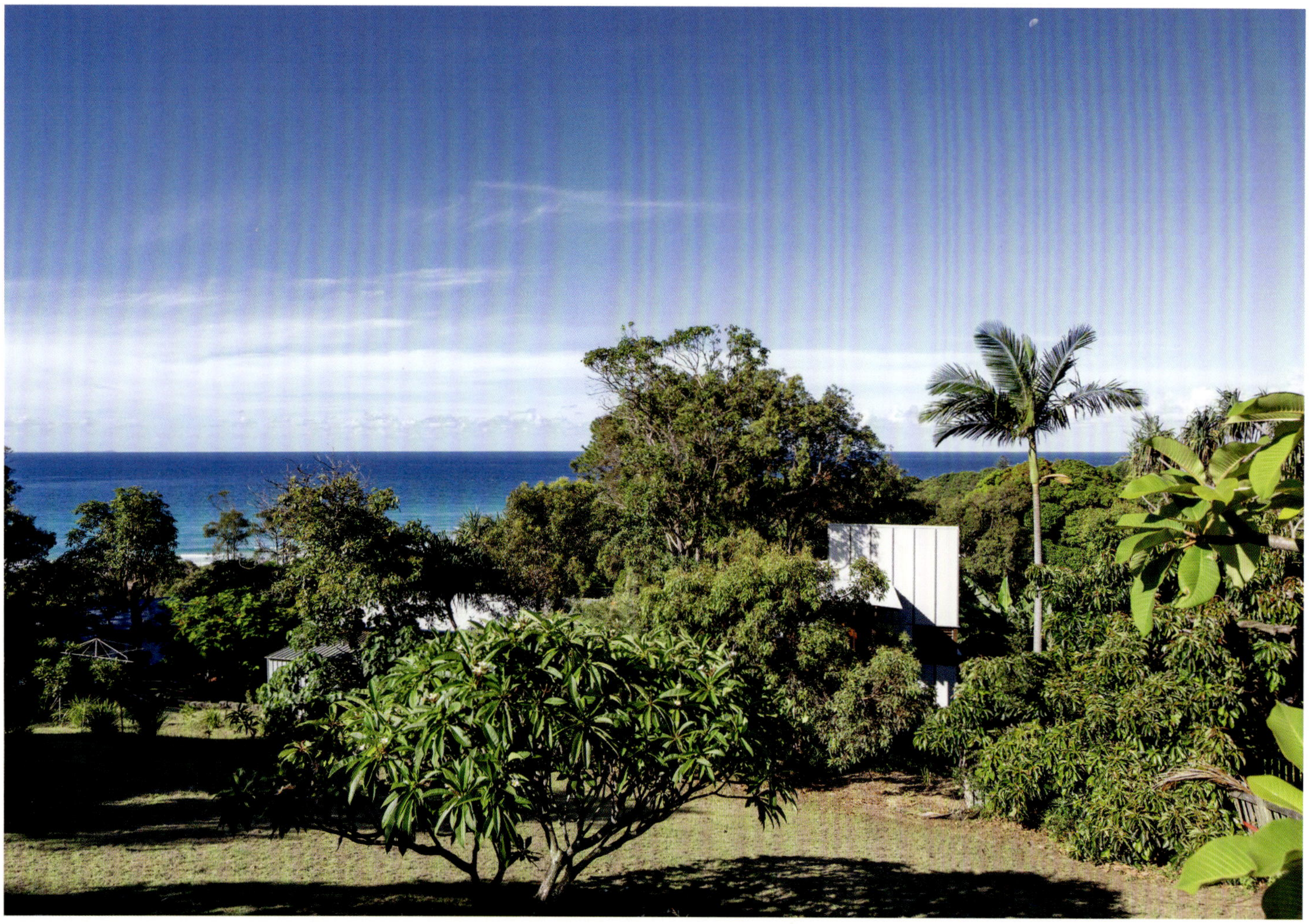

The architectural setting

The calm waters of Moreton Bay are sheltered from the Pacific Ocean's Coral Sea by Moreton, South Stradbroke and North Stradbroke islands. The 2000-square-kilometre bay is home to a rich array of flora and fauna and a significant area is recognised as a wetland of international significance under the Ramsar Convention on Wetlands. North Stradbroke Island is the world's second largest sand island and is known as Minjerribah by the Quandamooka people and laconically referred to as Straddie.

This idyllic coastal environment is home to vibrant local communities and is a discreet seaside holiday destination. Reached from the mainland by car or passenger ferry, this pristine setting is the canvas for a suite of internationally acclaimed and innovative beach houses, the most significant being the 1995 Mooloomba House at Point Lookout by Andresen O'Gorman (see page 293).

Point Lookout is on the north-eastern tip of the island and has a splendid ocean outlook that is animated by passing whales. Near Andresen O'Gorman's iconic house there are works by Donovan Hill, Jennifer Taylor and James Conner (see Dunbar, page 292), and Robert Riddel. Andresen's decades of architectural thinking, collaboration and research are deployed with a gentle hand to create her latest island building at Point Lookout: Moonshine.

Previous:
The dark timber-battened form of Moonshine nestles into its treed and steeply sloping site.

Opposite top:
The design takes cues from the nearby Mooloomba House, designed by Andresen O'Gorman in 1995.

Opposite bottom:
North Stradbroke Island's Point Lookout has ocean views of both Moreton Bay and the Coral Sea.

Above:
A covered deck cascades out into the landscape via terraced steps, removing the need for balustrades.

The lived experience

The dark timber–battened form of Brit Andresen's Moonshine recedes into its treed setting, deferring to the existing magic of Minjerribah. It is finely tuned with the unique experience of being in this subtropical paradise and is calibrated for the joys of a relaxed seaside escape. Resisting the urge to remove trees to enable clear views of the ocean, the home nestles itself into its steeply sloping bushy site and three timber living platforms closely follow this topography. The pavilions are linked by screened and covered external stairs, providing a continual awareness of the weather and seasons. The act of going outside to move from one zone to another clearly focuses the inhabitants' attention on the particular activity being performed – for example, the retreat to one of the bedroom pavilions indicates a transition to the sleeping phase.

Movement paths within the home are indirect and flow inside and outside with ease. A covered deck gently cascades out into the surrounding landscape via terraced timber steps, cleverly removing the need for balustrades. A room outdoors, this is a place to 'lean on ledges, perch on edges, recline on benches and gaze through the trees to the Coral Sea beyond'. The informality of its design invites habitation that suits the time of day, season or mood of the occupants themselves.

When cocooned within the home, a large oculus skylight above the dining table is another device to maintain the inhabitants' awareness of the vastness of the outside world. By day, it provides natural light deep into the plan and in the evening the moon's dim glow permeates into the centre of the home – hence why the owner has come to affectionately refer to the house as Moonshine.

Opposite:
The informality of the outdoor room invites habitation that suits the time of day or season.

Above:
Movement paths through the house indirectly flow inside and outside with ease.

Above:
Three timber living platforms step down the site, with a bunk room and laundry at the lowest level.

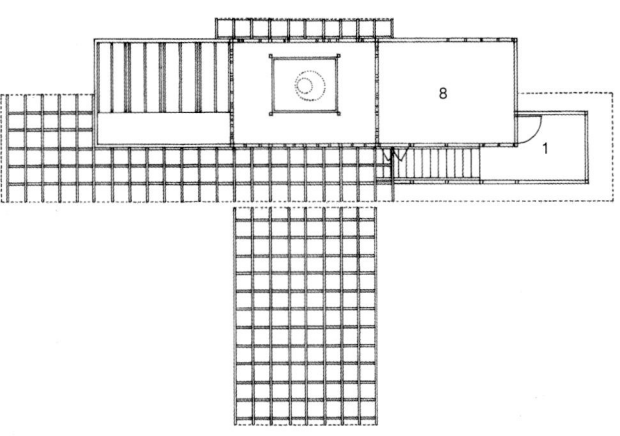

Upper level

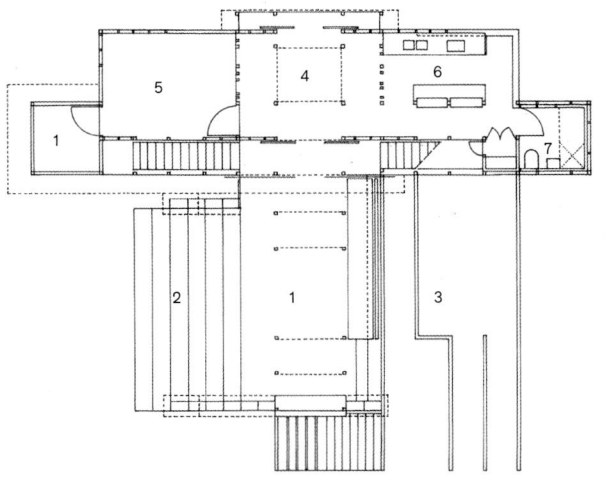

Middle level

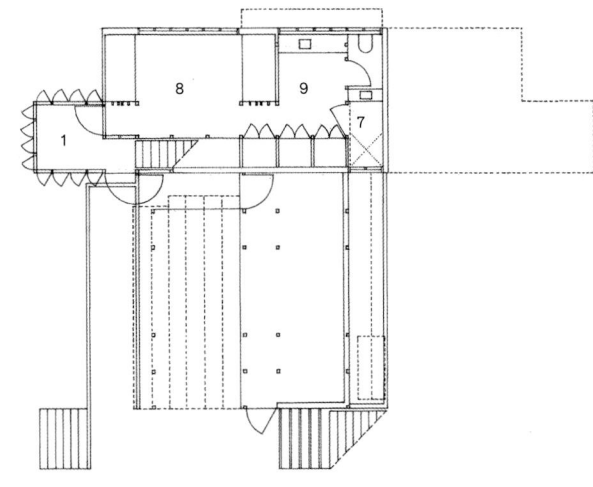

Lower level

1	Deck	6	Kitchen
2	Terraced steps	7	Bathroom
3	Garden	8	Bedroom
4	Dining	9	Laundry/store
5	Sitting		

1:250

0 ⊢——⊣ 5m

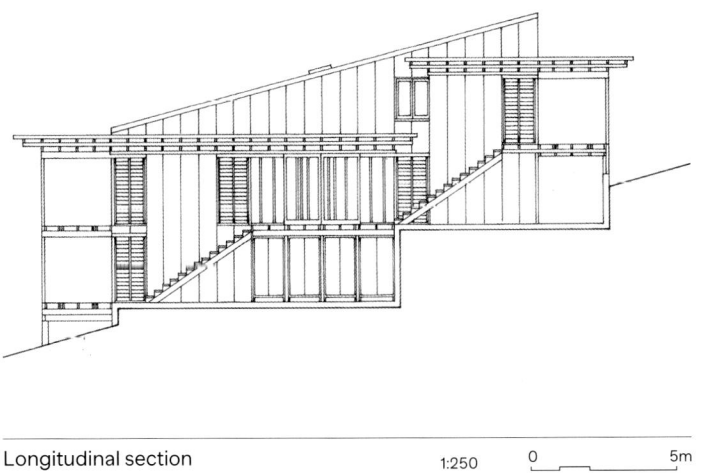

Longitudinal section 1:250 0 — 5m

Axonometric 1:500 0 — 5m

Architect — Brit Andresen Architect
Project team — Brit Andresen, Tony Mitchell, Michael Barnett
Contractor — Michael Lusis
Carpenter — Russell Specht
Concreter — Chris Wallace
Engineer — Rod Bligh
Blockwork — Elvis & Rose
Photographer — Dianna Snape

Bellbird Retreat

Killarney, Southern Downs
Steendijk

Completed – 2019
Project type – New build
Total site area – 315 acres
Internal area – 67 m^2
Number of residents – 2
Number of bedrooms – 2
Number of bathrooms – 1

Bellbird Retreat is built on the land of the Githabul people

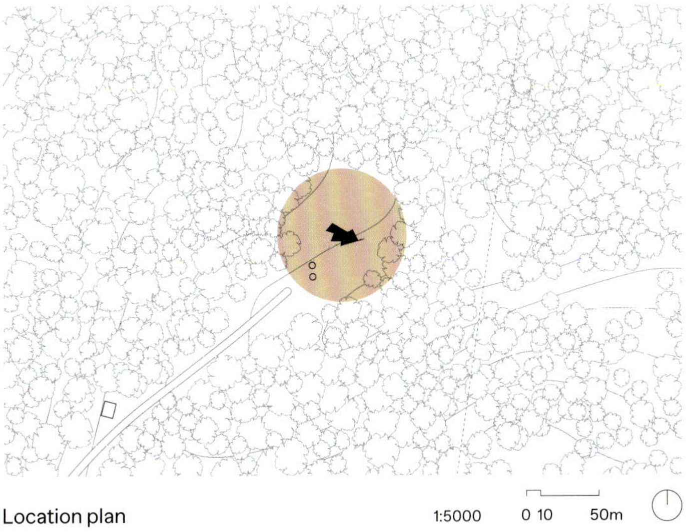

Location plan
1:5000

The architectural setting

Modernist ideas influenced the full spectrum of design – from the teapot and the chair and the building to the city plan. At the Bauhaus – the influential German art school founded by the architect Walter Gropius in 1919 and later run by architect Ludwig Mies van der Rohe – the vision for a unified expression for craft, art, design and architecture was implemented through an innovative and immersive pedagogy.

The European creativity that prospered across the continent in the first half of the 20th century profoundly shaped global architecture, art and design between the wars and in the postwar renewal. These ideas modestly influenced architecture in mid-century Brisbane and created a new generation of venturous architects and architectural educators. This interchange continues to have impact today via the increased internationalisation of architectural employment and education of the late 20th century. Global experiences have moulded the approach of the numerous contemporary Brisbane architects who have worked and studied abroad, and in the case of Brian Steendyk this has a direct association with the Bauhaus, with Steendyk having studied architecture at IIT (Illinois Institute of Technology) in Chicago, on a campus with renowned architectural works by Mies van der Rohe and education delivered by collaborators of the mid-century iconoclast.

Working across scales was a hallmark of the pioneering European modernists and Brian Steendyk's Brisbane-based studio practises in this tradition – designing furniture, buildings and urban infrastructure. Steendijk's Bellbird Retreat is a technically deft and materially rich building in the landscape that uses this thinking to create a house that simultaneously amplifies scale and celebrates intimacy.

Previous:
Bellbird Retreat is a materially rich building that simultaneously amplifies scale and celebrates intimacy.

Opposite:
Located on the edge of the Great Dividing Range, the home is subject to extreme weather contrasts.

Above:
A solid brick wall to the south and west protect the home from severe winds and bushfire.

The lived experience

Bellbird Retreat is located on an established nature refuge in Queensland's Southern Downs region at the edge of the Great Dividing Range – an area subject to extreme weather contrasts and, consequently, incredible biodiversity. 'Our house sits in a confluence of climatic conditions – the subtropics and the saddle of a mountain range,' says owner Craig Hodges. 'It has been known to snow at our property, but we are also susceptible to extreme bushfires.'

In order to withstand these extreme weather conditions, the home was designed by architect Brian Steendyk as a series of contrasts. A robust and solid brick wall to the south and west protect the home from severe winds, while a completely glazed edge opens out to the north and east. When the home opens up to the north, 'you feel like you're on a deck, rather than inside'. The home can be opened up or closed down as desired, depending on the time of day or season and the roof eaves are deep for protection from the summer sun, but allow the penetration of winter sun to warm the concrete floor. Locally grown hoop pine gives the interior carpentry details a rich golden hue and the sculptural steel roof opens up to frame immersive views of the mountain top.

Retreating from busy urban lives in Brisbane, the owners are keen environmentalists and, being on a nature refuge, there is an obligation to look after the landscape. 'We are part of a bushcare group – a wonderful community who work on each other's properties,' explains Craig. More recently, the bushcare group has been learning to control the threat of fire from traditional owners through cultural burning workshops. 'We wanted a place to look after. Our property is a nature refuge but also a refuge for us,' says Craig.

Opposite:
Glazed doors to the north and east slide away to transform the living area into a covered deck or platform.

Above:
Locally grown hoop pine gives the interior carpentry details a rich golden hue.

Above:
The compact home is designed as the owners' retreat from busy urban lives in Brisbane.

Above:
The sculptural steel roof of Bellbird Retreat angles up to the north, framing views of the surrounding mountains.

BELLBIRD RETREAT

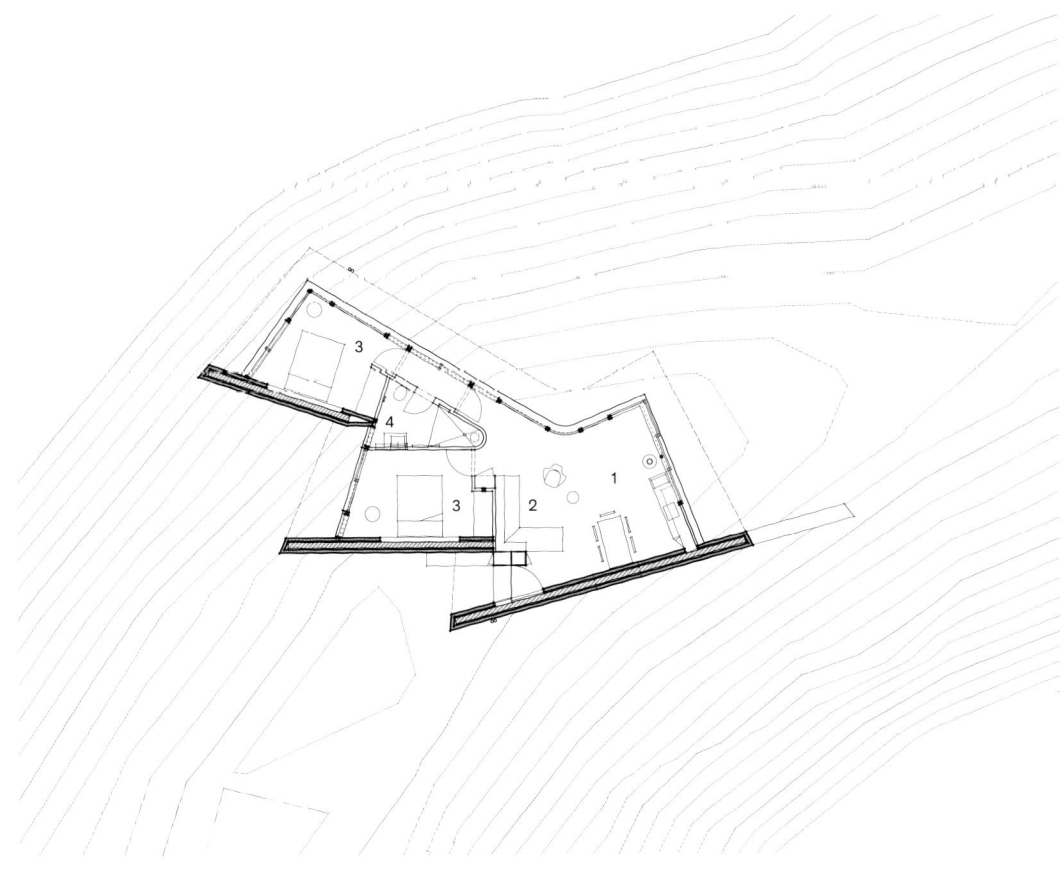

Plan

1. Kitchen
2. Living
3. Bedroom
4. Bathroom

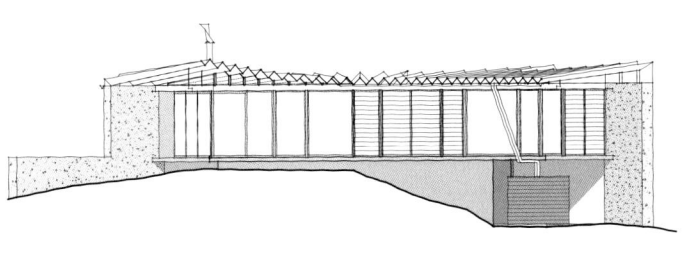

North elevation

Cross section

1:250
0 5m

Architect — Steendijk
Project team — Brian Steendyk, Shaun Crossman, Timo Lueck
Structural engineer — Westera Partners
Builder — EA & PJ Bell
Photographer — Christopher Frederick Jones; Craig Hodges (page 142)

Mount Coot-tha House

Mount Coot-tha, Brisbane
Nielsen Jenkins

Completed – 2019
Project type – New build
Total site area – 2524 m²
Internal area – 292 m²
External area – 24 m²
Number of residents – 4
Number of bedrooms – 3
Number of bathrooms – 2.5

Mount Coot-tha House is built on the land of the Turrbal and Yuggera peoples

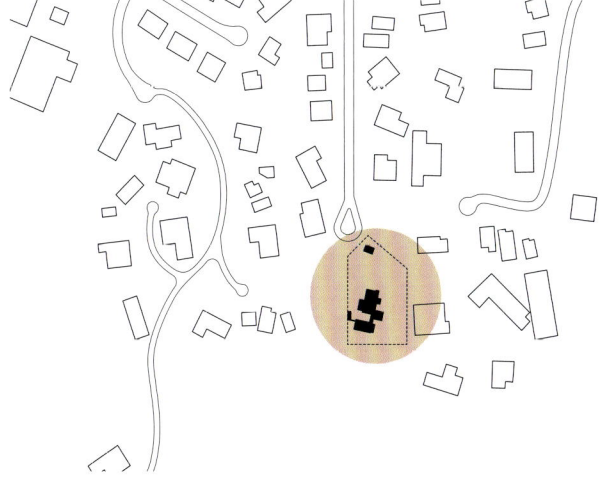

Location plan 1:5000 0 10 50m

MOUNT COOT-THA HOUSE

The architectural setting

Mount Coot-tha Reserve is a towering, topographical backdrop to the city of Brisbane. Development of the closest, suburban edges to the north and south of the parkland for house lots began in the 1960s and 1970s and this period saw the construction of exemplar work on both sides of the range, including Michael Keniger and Brit Andresen's Wirra House, a suite of innovative family houses by John Dalton (see Sun and Shadow House, page 294), and venturous architect–developer collaborations.

These projects are distinguished by their formal clarity, construction materials and resolute repose. Rooms gather under expressed gable and skillion roofs (sometimes asymmetrically figured) and they are primarily built of brick and blockwork, either left raw or painted. In response to the topography, they are benched and terraced into the (always) sloping terrain, and planned around courtyards and aspect.

The Nielsen Jenkins–designed Mount Coot-tha House confidently draws on the architectural ideas and strategies deployed in these late-modern buildings to create a home with a deep connection to its bushland setting. In section, the building is a series of stepped platforms under a singular roof that parallels the fall of the site. Views out into the bushland are ever present and the experience and activity of this robust but crafted house culminates in a partly enclosed courtyard room.

Previous:
Mount Coot-tha House is a robust but crafted house with a deep connection to its bushland setting.

Opposite:
In section, the home is a series of stepped platforms under a singular roof that parallels the fall of the site.

Above:
A spine of stairs runs up the side of the house to connect the series of staggered living platforms.

The lived experience

Mardi Jenkins's parents bought a hillside block of land in Brisbane's Mt Coot-tha forty years ago and, as children, she and her brother Morgan (now an architect) would spend hours scrambling up the slope of the eucalypt forest. 'We've always run through the bush. When we were younger it was just play – and now, as adults, we go on trail runs through the bush,' Mardi says. Since their childhood, the plot for Mount Coot-tha House has been divided off from the neighbouring property, where Mardi and Morgan's mum still lives. The familiarity and love of the bushy landscape was the starting point for the new home, designed by her brother and his co-director of Nielsen Jenkins, Lachlan Nielsen.

The stepped structure of Mount Coot-tha House climbs up the slope and embeds itself into the forest, periodically opening up to frame curated views of the surrounding landscape. A spine of stairs runs up the side of the house, extends to the series of living platforms and ensures you are always following the slope of the land as you move through the home. A semi-enclosed outdoor courtyard punctuates the plan halfway up and is the pivoting point between public and private zones.

As Mardi reflects, 'It's really all about the trees. They are so beautiful, comforting and protective. And the house just makes you feel a part of the forest.' In a similar view, the muted colour palette of the besser-block building surrenders itself to the natural elements. 'The gums drop their leaves, and the tea tree stains the building – and it just looks better.'

Opposite:
A semi-enclosed outdoor courtyard punctuates the house at a pivoting point between public and private zones.

Above left:
The kitchen sits below the main courtyard and is the central hub around which life revolves.

Above right:
Glimpses of intimate gardens are in contrast with expansive bushland views.

Following:
Connections between the house and the surrounding eucalypt forest are carefully curated by the architect.

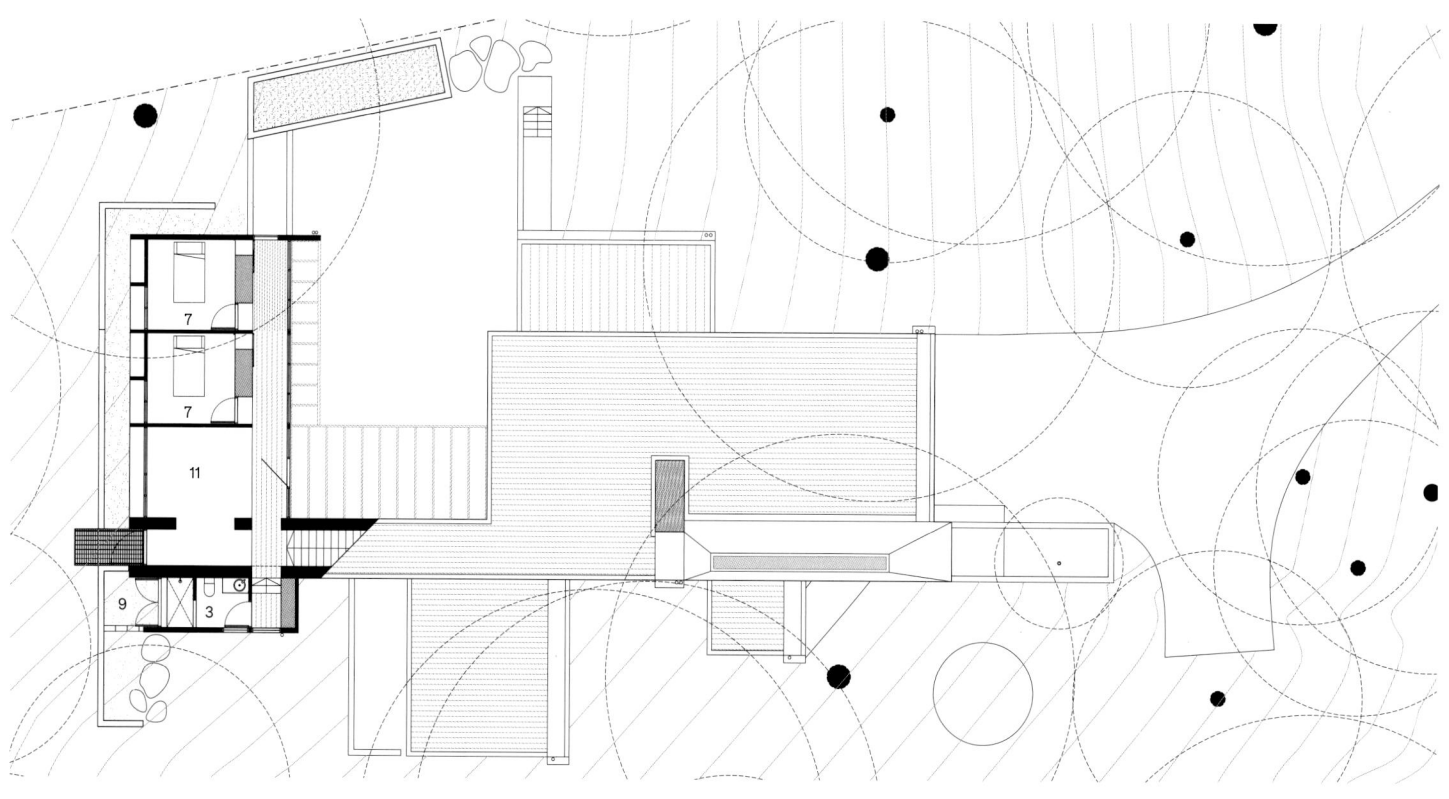

Second floor

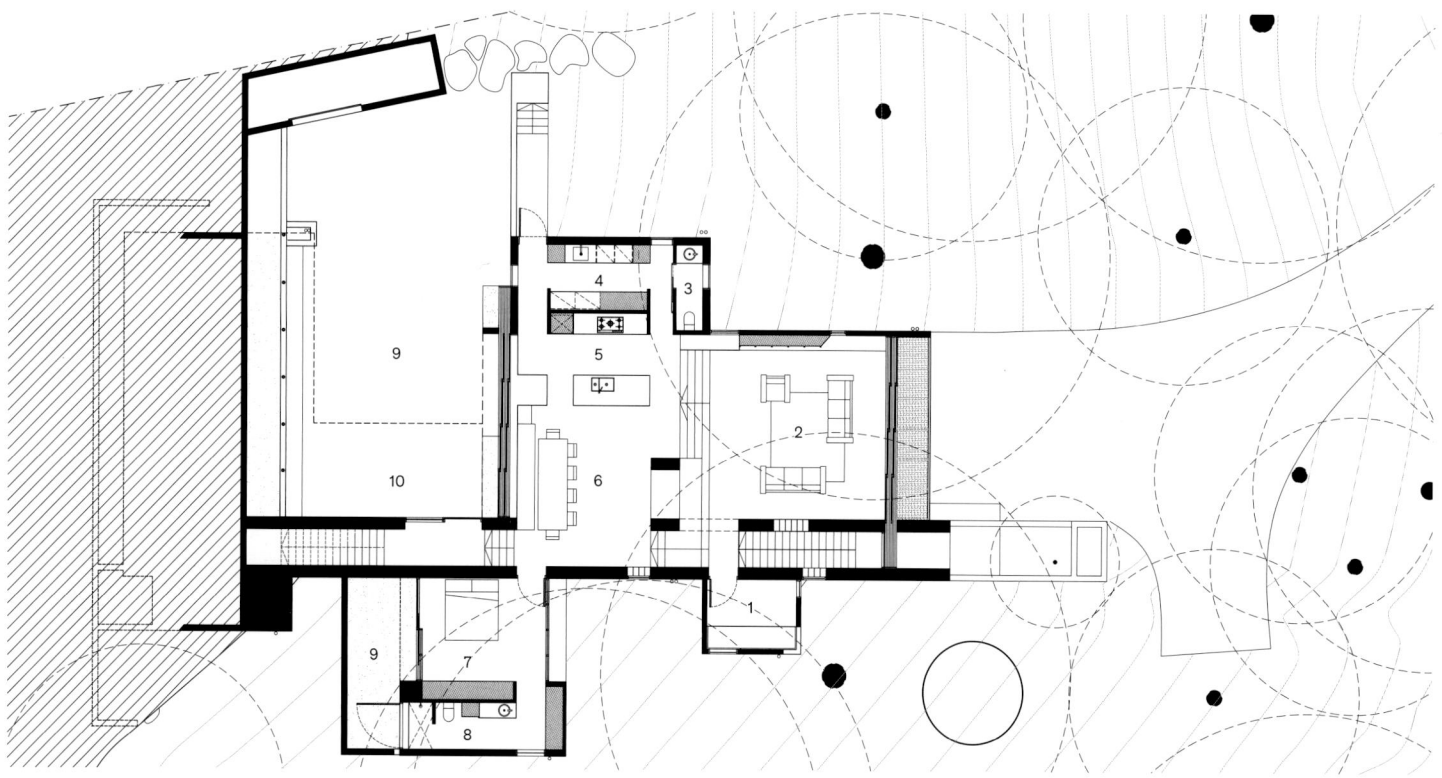

First floor

1	Study	7	Bedroom
2	Living	8	Ensuite
3	Bathroom	9	Courtyard
4	Laundry/pantry	10	Terrace
5	Kitchen	11	Rumpus
6	Dining		

1:250

0   5m

MOUNT COOT-THA HOUSE

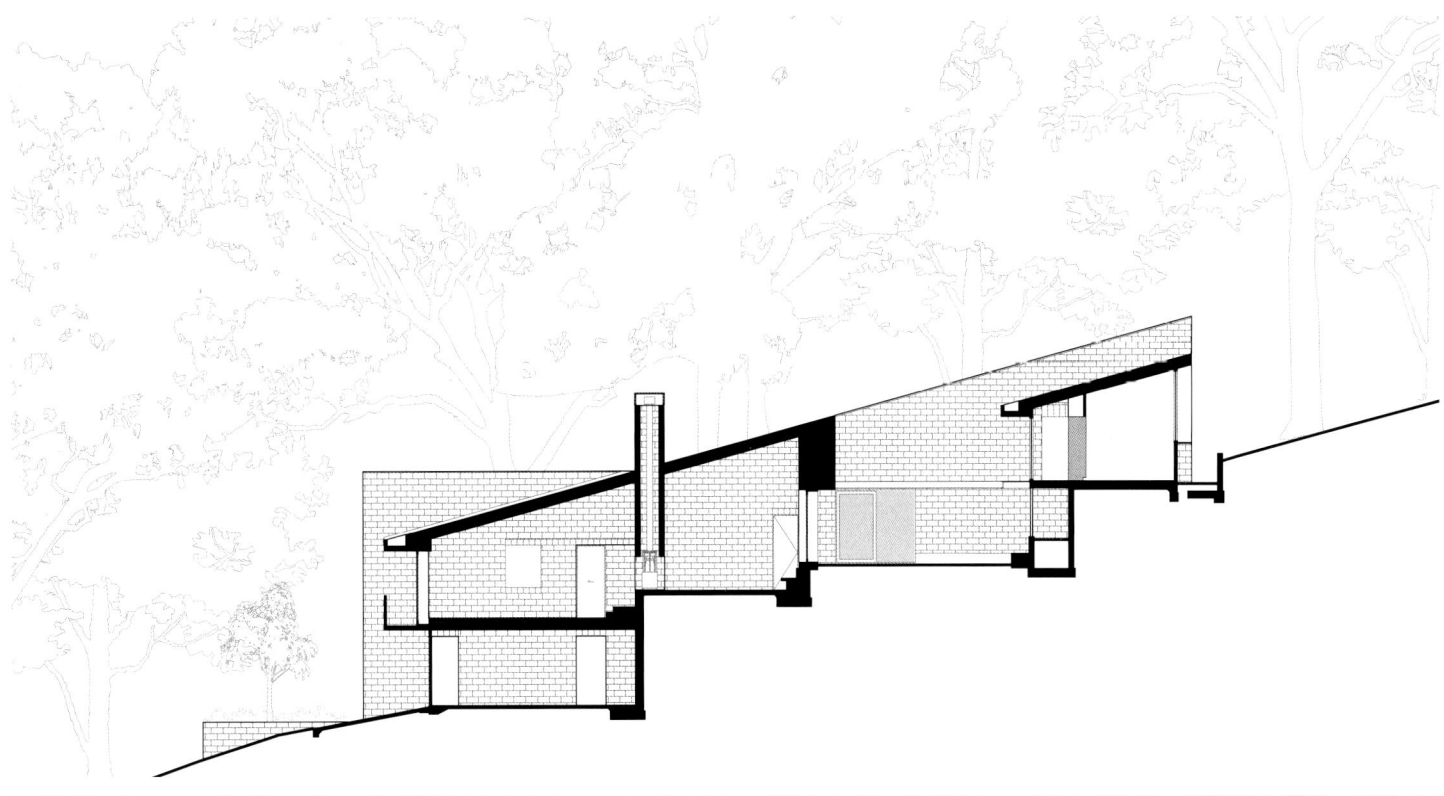

Longitudinal section

1:250
0   5m

Architect — Nielsen Jenkins
Project team — Lachlan Nielsen, Morgan Jenkins, Kelsey Homer, Michael Lumby, Nicholas Russell, Laura McConaghy, Jonathan Kopinski, Tanya Nielsen
Builder — Struss Constructions
Engineer — Westera Partners
Landscape — Jonathan Kopinski and Nielsen Jenkins
Town planner — Place Design Group
Cladding — Sustainable Cladding and Roofing
Bushfire consultant — Wollemi Eco-Logical
Photographer — Tom Ross

Sunrise Studio

Doonan, Noosa Valley
Bark Architects

Completed – 2021
Project type – New build (secondary dwelling)
Total site area – 5720 m²
Internal area – 74 m²
External area – 36 m²
Number of residents – 2
Number of bedrooms – 2
Number of bathrooms – 1

Sunrise Studio is built on the land of the
Gubbi Gubbi (Kabi Kabi) people

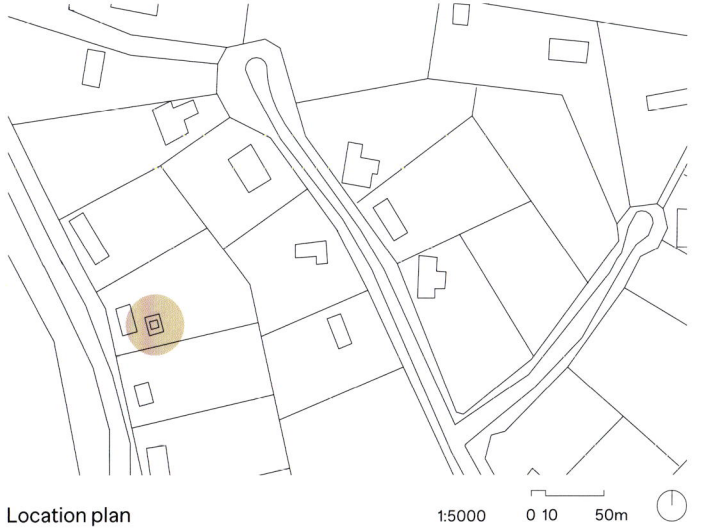

Location plan 1:5000 0 10 50m

Previous:
Sunrise Studio is a new companion for one of Gabriel Poole's innovative Quadropod houses.

Top:
The owners have spent over ten years repairing and nurturing their property's ecosystem.

Bottom:
The black steel box is nestled into the scenic Noosa Valley, looking out to the distant eastern coastline.

The architectural setting

Along an arris ridge in Doonan – a bushland suburb to the west of Noosa – two exemplary architect-designed houses, built over forty years apart, sit in gentle companionship. The most recent addition to this beautiful sloping site is the black-box Sunrise Studio by Bark Architects. This compact house sits alongside one of Gabriel Poole's innovative Quadropod houses. Both buildings are nestled into the scenic Noosa Valley setting and look out to the distant eastern coastline.

In the early 1970s the acclaimed architect Gabriel Poole, recipient of the Australian Institute of Architects Gold Medal in 1988 and the designer of the ground-breaking Tent House construction system – deployed for his own house in Eumundi and publicly exhibited in the Botanical Gardens Brisbane in the early 1990s (see The Courier Mail Tent House, page 294). From the 1970s to the 1990s Poole used the cost-effective Quadropod construction module to create a series of climate-responsive houses on Queensland's Sunshine Coast. Elevated on platforms supported by tree-like steel structures that are anchored to the site by four slender columns, these taut houses are sibling to the experimental American Case Study Houses of the mid–late 20th century, particularly the iconic 1949 Eames House by Charles and Ray Eames, and part of a global movement that resonates locally through ongoing experiments with steel construction – including the 2002 Clarke MacLeod House by Chris Clarke (see page 293).

The Sunrise Studio is in conversation with these local and international precedents – in its siting and architectural strategy – and both buildings speak to the distinctiveness of place.

Above:
The sounds and smells of the surrounding landscape permeate the interior of the home.

The lived experience

Ten years ago, David and Simone moved from their small, inner-city Sydney terrace onto 1.5 acres of lush Sunshine Coast rainforest. David reflects, 'When we first bought our Doonan house [designed by Gabriel Poole], Singapore daisy (*Sphagneticola trilobata*), a pest weed, was everywhere. We pulled them out by hand and planted new native shrubbery. This has encouraged the native wildlife to return to our block – wallabies, koalas, bush turkeys – and they are all here to stay.'

Repairing and nurturing the site's ecosystem over the years led David and Simone to their architectural brief for Sunrise Studio, a new secondary dwelling — 'There was to be no damage to the land or the trees.' Working with architects Lindy Atkin and Steve Guthrie from Bark Architects, clients David and Simone were assiduous in avoiding the removal of any existing trees. They recall how the siting of the new building was even slightly adjusted to avoid the breaking of a tree branch that was home to a resident tawny frogmouth. To this day, the same tawny frogmouth happily perches on the same branch.

The design of the Sunrise Studio, now home to David and Simone's daughter and grandson, was born from genuine respect for the landscape. Hovering on stilts above the now verdant scrub, the home's internal spaces wrap around a skywell, with two celery wood (*Polyscias elegans*) rainforest trees planted at the centre. In this secondary dwelling, landscape – both metaphorically and physically – is the heart of the home.

Opposite:
Hovering on stilts above the verdant scrub, the home's internal spaces wrap around a central skywell.

Above:
Fixed windows frame horizon views and gentle breezes pass through louvred panels.

Above:
A covered deck connects the two main internal living areas and forms an outdoor room.

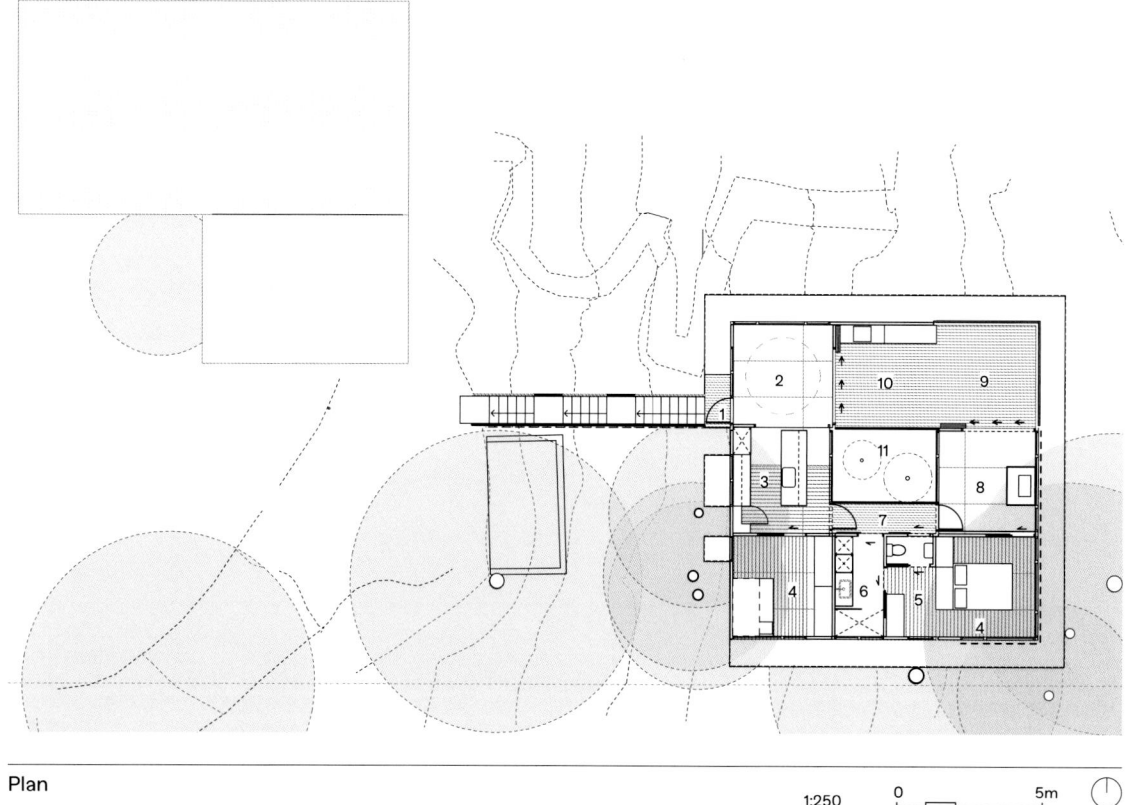

Plan 1:250 0 5m

1 Entry
2 Dining/study
3 Kitchen
4. Bedroom
5 Robe
6 Bathroom
7 Lightwell deck
8 Living
9 Yoga deck
10 Outdoor dining
11 Skywell

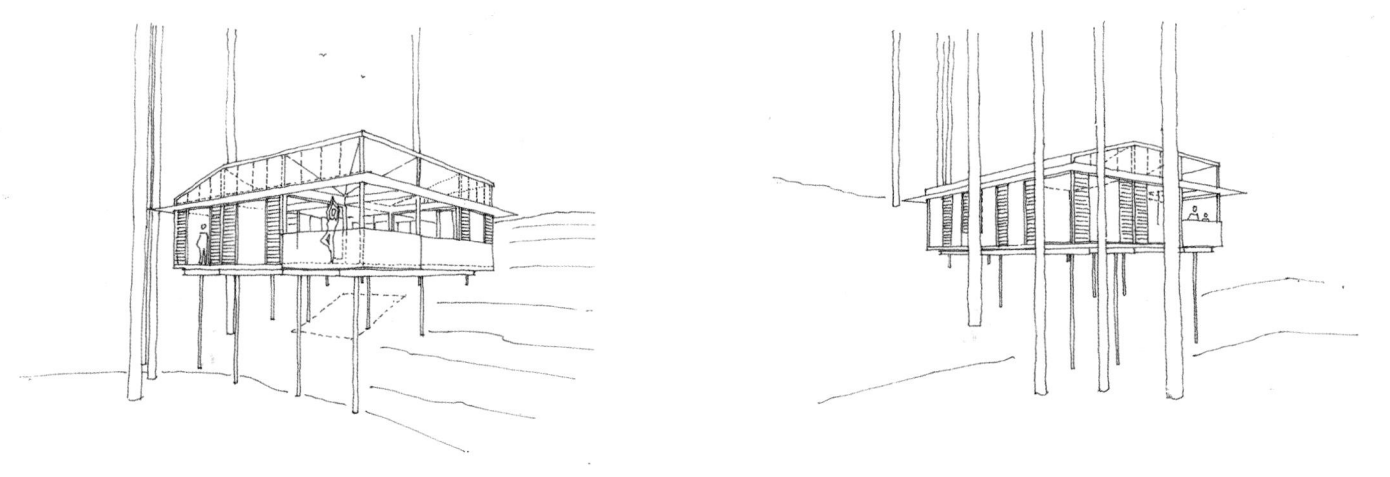

Sketches Not to scale

North elevation

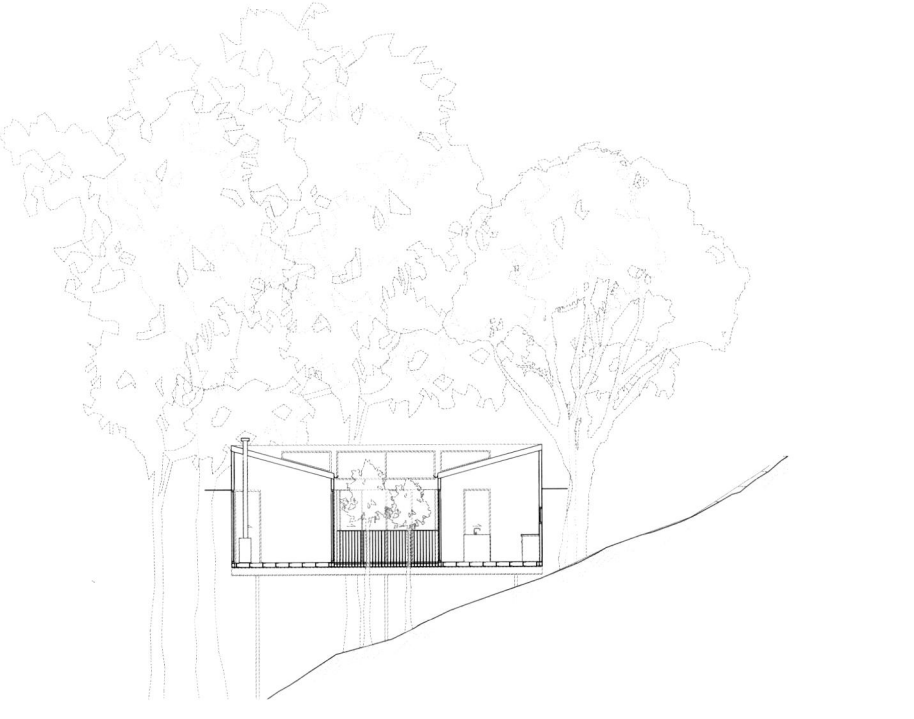

Cross section

1:250
0   5m

Architect — Bark Architects
Project team — Stephen Guthrie, Lindy Atkin, Tim Griffiths
Structural engineer and geotechnical investigator — SCG Consulting Engineers
Building certifier — Pacific BCQ
Detail survey — Hass Surveys
Photographer — Christopher Frederick Jones

Traditions reimagined

The challenge of celebrating and reimagining Queensland's architectural inheritance is exemplified in these projects. Two strategies characterise the approach of the architects. In the renovation projects the big challenge is connecting the much-loved, elevated building with the landscape, which is most often a generous and underused backyard. This is achieved with inventive extensions grafted onto the back of the existing house or burrowed underneath – and sometimes a combination of both. These techniques cleverly address the heritage protections that have been placed on the existing building fabric and envelope by local governments, ensuring that neighbourhood character is retained. In parallel, many of the architects have worked inventively to reinvigorate the techniques and materials of the timber building tradition of Queensland, embracing the contemporary sustainability agenda and developing new models for infill housing in the older suburbs.

Aperture House

Highgate Hill, Brisbane
Blight Rayner and Twofold Studio

Completed – 2013
Project type – Alteration and addition
Total site area – 524 m²
Internal area – 170 m²
External area – 320 m²
Number of residents – 4
Number of bedrooms – 3
Number of bathrooms – 2

Aperture House is built on the land of the
Turrbal and Yuggera peoples

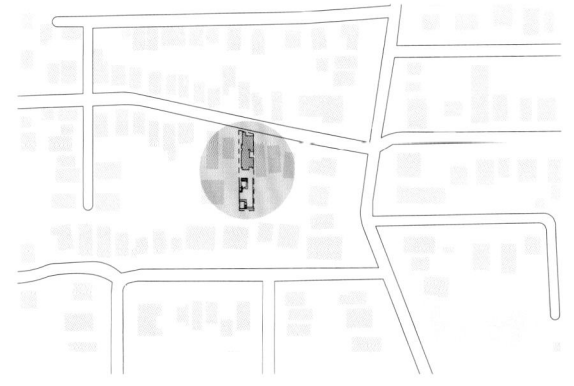

Location plan   1:5000   0 10   50m

The architectural setting

The history of brickmaking in Queensland extends back to the establishment of the Moreton Bay penal settlement in the 1820s. Local clay was sourced from across Brisbane for the manufacture of rudimentary convict-made bricks and these were used for the settlement's most important public and mercantile buildings.

The early clay pits were in what is now the city centre, before moving out to suburbs where this historic activity is now embedded in the naming of places like Clayfield and Virginia. By the end of the 19th century the mechanisation of brick production had replaced the local cottage industry and the early large-scale manufacturers of bricks in Brisbane included the builder and stonemason John Petrie, who was Brisbane's first mayor, and James Campbell and Sons, the operators of the Albion Brick and Pottery Works.

Aperture House by Blight Rayner and Twofold Studio reimagines a humble workers cottage in the suburb of Highgate Hill. Here, the original structure is unusual because it was partially constructed from bricks, including the foundations and a generous fireplace, and this condition informed the profound transformation. The close collaboration between the architect and the artisan bricklayers Elvis & Rose enriched the details, and this finely detailed and spatially rich renovation adds an engaging new layer to the story of brick architecture in Queensland (see Fulcher Residence, page 293, and Dyer Street House, page 293).

Previous:
Responding to the original split-level plan, the new spaces at Aperture House cascade into the backyard.

Opposite:
A transitional indoor-outdoor brick loggia hovers above the garden, allowing an occasional creek to flow through the site.

Above left:
A new section grafts to the original two-bedroom 1880s worker's cottage at the high point of the gabled roof.

Above right:
The owners' and designers' affinity with the original brick fireplace inspired the choice of materials for the extension.

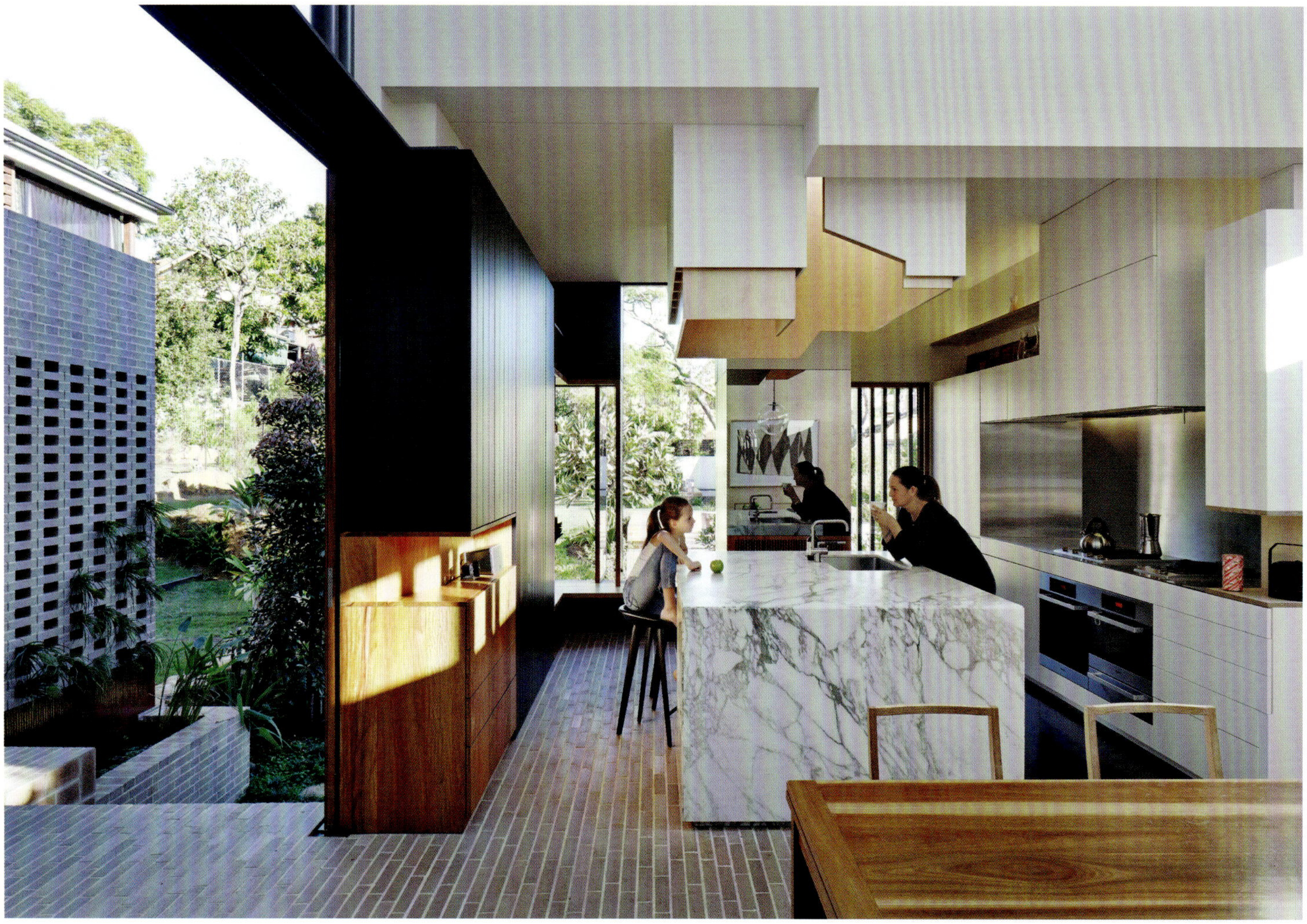

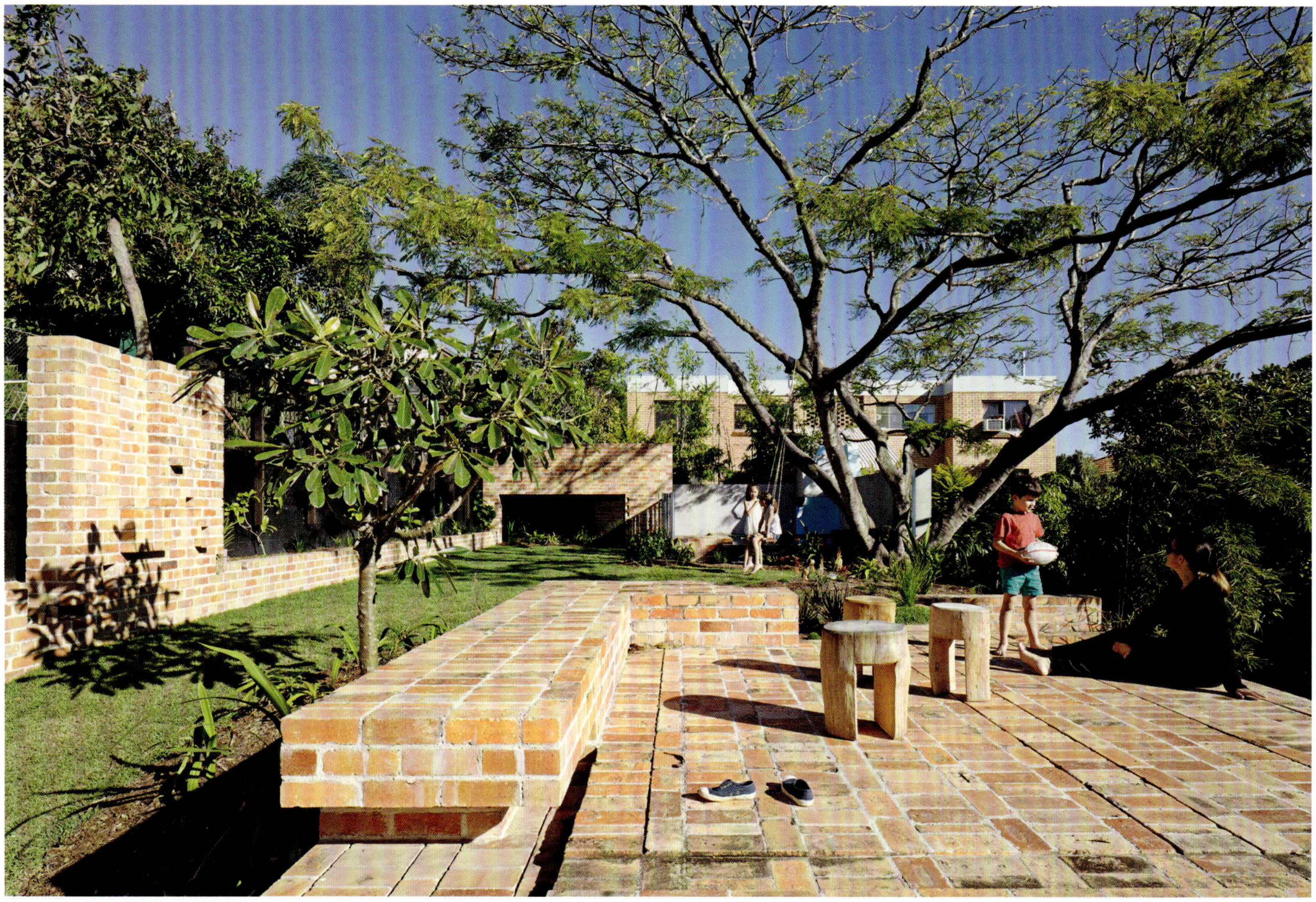

The lived experience

Architect and owner Jayson Blight and his wife Melissa, also a designer, lived in their two-bedroom 1880s worker's cottage until they had a 'clarifying moment of realisation that the youngest of our two children was about to start school and was still sleeping in a cot-sized bed'. Along with the pragmatic need for more space, there was a desire to establish a better connection with the backyard. The original cottage is split-level, leading to a simple decision by the design duo to continue the cascading of spaces into the garden at the southern end of the site. A transitional indoor–outdoor brick loggia hovers above the garden, allowing an occasional creek to flow through the property after subtropical downpours.

In response to the original cottage's unusual application of masonry construction and the couple's affinity with the old fireplace, brick was the chosen material for the addition. Sightlines to the brick fireplace are retained from the new living areas, providing regular reminders of the original home's spirit, and a mini museum of artefacts found during the excavation sit in a tiny slot behind the fireplace. Inspired by the beautiful volume generated by the existing house's double-gabled roof, the new section grafts itself to the old at a high point of the gable, bringing baffled northern light into the centre of the house and operable louvres vent hot air.

In adding a new layer of history to this Brisbane cottage, memories of the past are preserved and celebrated.

Opposite top:
Large sliding doors can be rolled back to connect the indoors with out and expand the living area.

Opposite bottom:
The use of masonry and brickwork extends into the garden composition that defines a series of outdoor rooms.

Above:
Sculptural elements in the pool strengthen the connection between house and garden.

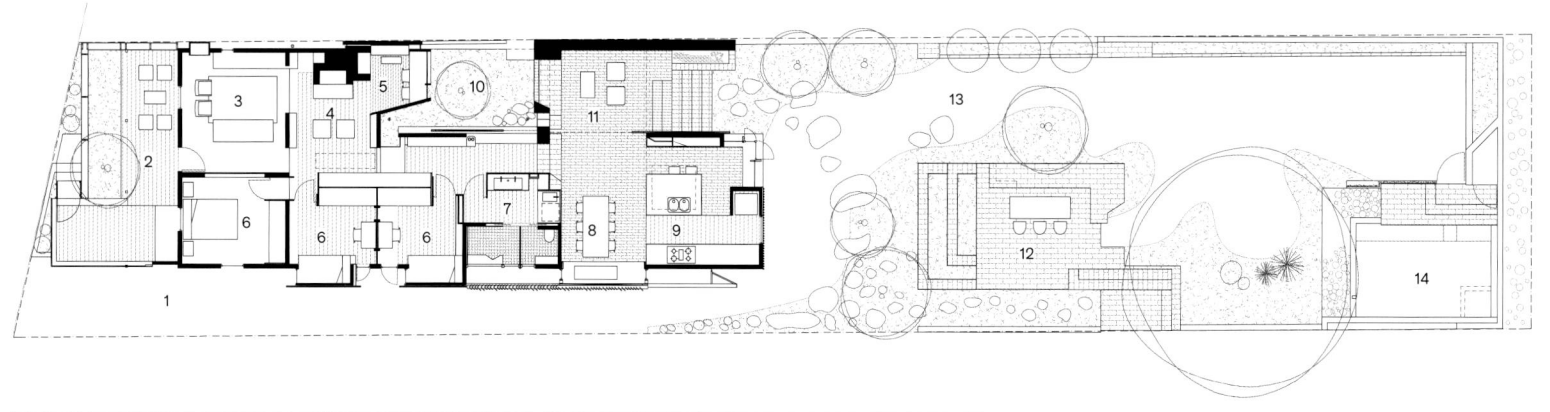

Upper level

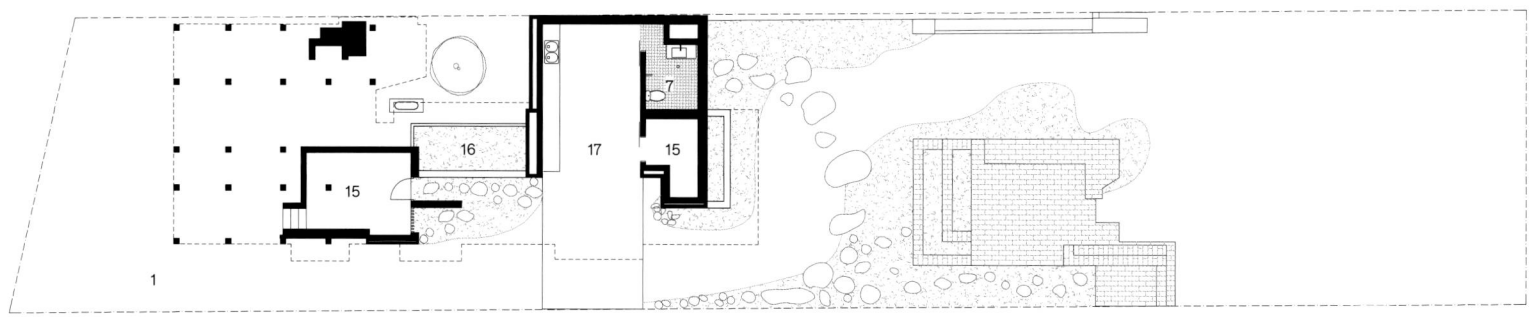

Lower level

1	Driveway	10	Courtyard
2	Verandah	11	Loggia
3	Lounge	12	Terrace
4	Library	13	Garden
5	Study	14	Pool
6	Bedroom	15	Store
7	Bathroom	16	Fernery
8	Dining	17	Garage
9	Kitchen		

1:250
0 5m

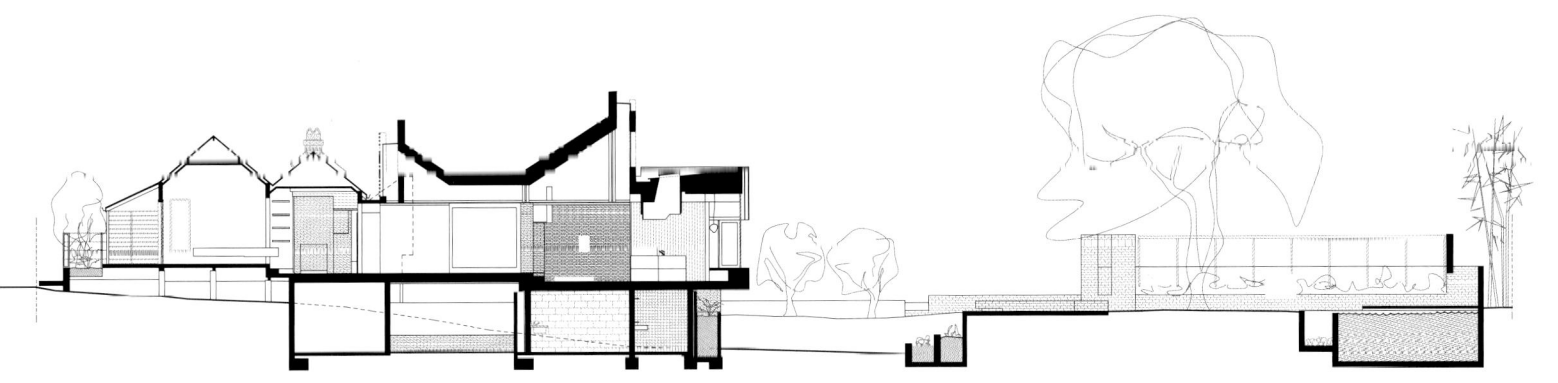

Longitudinal section

1:250
0   5m

Architect — Blight Rayner and Twofold Studio
Project team — Jayson Blight, Melissa Blight, Jasper Brown, Spyros Barberis, Michelle Fitzgerald, Troy Rafton
Architectural masonry — Elvis & Rose
Landscape architect — Steven Clegg Design
Structural engineer — Westera Partners
Hydraulic engineer — Thomson Kane Hydraulic Engineering Consultants
Certifier — Knisco
Builder — Frame Projects
Photographer — Christopher Frederick Jones

Shutter House

West End, Brisbane
Kim and Monique Baber

Completed – 2014
Project type – Alteration and addition
Total site area – 400 m²
Internal area – 140 m²
External area – 260 m²
Number of residents – 3
Number of bedrooms – 4
Number of bathrooms – 2

Shutter House is built on the land of the
Turrbal and Yuggera peoples

The architectural setting

Queensland's timber industry traces its history back to the 1840s, beginning in the Brisbane region and reaching Tropical North Queensland by the 1870s. The plentiful red cedar, kauri pine and hoop pine was veraciously and indiscriminately felled for the construction of buildings and infrastructure across the expanding colony and was a valuable export commodity.

The impact on the ancient, carefully managed landscape was rapid, and by the early 19th century one third of Queensland's hoop and bunya pine trees had been felled. The need for a more sustainable approach to the use of forest products was first identified in the late 19th century and this resulted in an ongoing, collaborative project that, in more recent years, has yielded significant land conservation and timber milling efficiency initiatives.

Architectural innovation has given form to this imperative and this future-focused challenge is embedded in the design approach deployed at the Shutter House by Kim and Monique Baber. The poised, screened extension is a gentle addition to the eclectic landscape of the neighbourhood's backyards and a research-informed nod to the timber construction traditions of Queensland.

Previous:
Shutter House is a screened extension to an existing cottage that offers a semi-outdoor space for year-round use.

Opposite:
The new part of the home responds to the eclectic landscape of the neighbourhood's backyards.

Above left:
The exterior staircase, traditional of Queenslander homes, has here been incorporated into the interior space.

Above right:
Built-in bench seats around the periphery of the extension allow occupation and enjoyment of the edges.

The lived experience

The deep and wide Queensland verandah has enduring and nostalgic appeal, offering a comfortable semi-outdoor space in most seasons. It provides shade, catches breezes and protects from subtropical afternoon storms. These verandahs are an elevated vantage point to surveil the neighbourhood, and timber lattice screens often provide additional shade and privacy to these transitional zones.

At the Shutter House, husband-and-wife architect duo Kim and Monique Baber have reinterpreted the traditional Queenslander verandah to create a habitable internal deck that is protected from the harsh western sun, while opening to views of Mount Coot-tha. The back wall of the original house has been peeled away to make way for the new hybrid space. The new is subtly demarcated from the old by narrow blackbutt boards abutting the original wide pine flooring – a reminder of the transition to a peripheral zone. The kitchen occupies the new deck territory and crafted timber joinery components offer the comforts of indoors, but with the benefits of outdoors. In a similar vein to the traditional lattice screens, a carapace of operable timber shutters shields the new internal verandah and allows for edited levels of shading and privacy.

The informality of the Brisbane cottage settlement is wholeheartedly embraced by the owners: 'We spend a lot of time on our indoor deck. We get great views and we like to watch people on the street. My dad and sister live next door, so we stick our heads out of the shutters to say hi to them.'

Opposite:
Operable shutter windows provide shelter from sun, wind or neighbours' eyes as desired.

Above:
The habitable internal deck is a vantage point to survey the neighbourhood and enjoy the views of Mt Coot-tha.

Above:
The new is demarcated from the old by narrow blackbutt boards abutting the original wide pine flooring.

Above:
The kitchen occupies the new deck territory and crafted timber joinery offers the comfort of indoors, but with the benefits of outdoors.

SHUTTER HOUSE

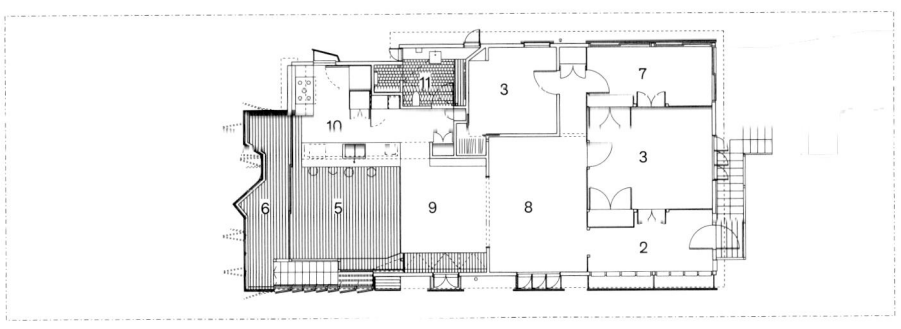

Upper level

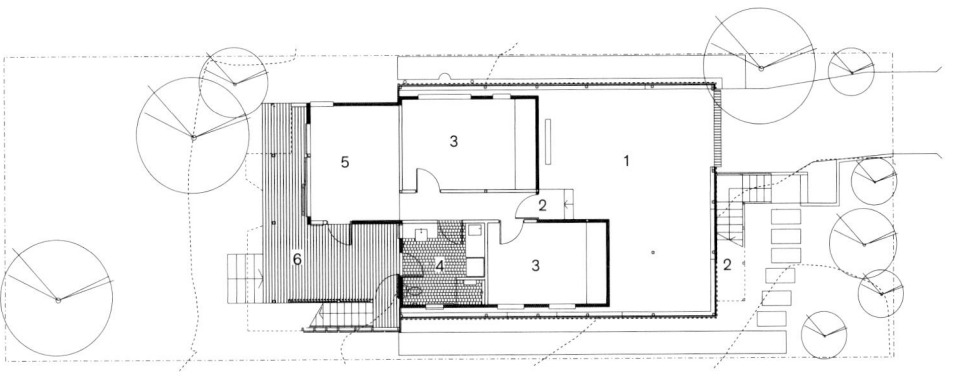

Lower level

1 Carport
2 Entry
3 Bedroom
4 Bathroom/laundry
5 Living
6 Deck
7 Sunroom
8 Lounge
9 Dining
10 Kitchen
11 Bathroom

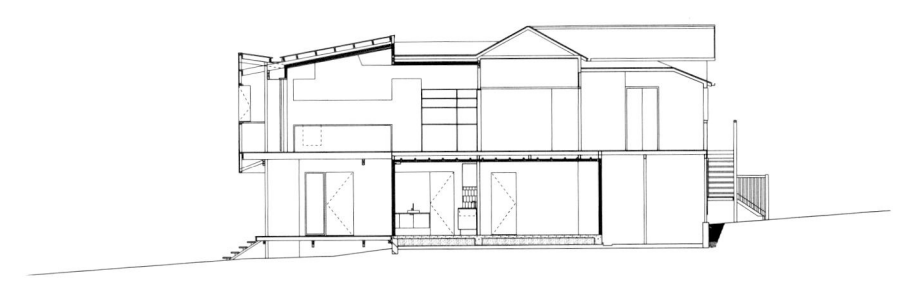

Longitudinal section

1:250
0 5m

Architect — Kim and Monique Baber
Project team — Kim Baber and Monique Baber
Structural engineer — AD Structure
Builder — John Rich
Photographer — Christopher Frederick Jones

Left Over Space House

Paddington, Brisbane
CultivAR Architecture

Completed – 2015
Project type – Alteration and addition
Total site area – 350 m² (80 m² buildable)
Internal area – 125 m²
External area – 80 m²
Number of residents – 5
Number of bedrooms – 4
Number of bathrooms – 2

Left Over Space House is built on the land of the Turrbal and Yuggera peoples

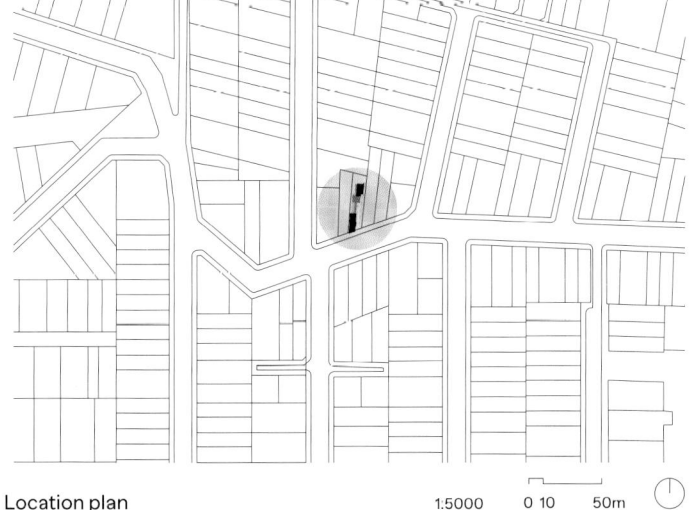

Location plan

The architectural setting

The timber building tradition that developed in Queensland in the early years of European settlement was used almost universally across the scale and function of buildings. The remarkable versatility of this construction technique was deployed for shops, churches, houses and schools. The little village of buildings that gather in the near vicinity of the Left Over Space House exemplify this versatility. Along this pretty street in the inner-city suburb of Paddington there is a former dance hall (with a welcoming portico front) and its caretakers' quarters, closely set cottages with open front verandahs, and local shops on the corners of the blocks, all built in timber.

The Left Over Space House by CultivAR Architecture reimagines the petite 100-year-old caretakers' cottage – which occupies a sliver of steep, overlooked and encroached land once deemed unsuitable for redevelopment – as a bespoke and enriching family home for its architect owners. In this work the practice studiously pursued an architectural language that has relevance across residential, public and commercial architecture, referencing the unique qualities of place. The project of renewing this marginalised building, beset by termite damage, asbestos sheeting, lead paint and damaged glazing and fixtures, was a work of personal passion, underpinned by a deep commitment to the intersection of architecture, building and faith.

Previous:
At the Left Over Space House, a wide, timber stair opens to an outdoor atrium and garden beyond.

Opposite:
The western facade illustrates the layering of spaces that cascade down a steep and narrow site.

Above:
The petite 100-year-old caretaker's cottage has been lovingly restored, reworked and extended.

Top:
A translucent roof and a continuation of the timber material palette grafts the new part of the home to the old.

Bottom:
The house is a series of intimate experiences, such as this book-lined daybed in the front library.

The lived experience

When designing their family's future home, architects Rebekah and Casey Vallance drew from a favourite design studio subject, led by Brit Andresen, that required them to design a corner related to a childhood memory. Rebekah recalls, 'I'd sit on some steps between the kitchen and a window with a view of the garden and talk to my mum. This moment had an outlook and provided refuge – I could see out to the world, but I also felt protected and nurtured.' For their own future children, Rebekah and Casey wanted to bring the essence of this memory into their home.

Just six months after completing their architectural studies, Rebekah and Casey Vallance bought their early 20th-century four-room cottage in Brisbane's Paddington. The timber cottage was lovingly restored, reworked and extended by the couple, bit by bit, over an eight-year period. During and since this time, the couple have had three little girls who have embraced the home and made it their own. 'We spent years anticipating and empathising how children might interact with the spaces and now we see them playing in it as we imagined.'

Beyond the inward-facing cottage, the timber addition opens up at the back and presents a wide, cascading stair down to the outdoor atrium and garden beyond. The stairs in this home share the same spatial qualities as the space in Rebekah's childhood memory and this covered, double-height atrium has become the centre of daily life for the family. 'We see the house as a series of intimate experiences, but our outdoor terrace can be transformed into a more public space to welcome in our wider community.' This new part of this home is formally distinct from the old cottage, but still spatially grafts itself to the old cottage via a translucent roof and a continuation of the timber material palette.

Above:
The home is designed to nurture family life, with childhood memories of the architect owners embedded into the design.

Upper level

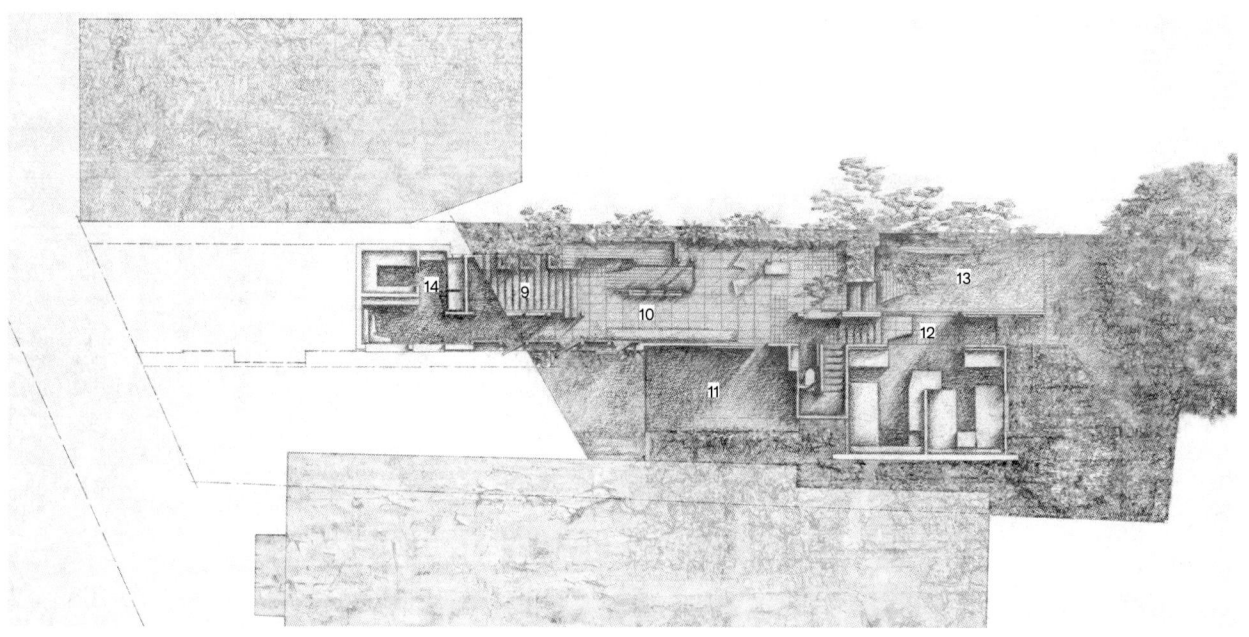

Lower level

1 Ecclesiastical library
2 Bathroom
3 Entry
4 Dining/meeting room
5 Bridge library
6 Living
7 Kitchen
8 Rooftop terrace
9 Garden stair
10 Garden terrrace/studio
11 Carport
12 Children's rooms
13 Garden
14 Laundry/store

1:250
0   5m

LEFT OVER SPACE HOUSE

Longitudinal section

1:250
0 — 5m

Architect — CultivAR Architecture
Project team — Rebekah Vallance and Casey Vallance
Structural engineer — Edmiston & Taylor Consulting Civil and Structural Engineers
Photographer — Christopher Frederick Jones

West End House

West End, Brisbane
KIRK

Completed – 2015
Project type – New build
Total site area – 272 m²
Internal area – 114 m²
External area – 20 m²
Number of residents – 4
Number of bedrooms – 3
Number of bathrooms – 2

West End House is built on the land of the
Turrbal and Yuggera peoples

Location plan

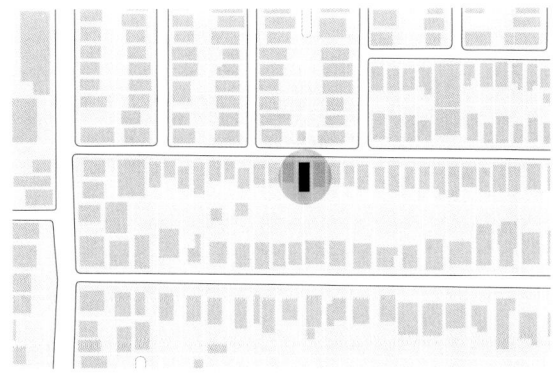

1:5000   0 10   50m

Previous:
Although a completely new house, West End House draws on the spirit of the traditional worker's cottage.

Top:
Rational timber structural systems, framing and cladding give the home formal clarity.

Bottom:
An appreciation of the streetscapes and heritage values of Brisbane's West End neatly stitch the home into its site.

The architectural setting

The culturally ubiquitous timber Queenslander house is a pre-modernist exemplar of an efficient, kit-of-parts architecture. This 19th-century building type was developed through a resource-informed use of locally available timber species and sawmilling techniques and this approach to construction is prescient of the contemporary interest in the provenance of building materials.

A reinterest in the possibilities of timber construction emerged in Queensland in the optimistic postwar era, informed by engagement with modernist ideas about industrialisation and prefabrication. A notable example of this is the competition-winning Plywood Exhibition House (see page 294), an innovative reinterpretation of the traditional Queenslander designed by Peter Heathwood and John Dalton and displayed at the Brisbane Exhibition from 1958 to 1963.

The West End House by KIRK is a detached, infill dwelling that draws on both these lessons from the story of Queensland architecture to create a contemporary, sustainable residence. The compact timber and plywood home sits on what was the last vacant site in the 1865 West End Estate and the design of the building is informed by a deep study of, and appreciation for, the streetscapes and heritage values of the much-loved Brisbane suburb. The formal clarity of the house is the outcome of a studious approach to materials and construction, achieved through a rationalisation of the structural systems, framing and cladding.

Above:
The lines of the exposed ceiling beams neatly extend to meet the exterior screening system.

Above:
A layering of openings allows the occupant to control the level of connection between inside and outside.

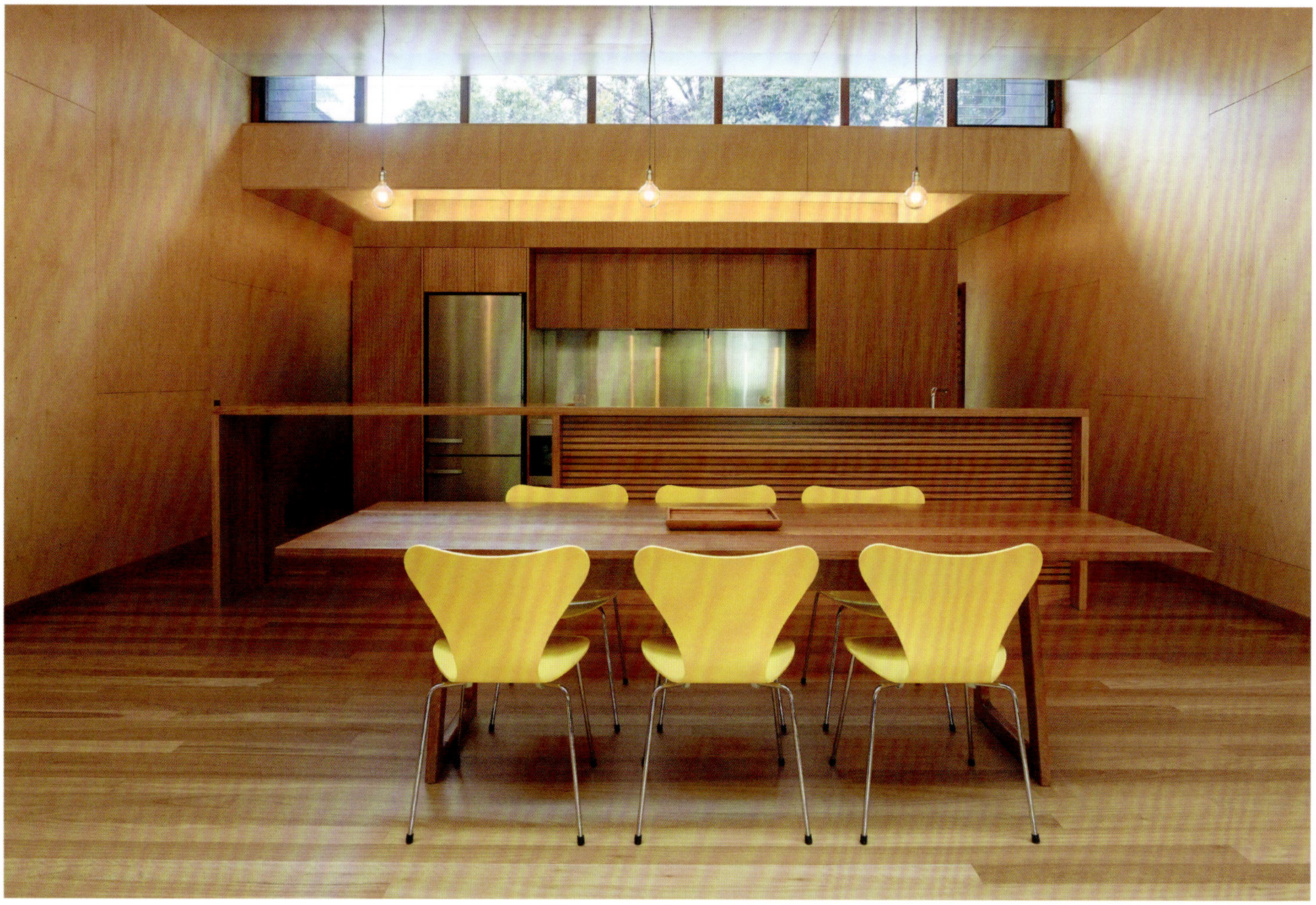

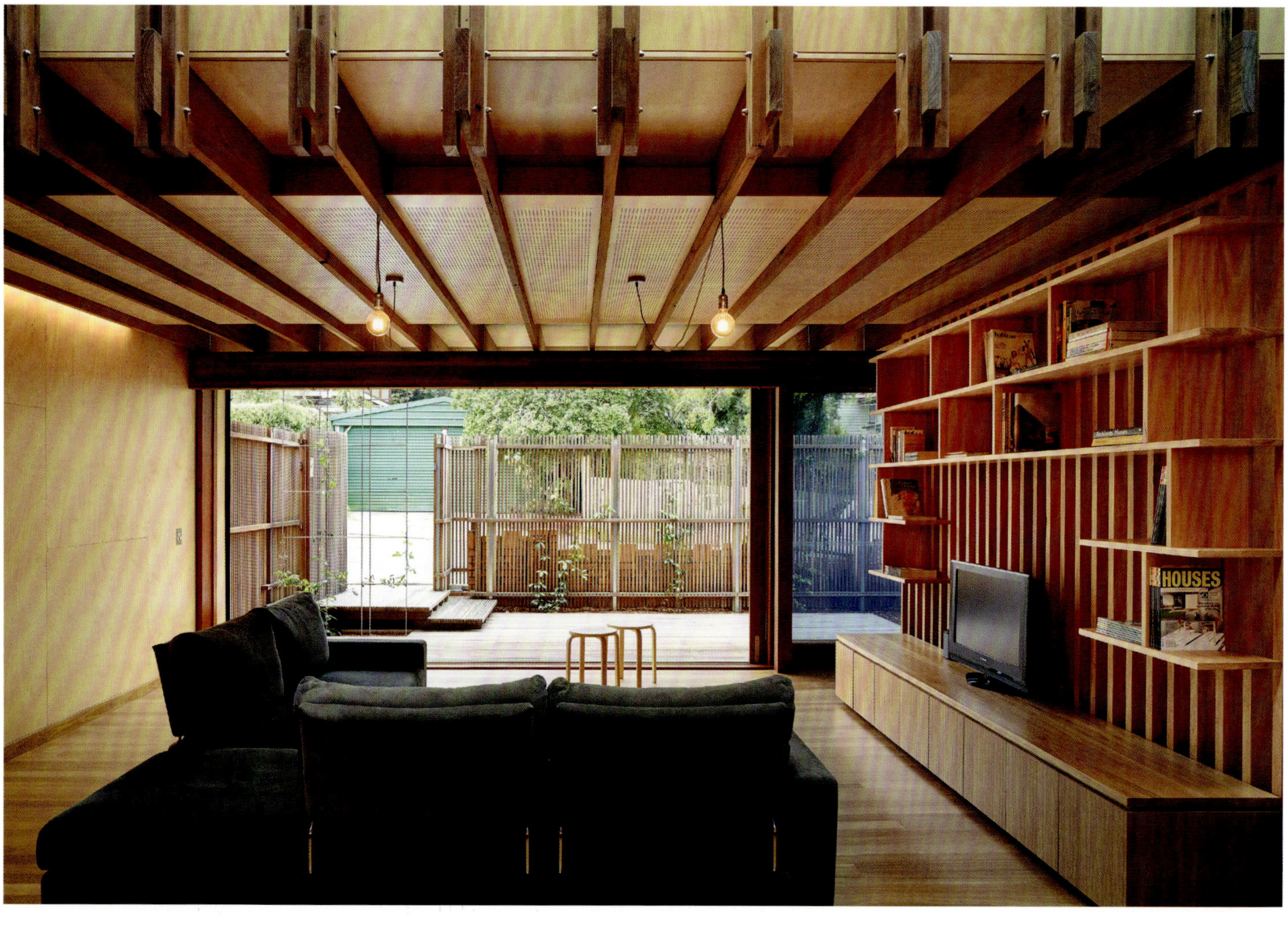
HOUSES

The lived experience

The owners of this house were enjoying living in Brisbane's West End when they came across an empty parcel of land within the highly regulated character neighbourhood. Although the couple were aware of the difficulties of the site, they were up for the challenge. After purchasing the small block, they approached architect Richard Kirk to design them a new home. Located in a typically narrow street of predominately prewar Queenslanders, Richard's design proposal is a contemporary reinterpretation of the architectural language of these timber-framed workers' cottages.

The form of the new house maximises the buildable area on a small site and, conforming to local council requirements, it has similar proportions to its neighbouring cottages. While it stitches neatly into the streetscape, the internal organisation of spaces responds better to the subtropical climate and family living than the traditional model of this housing type. 'When we first met Richard, we spoke mostly about how the house needed to engage with the street, with the living spaces having access to the northern light. We didn't have kids then, but now we have two children and the house has really come into its own. The kids now play out on the street with the neighbours and, while we have our privacy, we can still see out there from our living room.' In addition, timber screening to the upper north facade, now covered in flourishing vines, affords privacy to the north-facing main bedroom suite, while maintaining views, light and ventilation. Although a completely new house, the spirit of the traditional worker's cottage is palpable at the West End House.

Opposite top:
The kitchen features joinery elements that slide, pull, pivot and fold open when required.

Opposite bottom:
The living space is orientated north towards the street, encouraging community engagement.

Above:
The main bedroom overlooks the street, encased in timber screening, now covered in flourishing vines.

TRADITIONS REIMAGINED

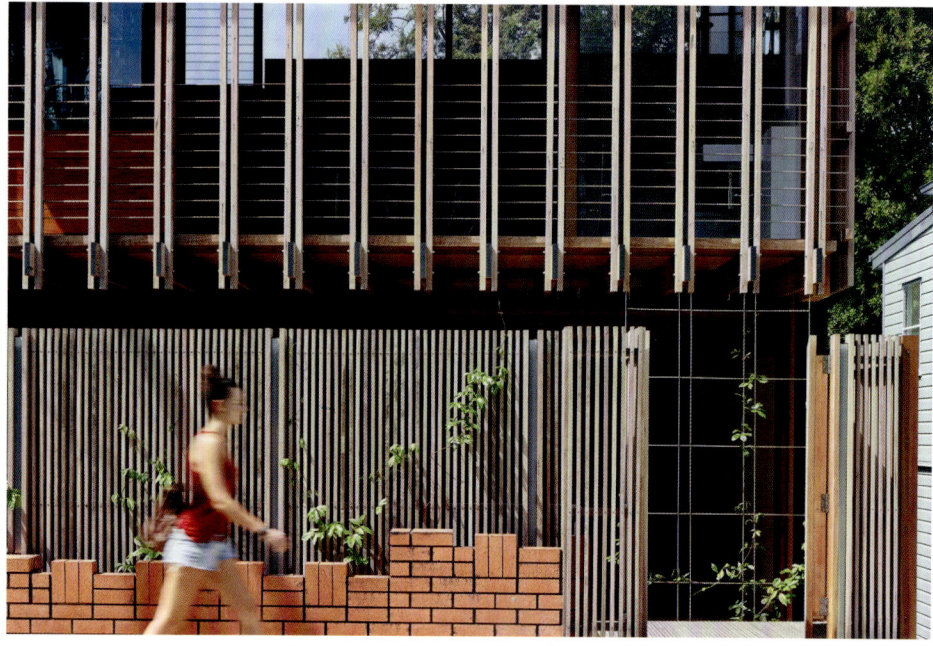

Top:
The repetitive patterns of the timber construction is echoed in the design of the inbuilt joinery units.

Bottom:
The new compact infill dwelling sits on what was the last vacant site in the 1865 West End Estate.

WEST END HOUSE

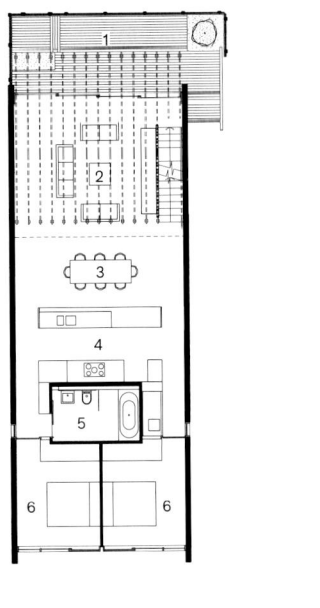

Lower level

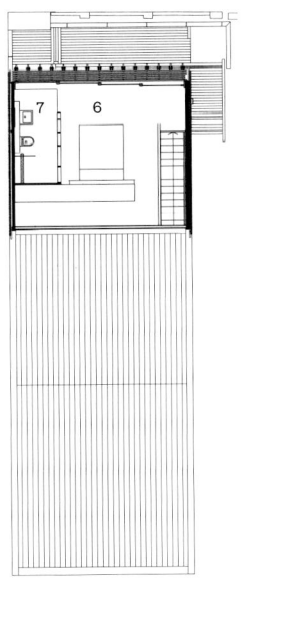

Upper level

1 Terrace
2 Living
3 Dining
4 Kitchen
5 Bathroom
6 Bedroom
7 Ensuite

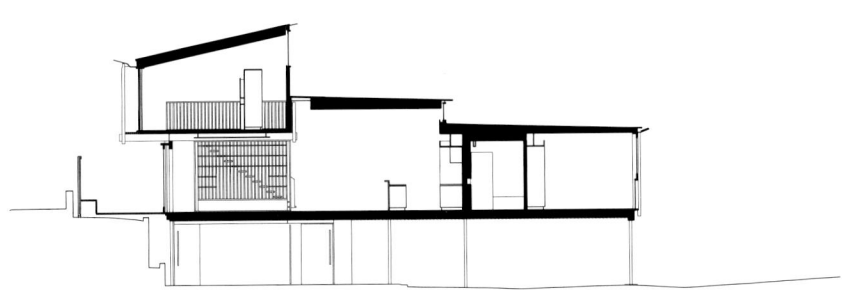

Section

1:250
0   5m

Architect — KIRK
Project team — Richard Kirk, Matthew Mahoney, Yee Jien, Jonathan Ward
Structural engineer — NJA Consulting
Hydraulic engineer — Neil Blair and Associates
Contractor — Owner and Artisan Carpentry
Photographer — Scott Burrows

Camp Hill House

Camp Hill, Brisbane
Twohill & James

Completed – 2016
Project type – Alteration and addition
Total site area – 607 m²
Internal area – 196 m²
External area – 22 m²
Number of residents – 4
Number of bedrooms – 3
Number of bathrooms – 2

Camp Hill House is built on the land of the Turrbal and Yuggera peoples

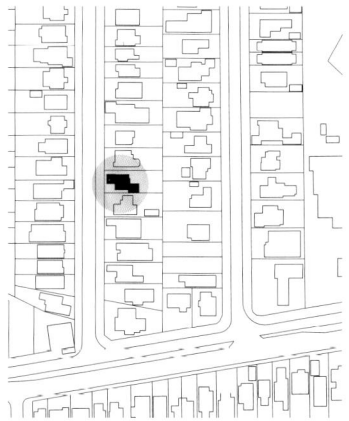

Location plan

1:5000 0 10 50m

CAMP HILL HOUSE

The architectural setting

The Brisbane suburb of Camp Hill was developed on farmland to house lots from the late 1800s through to the mid-1920s. One of Brisbane City Council's iconic electric tram routes, which criss-crossed Brisbane from 1948 to 1969, ran along the bisecting line of Old Cleveland Road from west to east. Camp Hill is six kilometres south-east of Brisbane's CBD and the 170-hectare Whites Hill Reserve – a significant bushland remnant with sections of open eucalypt forest and rainforest – occupies the southern wedge of the residential suburb.

The existing Camp Hill House was a modest, but well-loved interwar timber building and Twohill & James's sensitive alterations and additions respect and amplify the special relationship between people and place. In the alterations there is the deployment of a purposeful functionality that focuses on the way the home supports daily life alongside the project of creating meaningful connections with the landscape of the site and the suburb.

The finely detailed additions add a new and enriching layer to the architectural story of this house and its setting. The prosaic and suburb-defining quality of the original cottage is carefully preserved, and the new work at Camp Hill House has a distinguished and elevated level of detailing and materiality that thoughtfully responds to memory and experience.

Previous:
Meaningful connections with the site and suburb are created in the additions to the Camp Hill House.

Opposite:
The finely detailed additions to the home respect and preserve the modesty of the original cottage.

Top:
Terracotta steps at the end of the long, open living and dining room act as a miniature amphitheatre.

Bottom:
Cooling breezes move through the generously sized openings, embracing the subtropical climate.

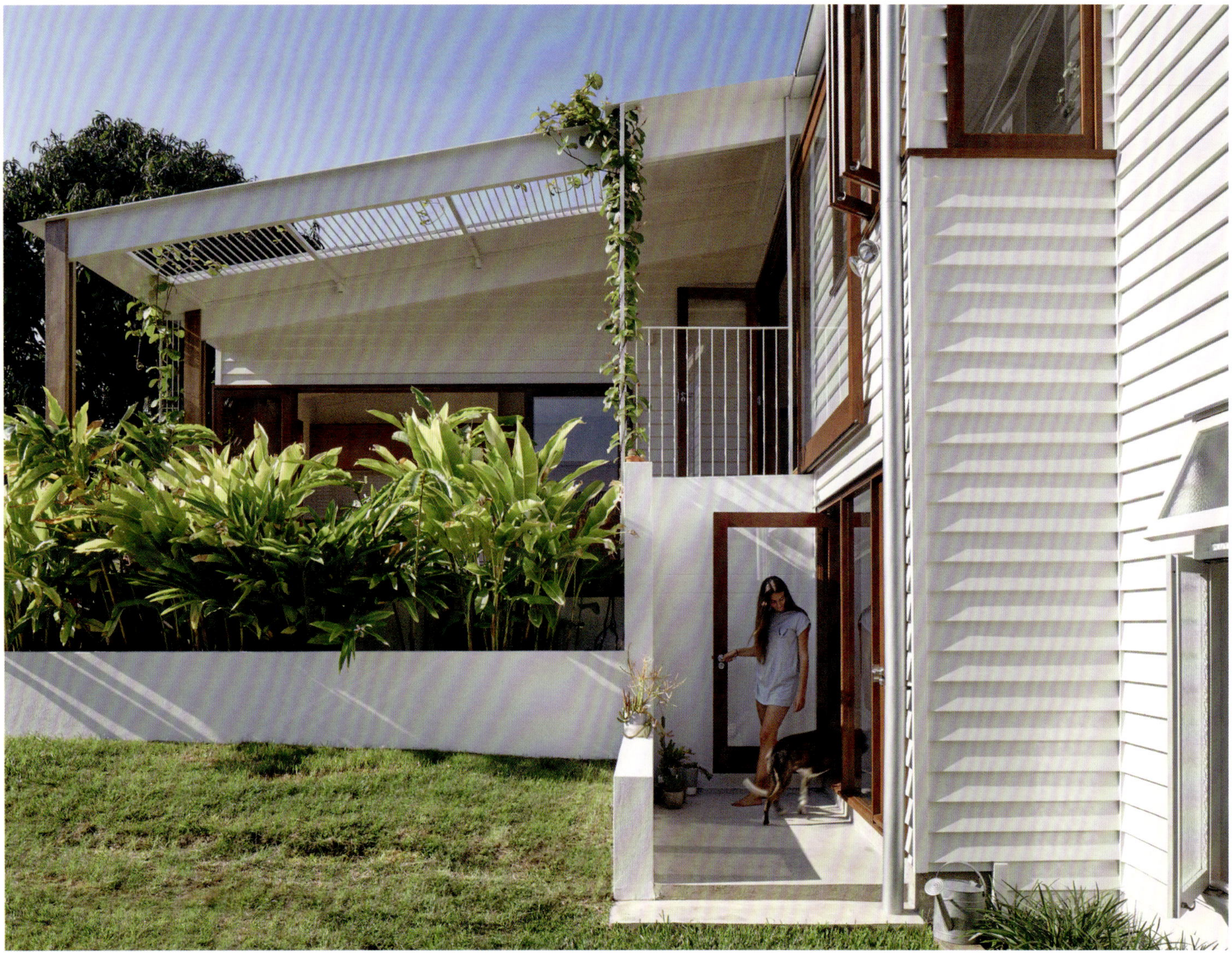

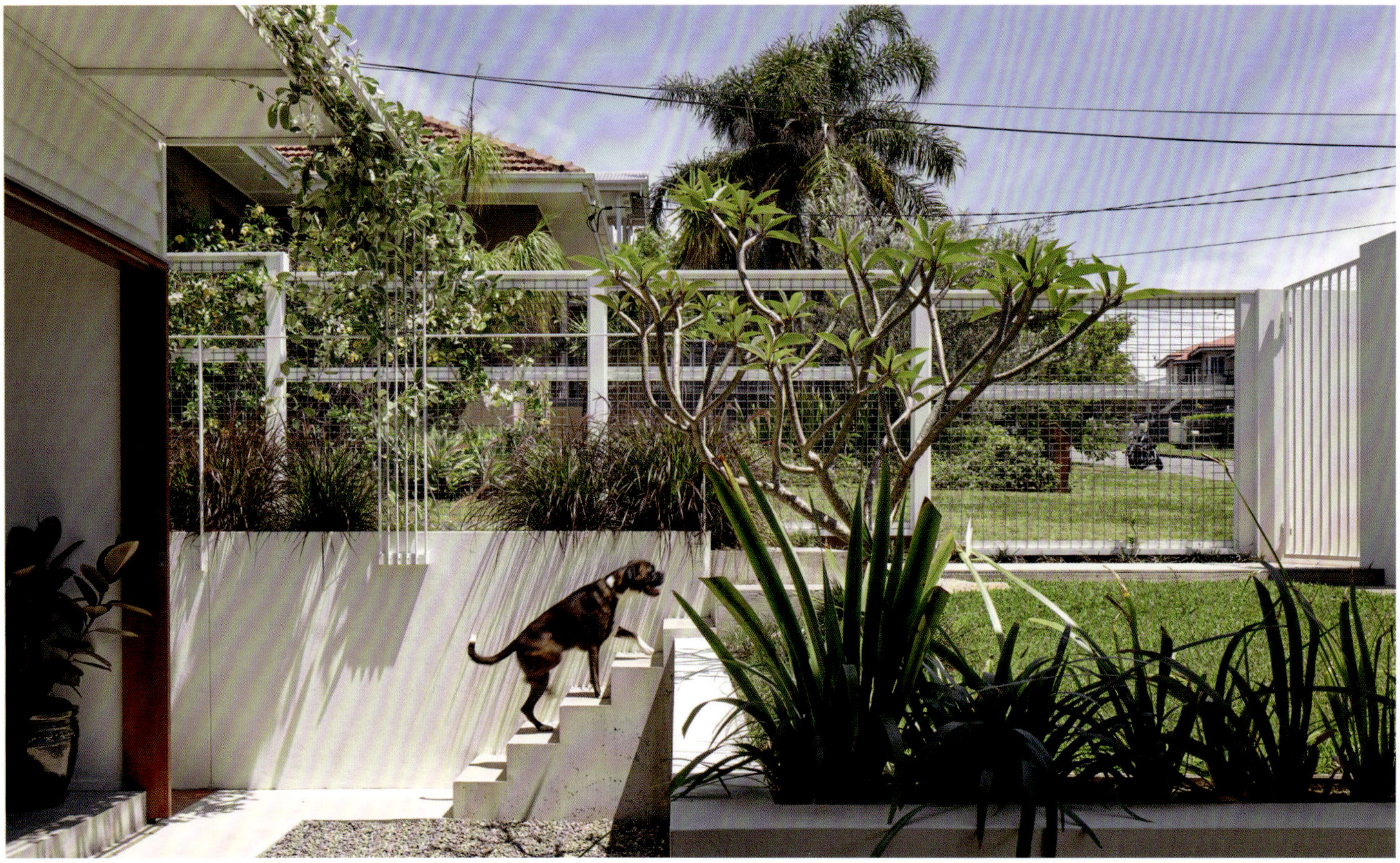

The lived experience

Israel Rivera bought his family's home in Brisbane's Camp Hill in 1993 when he was 21 years old. He and his wife now have two adult children and still live at the same address but, through working with architect Emma James of Twohill & James, the home has been updated to suit a contemporary lifestyle. 'The house spoke to us, it wasn't something we wanted to part with,' says Israel of his decision to alter and add to the existing timber cottage.

Israel is a creative person himself; he is now a director and photographer, and in a previous life he ran his own house-painting business. During this time, he was fortunate to spend some time on site at Donovan Hill's seminal C House, maintaining the custom timber panelling and joinery around the structure's formwork, many years after it was built. He was privy to a rare insight into architectural craftsmanship and he gained an understanding of how architecture can elevate daily life.

When renovating his own house, Israel lovingly restored as many of the timber elements as possible. The new addition grafts itself to the old, without clear delineation between the two parts. 'It's all blended in,' says Israel. 'Some visitors ask us which bit is old and which is new.' The roof of the existing cottage extrudes downwards over the new extension, with a trellis for climbing plants extending over the terrace and a new sequence of rooms connecting to the interior and garden. With cooling breezes moving through the generously sized openings, a variety of window seats and steps to perch on and a humble design quality, the informality of the Brisbane lifestyle permeates every inch of this home.

Opposite top:
Taking advantage of fall across the site, a third bedroom and studio is tucked in the space beneath the home.

Opposite bottom:
As the vines grow, an elegant metal trellis will create a series of shaded green enclosures.

Above:
The new kitchen is one part of a sequence of rooms that connect the interior to the garden.

Following:
The level of detail and materiality of the new work thoughtfully responds to memory and experience.

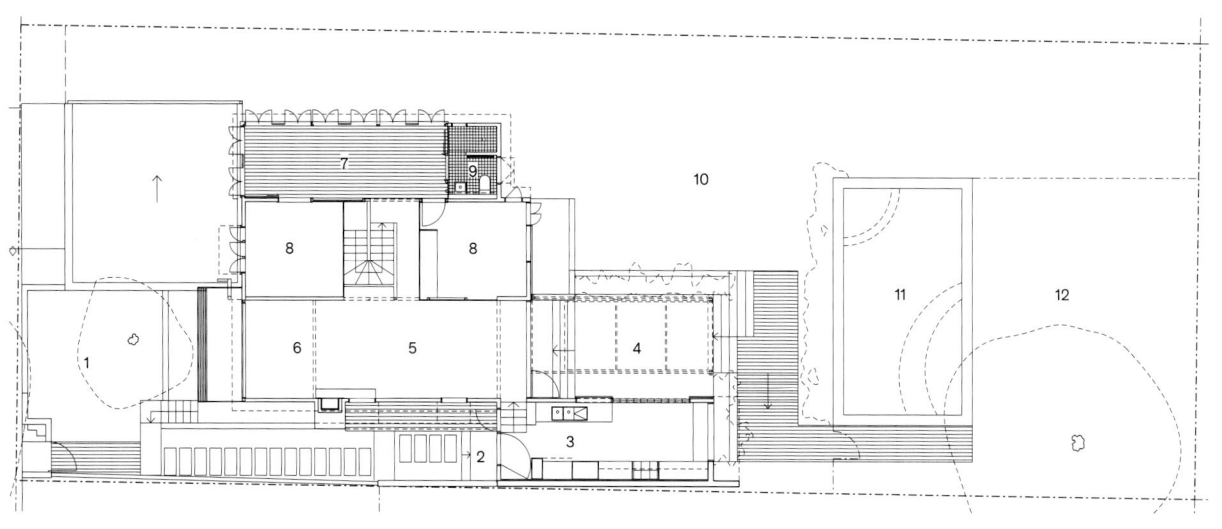

Upper level

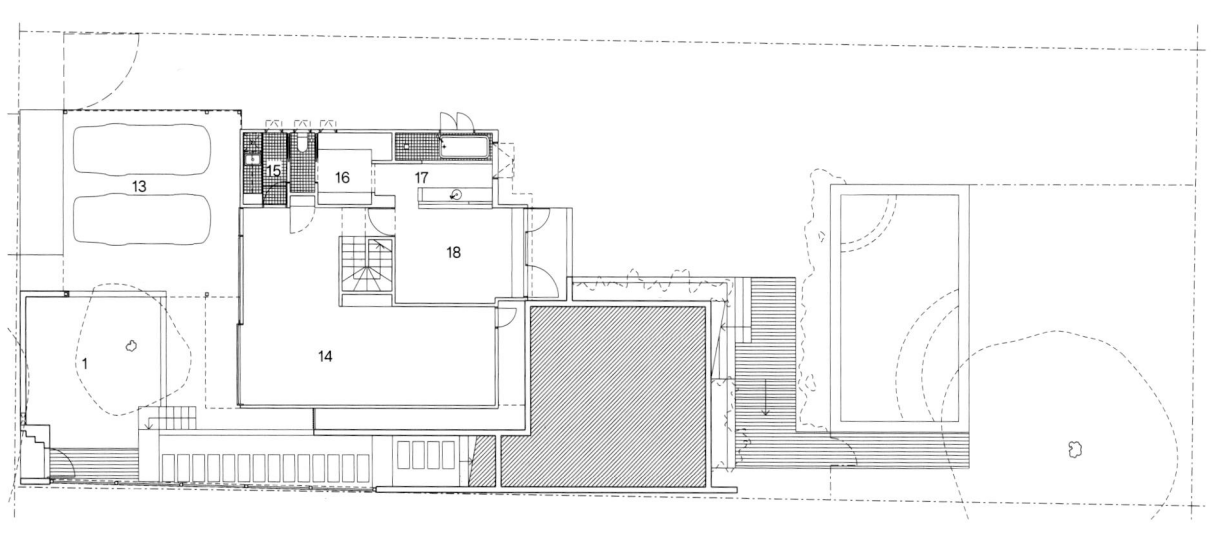

Lower level

1	Courtyard	10	Lawn
2	Entry	11	Pool
3	Kitchen	12	Pool court
4	Terrace	13	Carport
5	Dining	14	Studio
6	Living	15	Laundry
7	Sunroom	16	Walk-in robe
8	Bedroom	17	Ensuite
9	Bathroom	18	Main bedroom

Longitudinal section

1:250
0 5m

Architect — Twohill & James
Project team — Emma James, David Twohill, Sophie Benn
Builder — Robson Constructions
Structural engineer — AD Structure
Pool — Rogers Pools
Photographer — Christopher Frederick Jones

Terrarium House

Highgate Hill, Brisbane
John Ellway Architect

Completed – 2017
Project type – Alteration and addition
Total site area – 215 m²
Internal area – 105 m²
External area – 15 m²
Number of residents – 3
Number of bedrooms – 3
Number of bathrooms – 2

Terrarium House is built on the land of the
Turrbal and Yuggera peoples

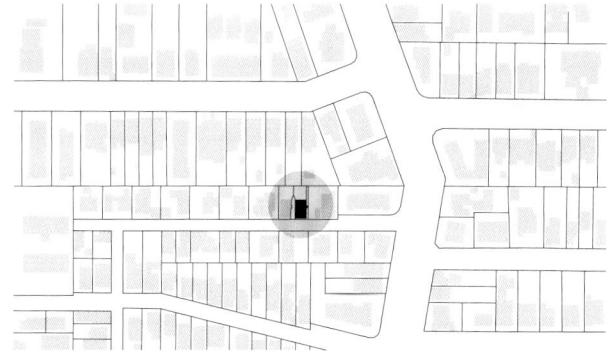

Location plan 1:5000 0 10 50m

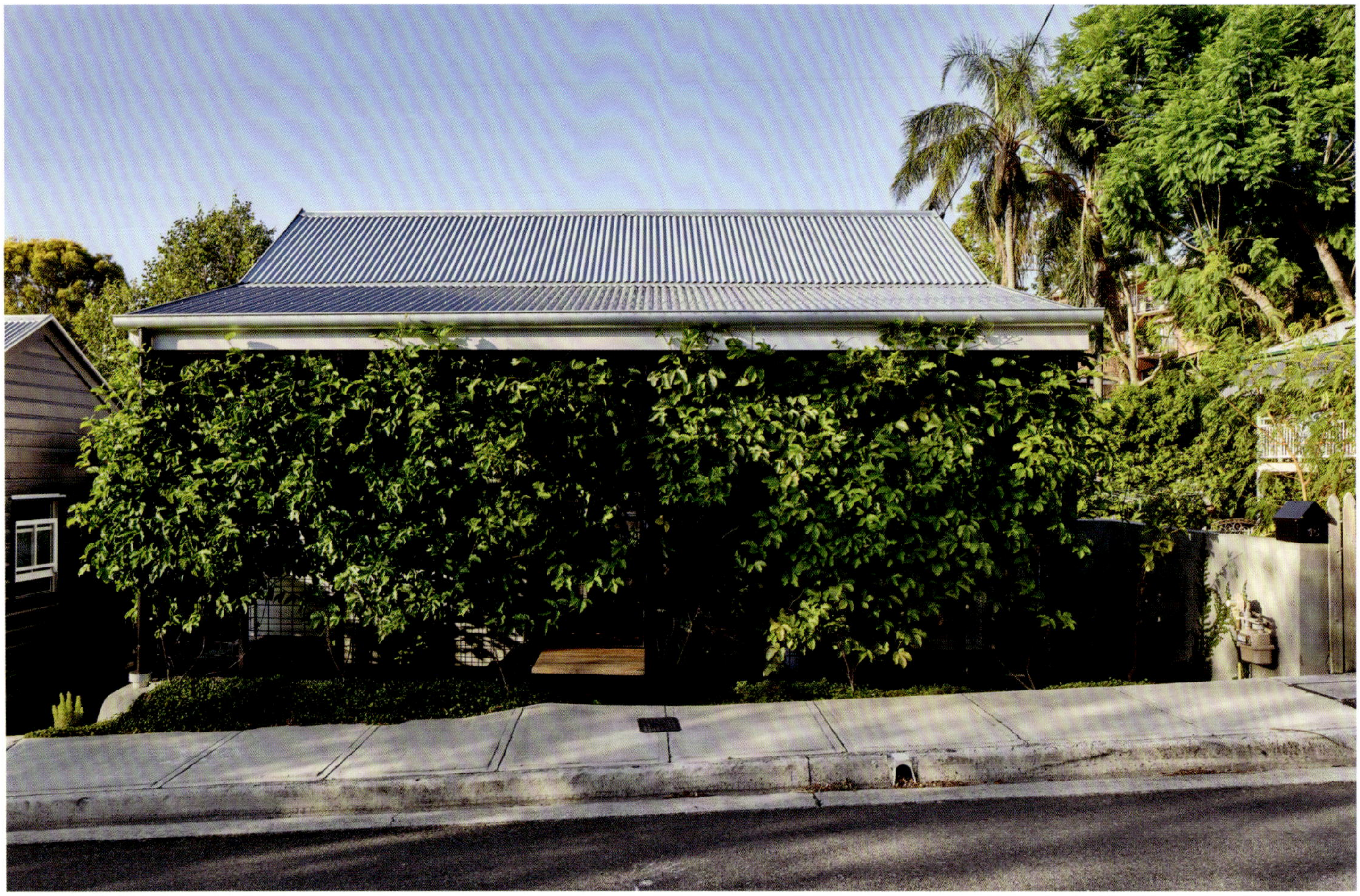

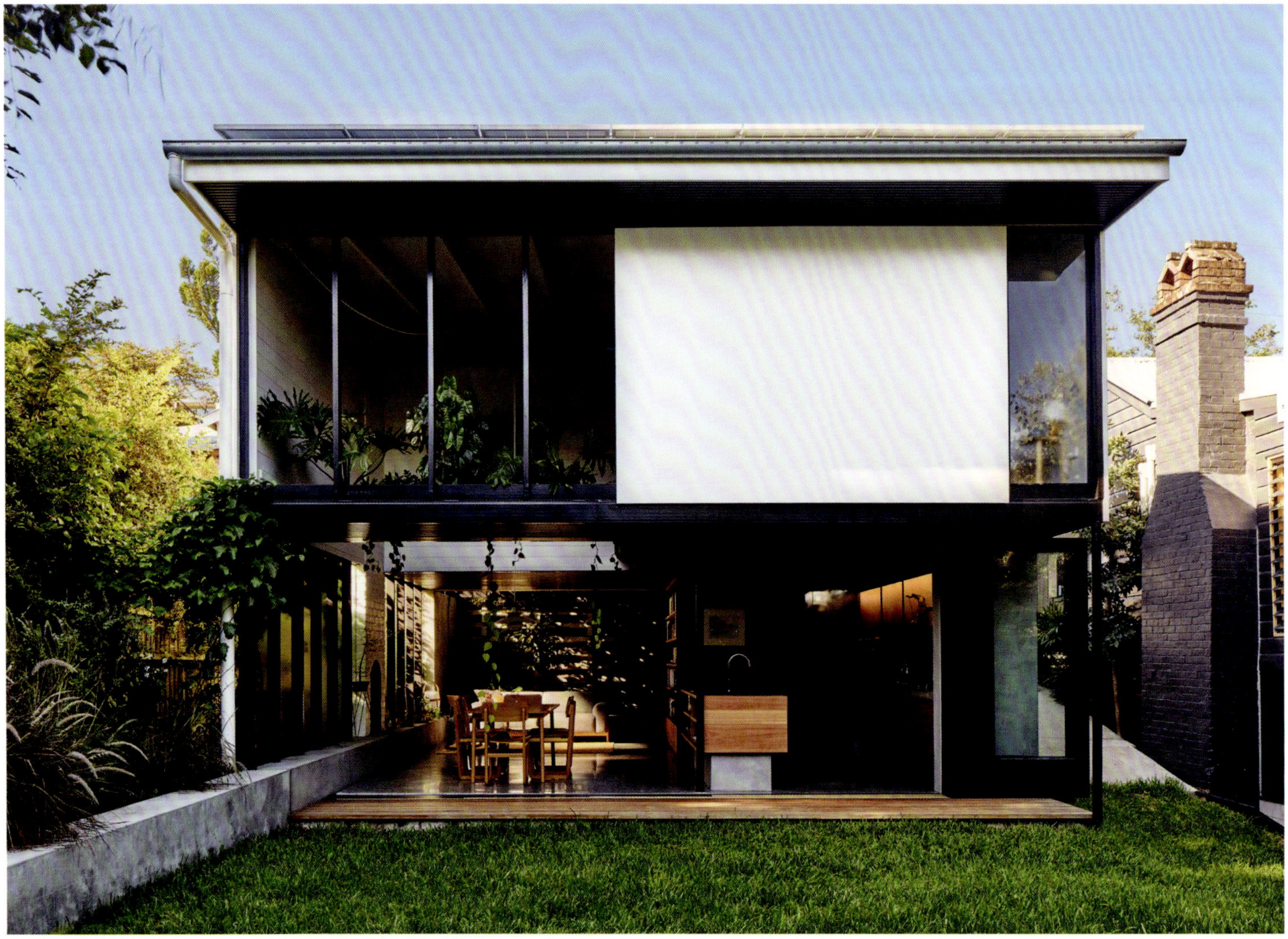

The architectural setting

The inner-city Brisbane suburbs of Highgate Hill, West End and South Brisbane sit on a topographically rich peninsula within a serpentine sweep of the Brisbane River. The architecturally diverse streetscape of Dornoch Terrace, which runs along the ridge of Highgate Hill, offers glimpses down into the enveloping remnant vegetation in the gullies that drop to the river below and across the suburban hinterland to the skyline of the city centre. The Terrarium House by John Ellway Architect sits in the intimate middle ground of this landscape.

Building-in the stumped under space of a Queenslander House to create extra accommodation is a somewhat ubiquitous home improvement project in the suburbs, and in many instances the original building is thoroughly compromised by an unsympathetic infill. In confident architectural hands the task provides ample opportunity for architectural invention and urban activation, and this is exemplified by John Ellway's approach to the design and construction of his own. Other examples in the nearby suburbs include the 3 House in New Farm by by Burton Architects and Channon Architects (see page 292) and the Banney Residence in Red Hill by m3architecture (see page 292).

Terrarium House is a striking reimagining and reconfiguration of an existing cottage that is simultaneously respectful and inquiring and where the new relationship with the landscape is profound. At Terrarium House the subtropical landscape is experienced up close, and the detailing and materiality of the additions celebrate the spatial capacity of the voracious vegetation.

Previous:
A covered outdoor stair marks the threshold between the old cottage and the new at Terrarium House.

Opposite top:
The form of the original gable-roofed worker's cottage has been preserved, but has been camouflaged in greenery.

Opposite bottom:
The rear elevation is composed of a series of openings that allows the occupants to exist in tune with the outside weather.

Above:
The open undercroft of the former one-bedroom cottage is now occupied with shadowy and breezy living spaces.

The lived experience

In rethinking the 'raise and build under' renovation strategy so often applied to Queenslander houses, architect and owner of Terrarium House, John Ellway has innovatively responded to the possibilities of the sloping topography of his site in Highgate Hill. The open undercroft of the former one-bedroom cottage is now occupied with shadowy and breezy living spaces, with the private bedroom spaces cocooned within the existing timber cottage. As John's wife Amber Winter says, 'It feels like you are living under the footpath, sheltered from the street, yet connected to it.'

The treatment of the street frontage retains the form of the original gable-roofed cottage but it has been camouflaged in the greenery of a dense vine. Behind the planted trellis layer, the verandah of the cottage has been removed, allowing light, air and access between levels via a covered outdoor stair. This space marks the threshold between the old cottage and the new, as well as the connecting point between the private and public spaces of the home. 'The stair becomes the transition from one time of day to the next – for example, you retire upstairs to the cottage to go to bed in the evenings.'

A unique benefit of living in such a benign climate like Brisbane's is the way homes can be designed so that inhabitants can exist deeply in tune with the outside weather. 'When it's hot, the house is like a tent – we have the doors wide open to encourage air flow. In the mild Brisbane weather, you get a breeze by opening portions up. And then when it's cooler, it can be completely closed down to be cosy and warm.'

Opposite:
The open-plan kitchen is a highly functional composition of custom cabinetry and cast concrete elements.

Above:
Upstairs, the private bedroom spaces are cocooned within the existing timber cottage.

Following:
Frosted glass washes the main living area in gentle daylight while ensuring the presence of greenery is always felt.

Above:
A double-height volume rises over the dining table, filling the lower level with northern light.

TERRARIUM HOUSE

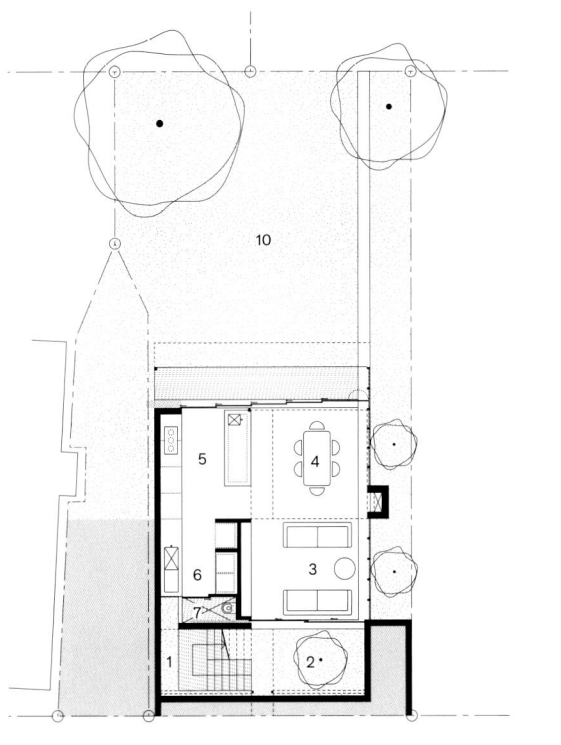

Lower level

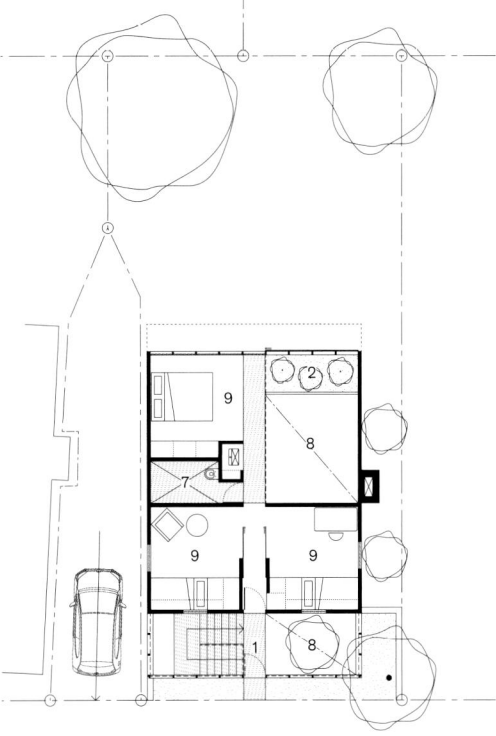

Upper level

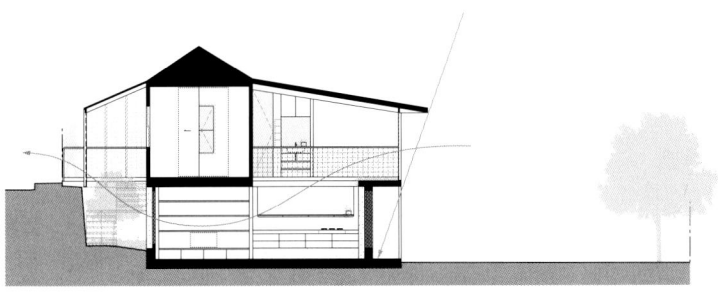

Longitudinal section

1 Entry
2 Garden
3 Living
4 Dining
5 Kitchen
6 Laundry
7 Bathroom
8 Void
9 Bedroom
10 Lawn

1:250
0   5m

Architect — John Ellway Architect
Project team — John Ellway
Builder — Mat Saggers
Engineer — Westera Partners
Photographer — Toby Scott

Annerley House

Annerley, Brisbane
Zuzana&Nicholas

Completed – 2020
Project type – Alteration and addition
Total site area – 412 m²
Internal area – 86 m² (existing)
plus 33.5 m² (extension)
External area – 29 m²
Number of residents – 3
Number of bedrooms – 3
Number of bathrooms – 1

Annerley House is built on the land of the
Turrbal and Yuggera peoples

Location plan

1:5000 0 10 50m

The architectural setting

Experiments with the roof form are a defining and identity-making characteristic of recent Queensland residential architecture. The iconic, pyramidal roof of the Queenslander house inspired the most venturous architects of the 1970s and 1980s to experiment with its expression and geometry, and this is exemplified by the ground-breaking Addison House in Taringa by Rex Addison, the enigmatic Carpenter Hall House by Russell Hall (see page 293), and the remarkable Campbell House by Don Watson, which was the recipient of the Australian Institute of Architects Robin Boyd Award for residential architecture in 1989.

In parallel to this cross-pollination of international postmodernism and an emerging new regionalism, there was the development of a sophisticated skillion roof form architecture in the 1990s. These lightweight, innovatively detailed houses gained national and international attention at the time and produced two Robin Boyd Award winners – the 1994 Fifth Avenue House in St Lucia by Bud Brannigan Architects (see page 293) and the 1996 Chapman House in Noosaville by John Mainwaring Architects (see page 293), plus Dragon House (see page 292).

At the Annerley House by Zuzana&Nicholas a bold new chapter is added to this story with a modest wedge-shaped extension that merges roof and wall in deference to the character of the existing house. This structure is experienced as a porous outdoor room and tucks neatly into the rear of the cottage, rising to a double-height volume that has a discreet loft in its apex.

Previous:
Annerley House is a modest, wedge-shaped extension that tucks neatly into the rear of an existing cottage.

Opposite:
The new connectivity to the garden is established via a series of inserted 'edges' or thresholds between inside and out.

Top:
Greenery abuts the concrete ledge perimeter of the extension, firmly embedding the home into the garden.

Bottom:
A mezzanine nested beneath the roof of the extension is a nook for reading and playing.

ANNERLEY HOUSE

The lived experience

Tamsin Cull purchased her cottage in Brisbane's southern suburb of Annerley fourteen years ago. The pragmatic need to update the home became apparent as she had a family and she approached Zuzana Kovar and Nicholas Skepper of multidisciplinary practice Zuzana&Nicholas. Her brief to this deep-thinking design duo wasn't about substantially increasing the internal floor area. Instead, it was about including the garden as part of the primary living area.

For Tamsin, this alteration and addition is all about the 'edges' or thresholds – between old and new, and house and garden. Although there is a clear distinction between what is old and what is new, particularly in the differing geometry of the two parts, the spirit of the humble worker's cottage is carried through the updated home. It is as much about what has been retained as it is about what has been added. The front rooms and enclosed verandah of the cottage were restored, but the fabric of the existing living area was edited predominantly to establish a new spatial order of connectivity to the garden.

Although the existing parts of the home have been opened to the backyard, a new double-height pavilion grafted to the eastern edge of the cottage is the primary transitional zone to the outdoors. A series of window seats at the threshold between house and garden invite occupation. 'With the sliding doors peeled back, it gives the feeling that you've hovering in the garden,' says Tamsin.

Opposite top:
A series of window seats invite occupation to further amplify the feeling of living in the garden.

Opposite bottom:
Stackable sliding doors create wide and unobstructed openings to the backyard.

Above:
Sightlines between old and new parts of the house have been orchestrated to create a new spatial order.

Above:
Although modest in area and materiality, the new room adds spatial luxury to the home.

ANNERLEY HOUSE

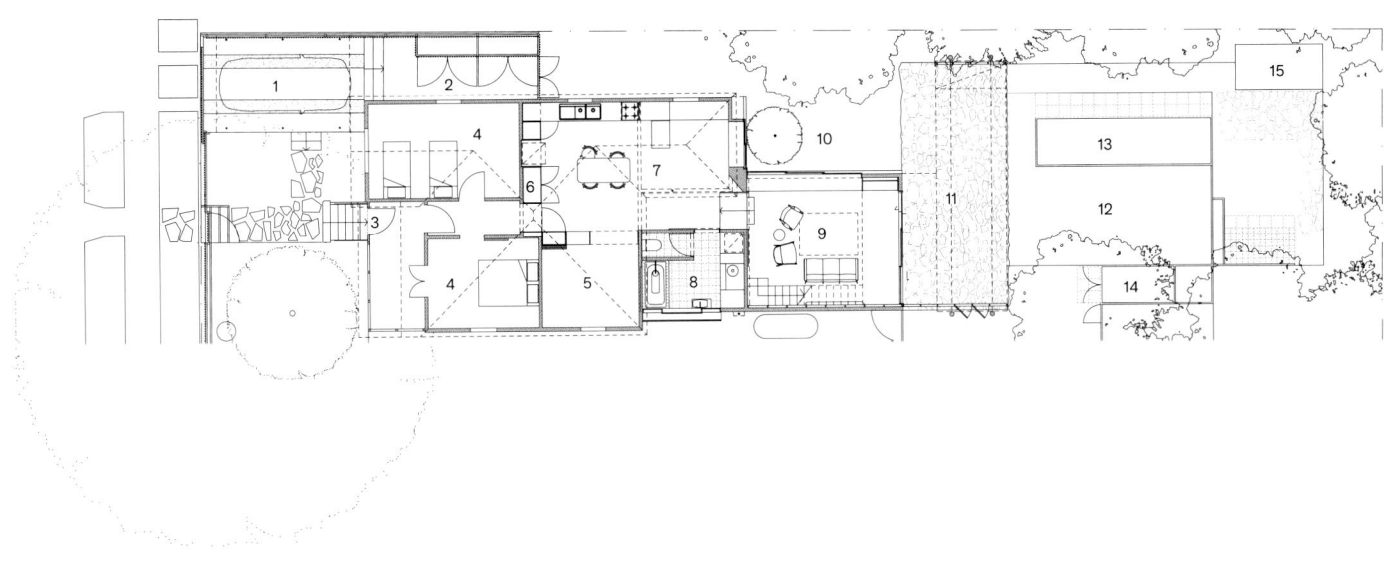

Plan

1 Carport
2 Services
3 Entry
4 Bedroom
5 Playroom/guestroom
6 Study nook
7 Kitchen/dining
8 Bathroom
9 Living
10 Courtyard garden
11 Terrace
12 Lawn
13 Productive garden
14 Chook house
15 Shed

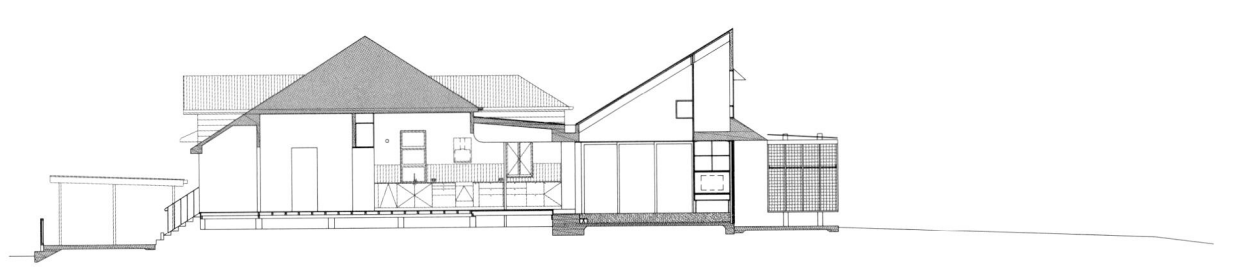

Section

1:250
0   5m

Architect — Zuzana&Nicholas
Project team — Zuzana Kovar and Nicholas Skepper
Structural engineer — NGS Structural Engineers
Landscape design — Jonathan Kopinski
Photography — Christopher Frederick Jones

Suburban ensembles

The small, detached outbuilding – a kitchen, lavatory, car garage, workshop or chook shed – is a part of the suburban landscape of Queensland's cities and towns. This informal urban condition is the inspiration for a contemporary architectural approach that studies and elevates this suburban utility to create engaging ensembles of buildings. In these projects the architect has shown great deference to the existing building (or buildings) on the site, often peeling back and removing layers of past, insensitive renovations to reveal the original form and adding new structures with strong urban legibility. The new buildings are designed as linked but architecturally independent structures that strategically re-plan the existing house or create secondary dwellings (or studios) that address the urgent need to increase the density and occupation of the suburbs.

Keperra House

Keperra, Brisbane
Atelier Chen Hung

Completed – 2012
Project type – New build (secondary dwelling)
Total site area – 600 m²
Internal area – 35 m²
External area – 10 m²
Number of residents – 2
Number of bedrooms – 1
Number of bathrooms – 1

Keperra House is built on the land of the Turrbal and Yuggera peoples

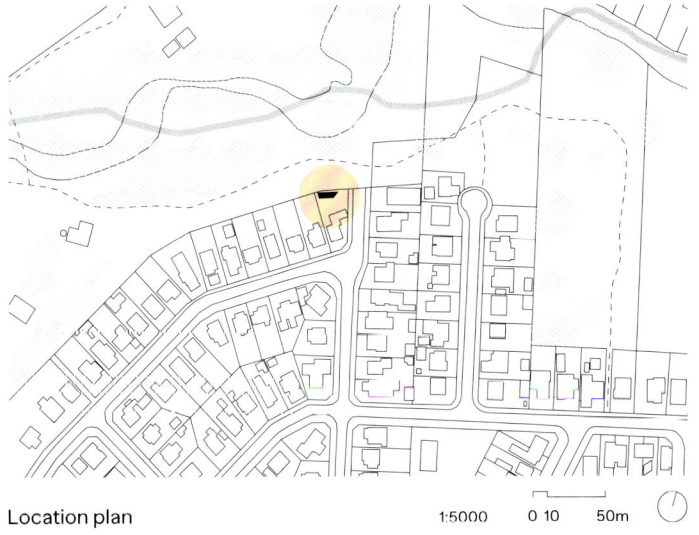

Location plan 1:5000 0 10 50m

The architectural setting

Queensland's postwar housing shortage escalated the development of new fringe suburbs and saw the construction of large tracts of War Service Homes Commission and Queensland Housing Commission dwellings. In these now middle-ring Brisbane suburbs, including Inala, Stafford, Zillmere, Norman Park and Keperra, these sturdy timber buildings of the 1940s and 1950s, some of which used prefabricated construction, sit on generous 10 x 40 m, quarter-acre blocks.

Across Brisbane this low-density suburbia offers opportunities for the addition of secondary dwellings, often referred to as a granny flat and more recently taking on the housing affordability and supply challenge in the guise of multi-generational living. This development approach, which responds to changing household demographics, requires serious architectural invention if it is to preserve the desirable character and qualities of the neighbourhood. Recent experiments of this nature in Queensland include the Garden Bunkie by Reddog Architects (see page 292), the West End Granny Flat by Jeremy Salmon Architect in Brisbane and Granny Flat on the Gold Coast by Clare Design.

Keperra House by Atelier Chen Hung is a replicable model for this much-needed socially, economically and environmentally sustainable suburban densification and a building that is delivered with an architectural rigour that embraces and amplifies its setting.

Previous:
Keperra House hovers above an unkempt suburban creek reserve and acts as a viewing platform.

Opposite:
The compact, 45 m² building is a secondary dwelling to an existing timber bungalow.

Above:
The robust building is autonomous to the existing home, with a private courtyard garden between the two.

The lived experience

Shakkei is the Japanese technique of borrowing scenery by framing elements of the surrounding landscape. Editing views and sightlines in this manner is a strategic way of giving interior spaces the impression of more space. Keperra House effectively appropriates the wilderness of an unkempt suburban creek reserve as its own private forest. In turn, the new 45 m² secondary dwelling is a dominant form hovering above the nature reserve. 'A lot of people walk past and say hello,' says owner Michael Alroe.

This approach of opening out to the surrounding landscape is in contrast to the existing single-storey timber bungalow that 'looks in on itself,' as Michael says. The placement of the new building creates a private courtyard garden between itself and the existing house, reinforcing the autonomy of each. Interaction between the two buildings occurs when the sliding walls of the semi-outdoor deck of the new addition are open, framing the lush foliage of the creek reserve in one direction and framing an existing jacaranda tree and the main house in the other direction.

Originally Michael intended to rent out the studio while living in the primary house himself, yet the reverse is now true. Adding functional amenity to the property, the flexible standalone structure allows for a number of arrangements, such as multigenerational living or conversion into a home office or studio. Whatever it's used as, this permeable pavilion is always 'a viewing platform to enjoy the lush natural habitat'.

Opposite:
The house borrows scenery by framing elements of the wilderness in the neighbouring nature reserve.

Above left:
The low-maintenance skin of concrete and galvanised steel is internally lined with plywood to add warmth.

Above right:
The small-footprint home has been carefully configured to ensure it doesn't feel cramped.

Following:
Large sliding doors transform the bunker-like home into a light-filled permeable pavilion.

Above:
A bend in the kitchen wall draws the attention outward towards the landscape view.

KEPERRA HOUSE

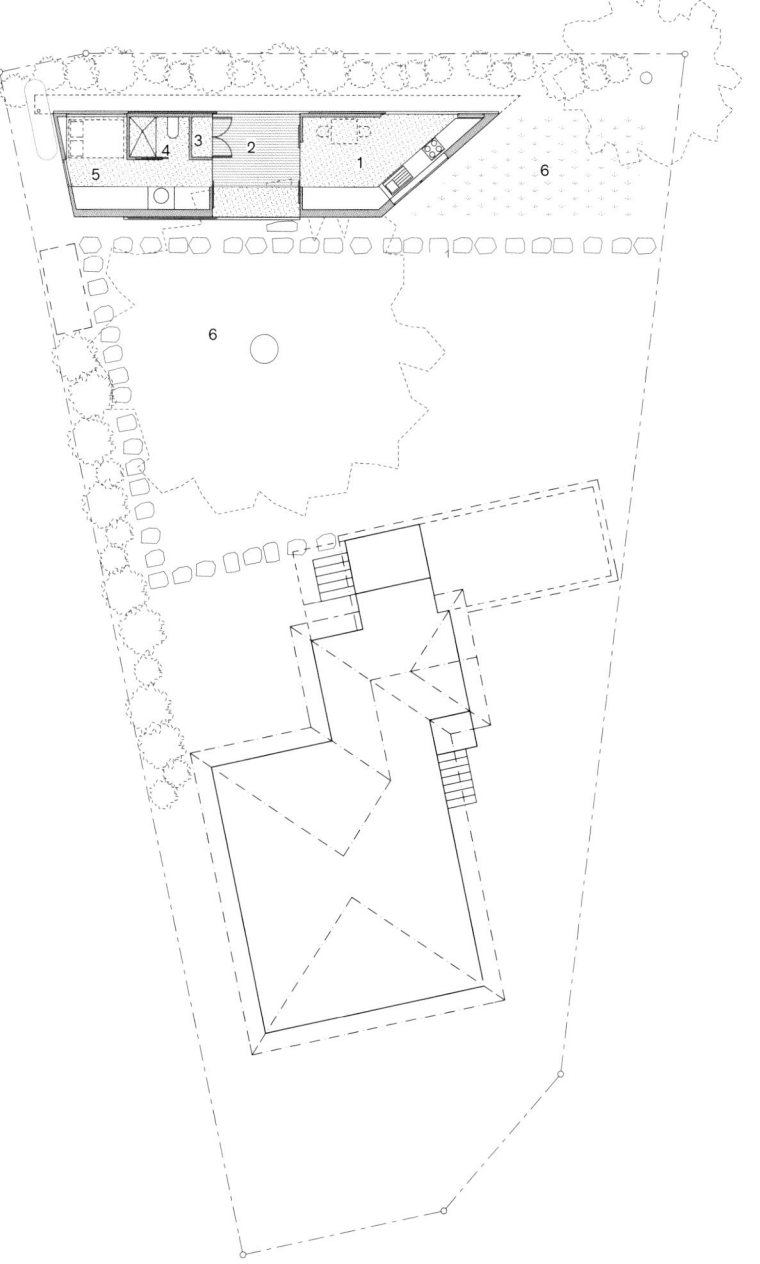

Plans

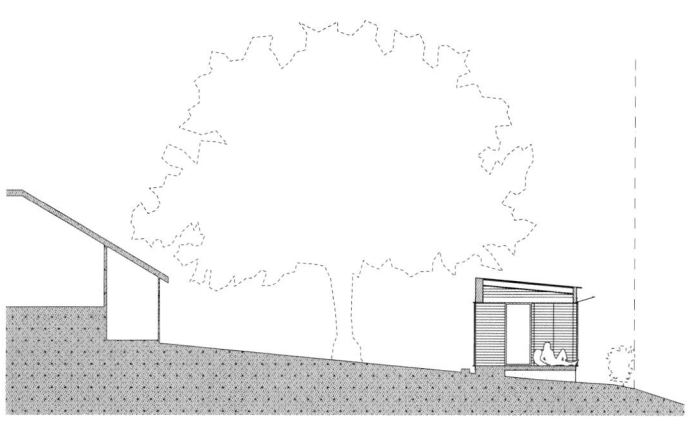

Cross section

1 Living/kitchen
2 Deck
3 Store
4 Bathroom
5 Bedroom
6 Garden

1:250

0 5m

Architect — Atelier Chen Hung
Project team — Melody Chen, James Hung, Renee Popovic
Engineer — Northrop Consulting Engineers
Photographer — Alicia Taylor; James Hung (page 230)

Granny Flat

Burleigh Heads, Gold Coast
Clare Design

Completed – 2014
Project type – Alteration and addition
Total site area – 400 m²
Internal area – 98 m²
External area – 25 m²
Number of residents – 2
Number of bedrooms – 2
Number of bathrooms – 2

Granny Flat is built on the land of the Kombumerri people

Location plan 1:5000

The architectural setting

The highest industry honour bestowed upon Australian architects is the Gold Medal. Established in 1960 and awarded annually by the Australian Institute of Architects, this gong recognises distinguished contributions to practice and the advancement of the discipline. Eight architects who have practised in Queensland have received the Gold Medal, with the first being Frederick Bruce Lucas in 1971 and the most recent being Don Watson, who was awarded in 2021. Across the national rollcall of Gold Medallists there is a threading of residential architecture practice – as the early, foundational work that established a prodigious career in public and commercial architecture; as a parallel endeavour to larger-scale work that sustains new ideas; and in several cases as the primary focus of the architect's practice.

Lindsay Clare and Kerry Clare, the 2010 joint recipients of the Gold Medal, present as something of a hybrid of this trilogy, having worked successfully across scales, locations and types, and from the realisation of exemplary built work across to the level of advocacy and policymaking. Their eponymous practice, Clare Design, emerged in the early 1980s under the mentorship of Gabriel Poole (the 1998 Gold Medallist) with a slew of innovative homes on the Sunshine Coast. With the ongoing project of developing the site of the Granny Flat as a multi-generational residential compound, the Clares have deployed a rigorous, first-principles approach to create a model for 21st-century subtropical living.

Previous:
Granny Flat is part of a multi-generational residential compound on the Gold Coast.

Opposite:
The studio invites an informal and relaxed lifestyle and a robust material palette requires little maintenance.

Top:
The character and scale of the neighbourhood beach shacks are referenced in the design.

Bottom:
Yellow pivot doors along the north-east elevation add a sense of play to the studio.

GRANNY FLAT

The lived experience

The modesty of the traditional mid-century beach shack is distinctive of Gold Coast's suburbia, but unfortunately many of these houses have been knocked down to make way for larger contemporary homes and apartment buildings. Architects Kerry and Lindsay Clare were keen to acknowledge the character and scale of the neighbourhood beach shacks in the design of the Granny Flat – a secondary dwelling that sits behind a 1950s fibro house on a 10-metre-wide 400 m^2 suburban block on the Gold Coast. The two-storey, 7 x 7 m studio adjoins the original dwelling via a roofed deck, with battened doors sliding to screen between the two to allow for privacy and retreat as required.

Having spent forty years living and working in South East Queensland, Kerry and Lindsay are acutely familiar with the low-density beachside suburb housing and saw an opportunity to make better use of resources by increasing the amenity of the site. The new pavilion is intentionally uncomplicated and flexible to cater to the varying needs of an intergenerational family. Passive solar and ventilation strategies inform the design, lightweight materials respond to the Gold Coast context, and a pop of yellow to the pivot doors to the north-east adds a sense of play. This is a studio that invites an informal and relaxed lifestyle – and its robustness means it could easily handle the return of wet and sandy beachgoers, requiring only a quick sweep of the floor.

Opposite:
The new secondary dwelling is intentionally uncomplicated and flexible to cater for varying needs.

Above:
The two-storey studio connects to the existing dwelling via a roofed deck, with a battened screen for privacy.

Above:
On the upper level, a flexible study space runs along one edge of the open living/sleeping area.

Above:
Passive solar and ventilation strategies inform the design and lightweight materials respond to the context.

First floor

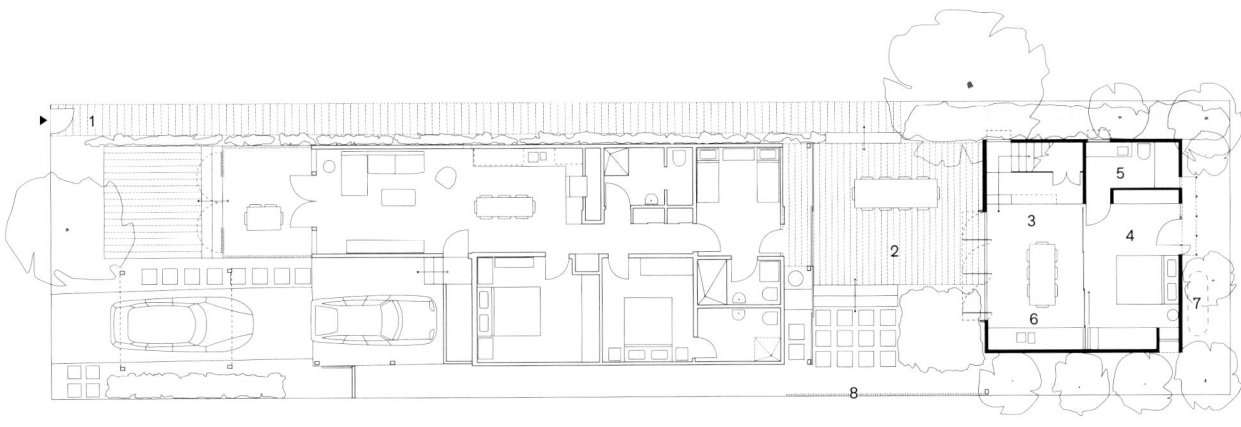

Ground floor

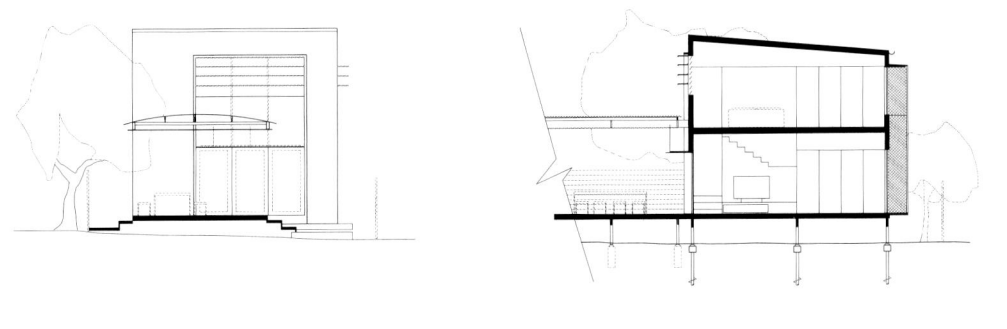

Elevation and section

1 Entry
2 Connecting deck
3 Dining
4 Living/guest
5 Bathroom
6 Kitchen
7 Water tank
8 Screen wall
9 Sitting
10 Bedroom
11 Study
12 Ensuite

1:250

0   5m

Architect — Clare Design
Project team — Lindsay Clare, Kerry Clare, David Currie, Dritta Wingender
Builder — ClareBuild
Structural and civil engineer — Mark Traucnieks
Photographer — Peter Hyatt

Bath House

Hermit Park, Townsville
Stephen de Jersey Architect

Completed – 2015
Project type – Alteration and addition
Total site area – 809 m²
Internal area – 108 m²
External area – 48 m²
Number of residents – 2
Number of bedrooms – 2 (plus sleep-out space)
Number of bathrooms – 1

Bath House is built on the land of the
Wulgurukaba people

Location plan

1:5000   0 10   50m

BATH HOUSE

The architectural setting

One of the very special characteristics of the timber and tin Queenslander houses is that they are relocatable. The contemporary process of moving a house is a well-organised and relatively fast exercise, with the building propped up and then lowered onto a house trailer the house is trucked overnight under police escort to its new site. If the house is very large it will be cut into pieces and then rejoined once in place.

In the major North Queensland coastal city of Townsville some of the city's most historic suburbs have more Queenslander houses today than they did a century ago because people moved homes here from their original locations in inland mining towns that went into decline in the early 20th century.

The Bath House by Stephen de Jersey Architect adds a crisp new building at the rear of an impressively intact and much-loved Queenslander house in Hermit Park, a Townsville suburb which was subdivided for housing lots in the 1880s. In this modest, exemplary project the architect has been respectful and responsive to the structural clarity, spatial organisation and siting strategy of the original 1930s building, skilfully augmenting its enduring functionality and updating it for an everyday and uplifting lifestyle in the dry tropics.

Previous:
With solid balustrades and a canopy overhead, Bath House is an extension that functions as an outdoor room.

Opposite:
The new building is respectful and responsive to the original 1930s four-room Queenslander cottage.

Above:
The outdoor room hovers above the garden, with stairs providing direct access to the backyard.

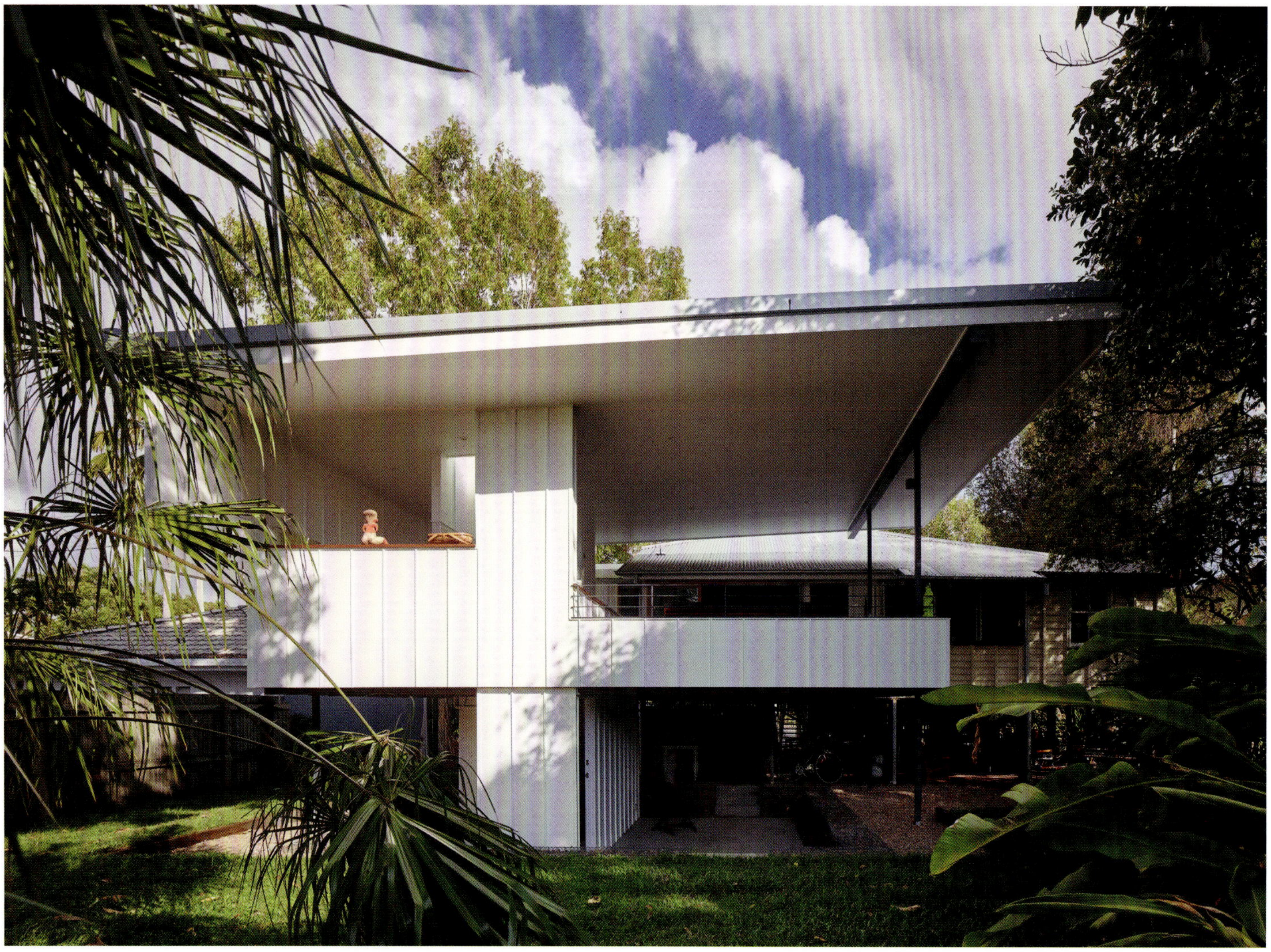

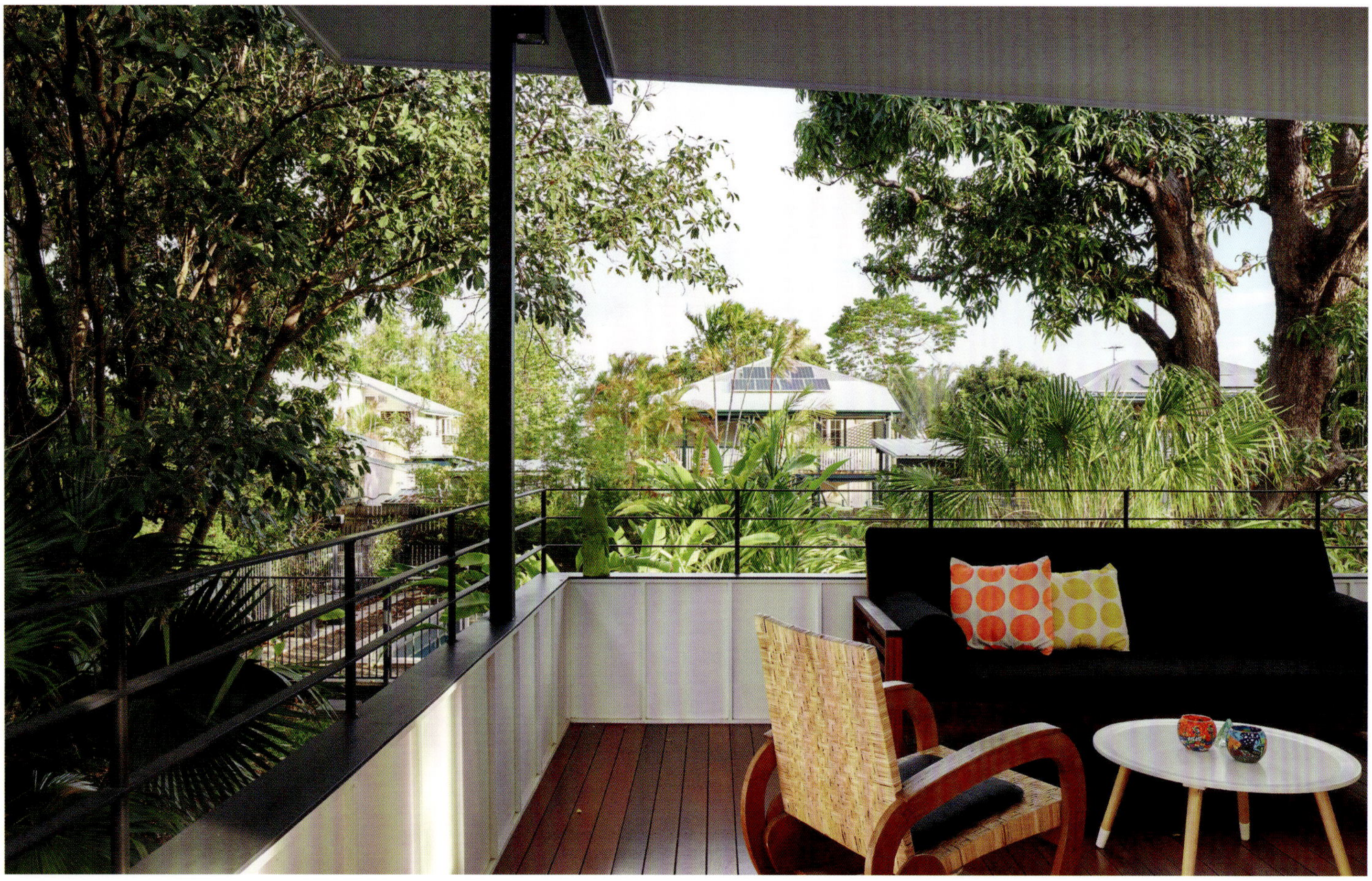

The lived experience

Sue Cole and Kerry McIlroy had lived in their four-room Queenslander cottage in Townsville for 30 years before approaching architect Stephen de Jersey to extend their home. 'We were reluctant to interfere with the integrity of the original house. It was built by a carpenter and still has a lot of the original features. Stephen was also quite charmed by it.' Thinking laterally about how the alterations could be accommodated, Stephen has essentially added a new indoor–outdoor pavilion that softly kisses the existing Queenslander.

The kitchen is the point of transition from old to new, with a long, sliding window that connects this space directly to the covered deck via a servery. The single shell, tongue-and-groove exterior of the original Queenslander house is retained and marks the transition from the early 20th century into the 21st century. The extension functions as an outdoor room, with solid balustrades and a canopy overhead. Kerry said, 'One of our friends calls our extension the "verdecchio" – a verandah, deck and patio all in one.'

Perched within a collection of trees endemic to the area, including a Burdekin plum (*Pleiogynium timoriense*), the outdoor room is regularly visited by various birds and butterflies. This space allows Sue and Kerry to be continually connected to the patterns of Townsville's dry tropical weather. An open-air bathroom continues this connection to the outdoors with views to the mango trees (*Mangifera indica*), while retaining privacy from the neighbouring block of flats to the west via a modesty screen. Hovering within the garden, this treehouse of sorts creates a sublime setting for dinner parties, reading, afternoon drinks or even somewhere to camp out for the night.

Opposite top:
The addition reinterprets the structural clarity and spatial organisation of the original Queenslander house.

Opposite bottom:
Perched within treetops, the outdoor room is regularly visited by various birds and butterflies.

Above left:
The kitchen is the point of transition from old to new and a long, sliding window that acts as a servery.

Above right:
An open-air bathroom has views to the mango trees, while maintaining privacy to the neighbours.

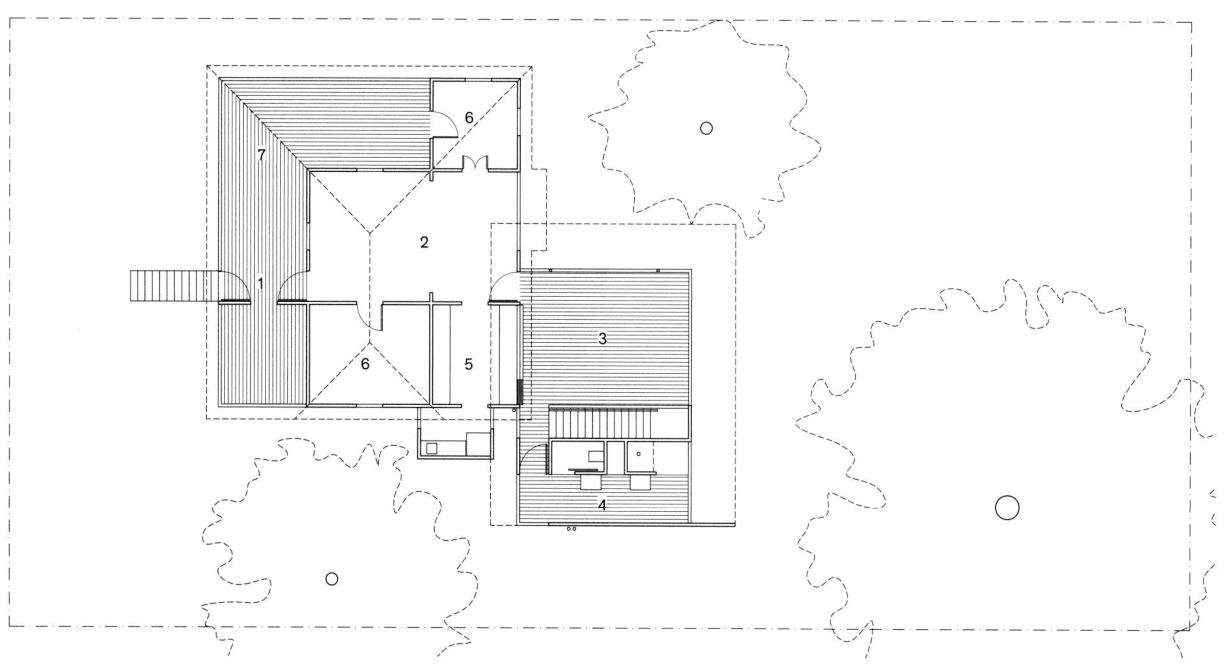

First floor

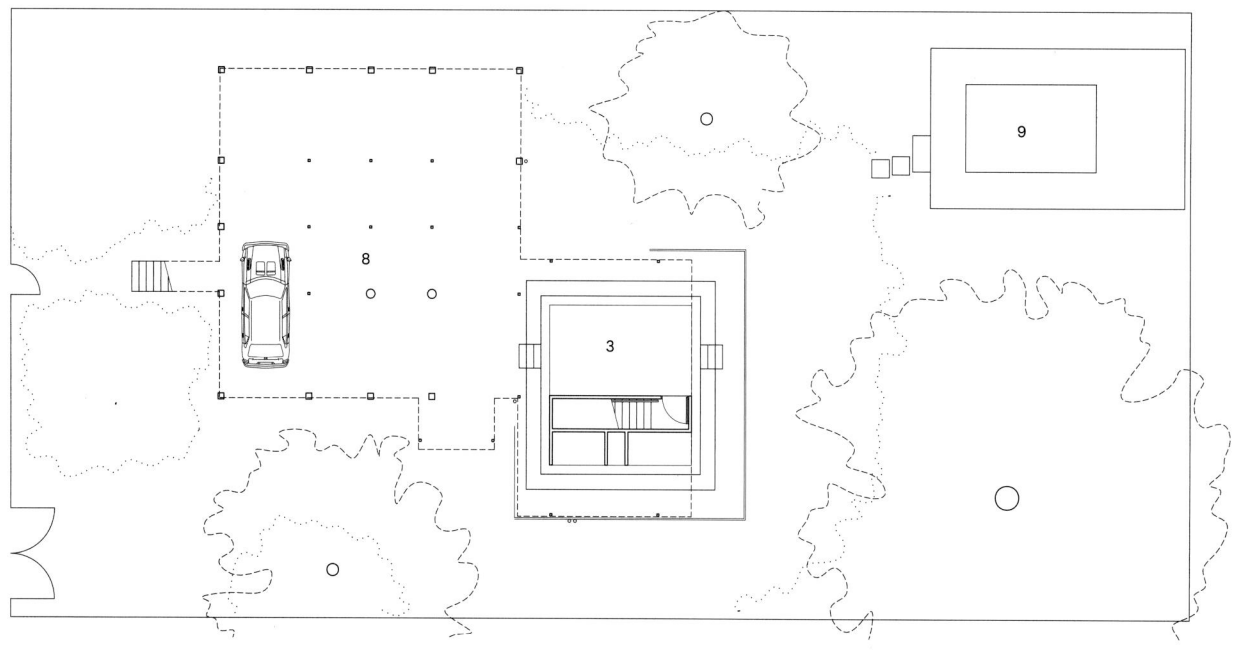

Ground floor

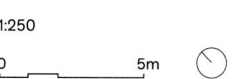

1:250

1	Entry	6	Bedroom
2	Internal lounge	7	Louvred verandah
3	External lounge	8	Undercroft
4	External bathroom	9	Pool
5	Kitchen		

BATH HOUSE

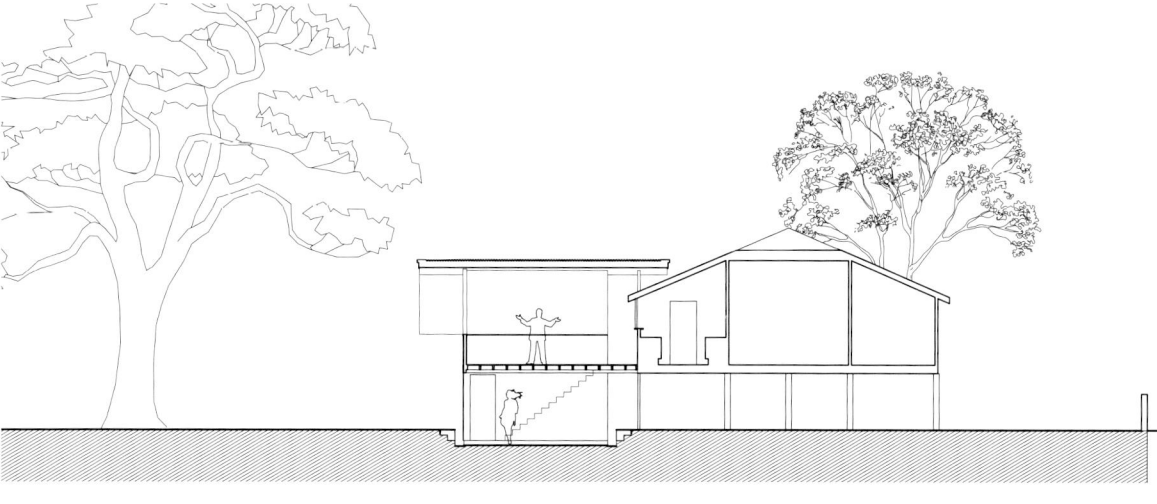

Longitudinal section

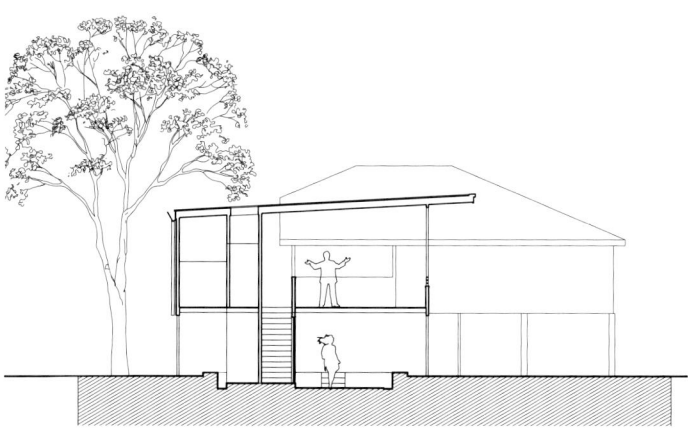

Cross section

1:250
0   5m

Architect — Stephen de Jersey Architect
Project team — Stephen de Jersey
Engineer — Glynn Tucker Consulting Engineers and Stark Consulting
Photographer — Scott Burrows

Auchenflower House

Auchenflower, Brisbane
Vokes and Peters

Completed – 2016
Project type – Alteration and addition
Total site area – 608 m²
Internal area – 174 m²
External area – 26 m²
Number of residents – 5
Number of bedrooms – 4
Number of bathrooms – 2

Auchenflower House is built on the land of the Turrbal and Yuggera peoples

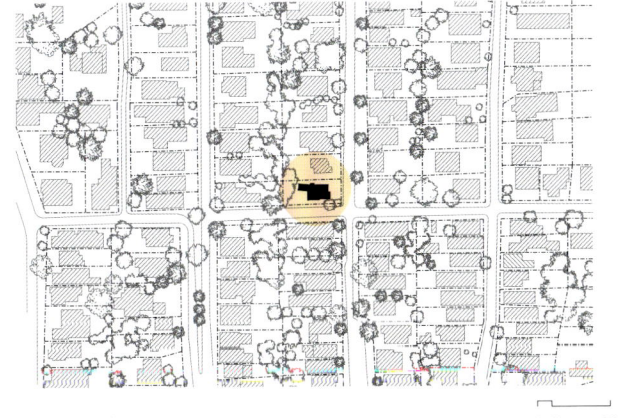

Location plan 1:5000 0 10 50m

The architectural setting

The Queenslander house has a special place in the arts and culture of the state. In the written form the texts of David Malouf, including *Johnno* and *12 Edmondstone Street*, are the most evocative and referenced in architecture. Malouf describes an authentic, place-based experience, writing in the period in which Brisbane was growing up, transforming from big country town to confident and ambitious metropolis and putting itself on the map by hosting global events like the 1982 Commonwealth Games and staging the 'Together We'll Show the World' World Expo on Southbank in 1988. The special, haptic qualities of these houses is also captured in visual art, from the painterly mid-century landscape and interior works of Margaret Olley to the perspectival, flyscreen experiments of contemporary artist Lincoln Austin.

The distinguished houses of Vokes and Peters are an artful response to the atmosphere and language of the Queenslander house that simultaneously critiques their imperfections and contested evolution. This thoughtful approach is deployed within an overarching and studious engagement with the unique nature of dwelling in this part of the world. At the Auchenflower House this has created a home that sits in gentle companionship with its built and natural context and adroitly connects its inhabitants with the seasons and the social life of the intimate neighbourhood.

Previous:
Auchenflower House captures the essence of Queensland living, connecting with the seasons and the neighbourhood.

Opposite:
The dwelling's triangular form makes a dramatic statement and reflects the steep slope of the landscape.

Above:
The entry sequence of the original 1930s home has been restored, adding contemporary detailing.

The lived experience

Brisbane is an adopted home for Michelle and Rick, owners of Auchenflower House. When searching for a place for their family of five to live, they were looking for an 'untouched Queenslander house' with 'gaps in the floorboards and a wide, breezy verandah'. When briefing their architects Stuart Vokes and Aaron Peters of Vokes and Peters, they were adamant that this interwar Queenslander house was to remain untouched. Stuart and Aaron's repeatedly proven subtle and sensitive approach to the intervening of a Queenslander house was perfectly suited to this brief.

Located on an exposed corner site in Auchenflower, the original 1930s home has an established civic presence. Similarly, the siting and form of the new living pavilion is in dialogue with the suburban street around the corner, using an architectural language that is informed by the existing structure without replication. Of note, the traditional battened back stair of the Queenslander forms the architectural motif for its elevation.

The small footprint and clever siting of the new pavilion reorients the home to the backyard and leaves space for a productive garden along the eastern street edge of the site. 'We love gardening and we are always out there,' explains Michelle. 'Sometimes we might give a pumpkin or another vegetable to a passing neighbour.' Genuinely fostering a neighbourhood connection, the home prompts Michelle and Rick to engage with what's happening beyond their fence line. The charmingly unassuming intervention acutely captures the essence of Queensland living – relaxed and open – with a sense of familiarity and nostalgia.

Opposite:
In an informal space that engages with the kitchen, green-painted floorboards reflect tones of the landscape.

Above:
At the front, the original Queenslander's verandah encourages engagement with the edge of the corner site.

Above:
At the back, a new staircase leads from the original home to a new semi-detached dormitory and studio.

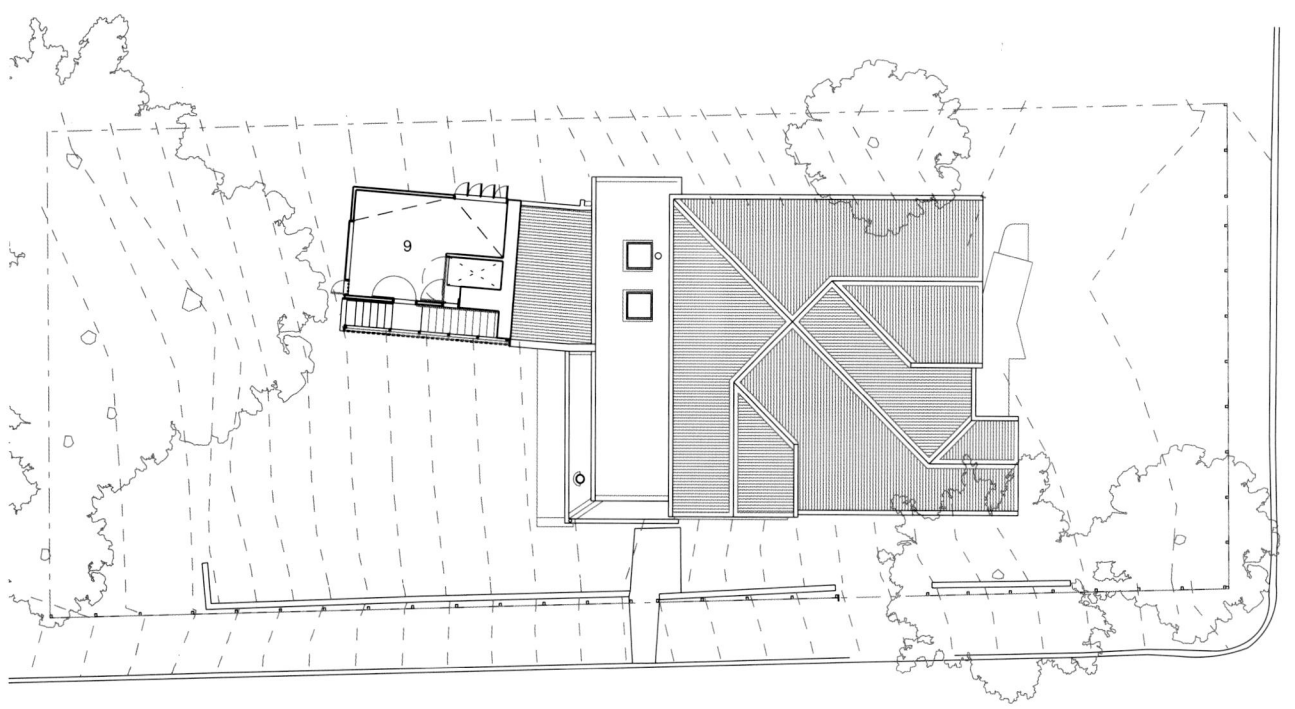

First floor

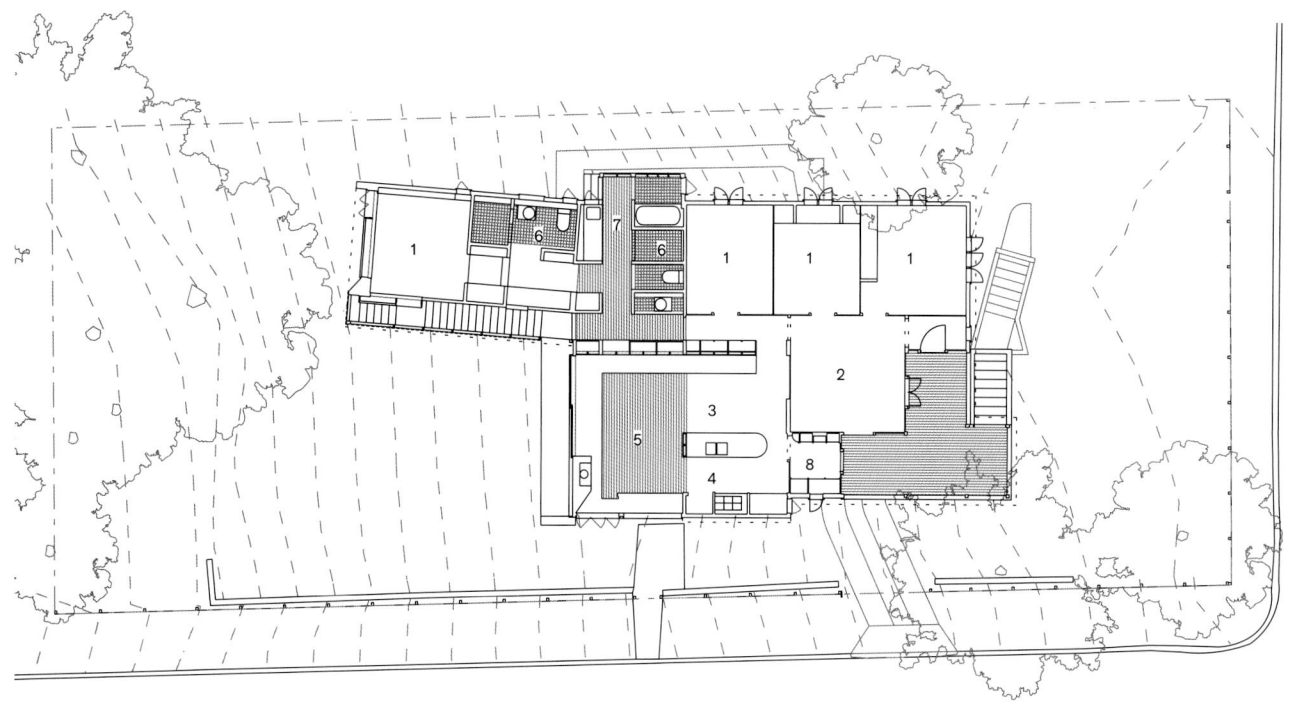

Ground floor

1:250

0   5m

1	Bedroom	6	Bathroom
2	Sitting	7	Laundry
3	Dining	8	Pantry
4	Kitchen	9	Studio
5	Family room		

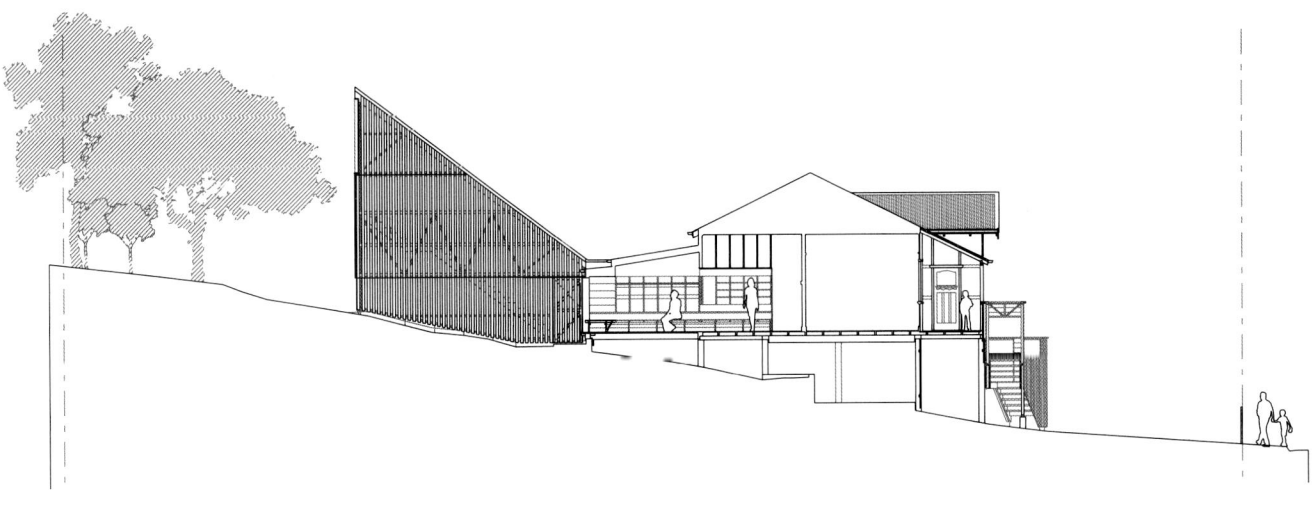

Longitudinal section

1:250
0 5m

Architect — Vokes and Peters
Project team — Stuart Vokes, Aaron Peters, Marty Said, Kirsty Hetherington
Structural engineer — Westera Partners
Hydraulic engineer — H Design
Builder — Bauen Projects
Photographer — Christopher Frederick Jones

Morningside Residence

Morningside, Brisbane
Kieron Gait Architects

Completed – 2017
Project type – Alteration and addition
Total site area – 886 m²
Internal area – 180 m²
External area – 39 m²
Number of residents – 5
Number of bedrooms – 4
Number of bathrooms – 2

Morningside Residence is built on the land of the Turrbal and Yuggera peoples

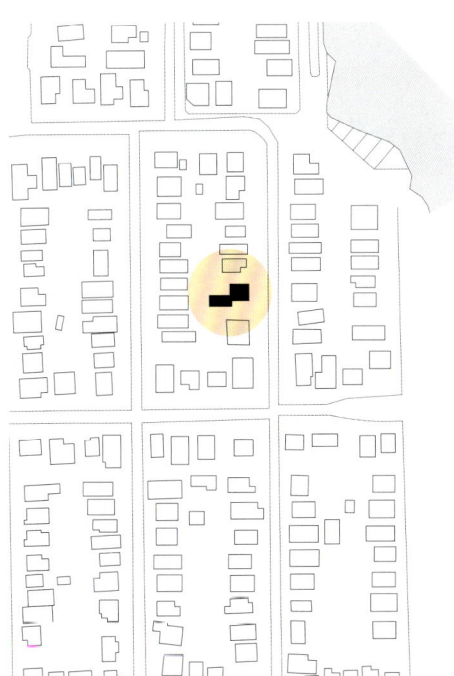

Location plan 1:5000 0 10 50m

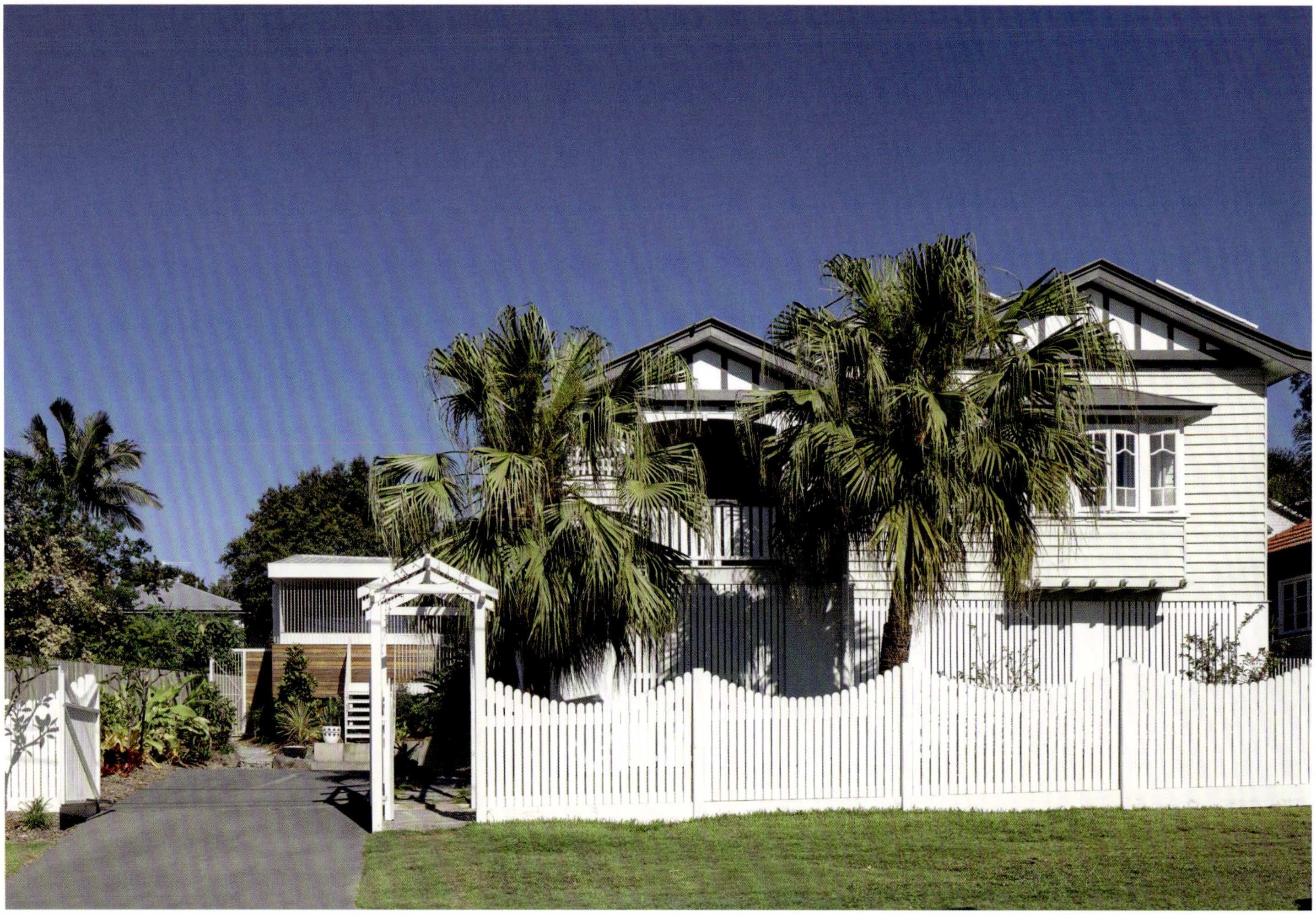

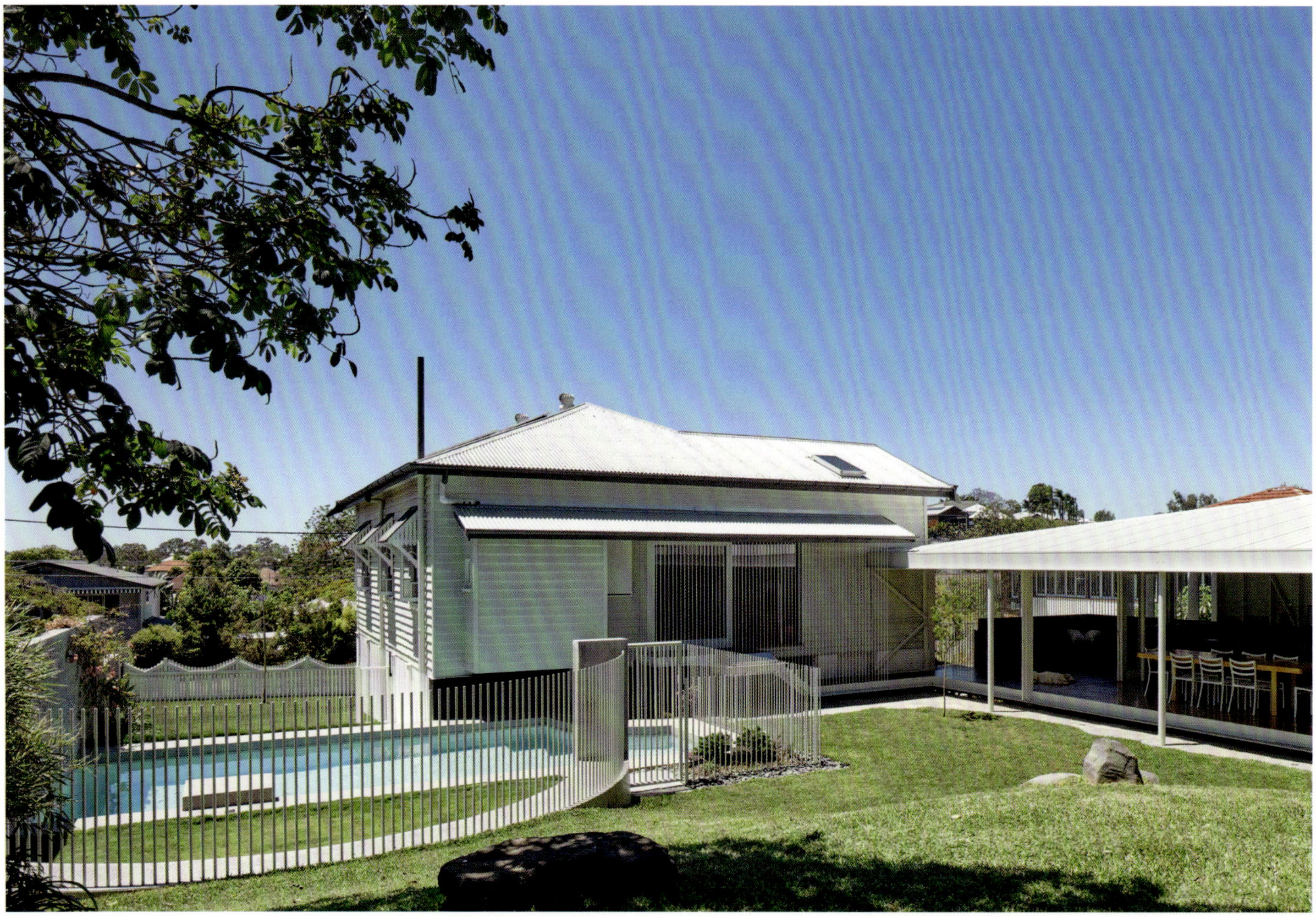

The architectural setting

The reimagining and enhancement of the relationship between building and landscape is a defining characteristic of recent Queensland residential architecture. The timber and tin Queenslander houses and the architecturally eclectic brick and timber housing of the suburbs are largely disconnected from the immersive and experiential qualities of their settings. Modernist principals of openness and transparency have scaffolded this aspirational connectivity in both new houses and renovations.

The new builds sit firmly on their sites, with terraces and courtyards that orchestrate the terrain as platforms for lightweight timber pavilions that discreetly feather into the setting and carefully frame views. Exemplary works of this architectural trajectory include the 1996 Grant House at Sunshine Beach by Gerard Murtagh (see page 292); the Alinghi Residence at Rocky Point in the coastal hamlet of 1770 by Grose Bradley BVN (see page 292); and the sophisticated Ogilvie House atop a seaside dune on the Sunshine Coast by Kerry Hill Architects (see page 294).

In the suburbs this strategy has been deployed to connect an existing house with the garden, and noted works include the Newmarket House by Owen Architecture (see page 294), which appends a crisp, white pavilion to the rear of a rare art deco gem. This architectural task underpins the work of Kieron Gait Architects and at the Morningside Residence a new, discreet pavilion creates a year-round living space that has a seamless relationship with the active backyard.

Previous:
The new pavilion of Morningside Residence is a family home characterised by openness and a sense of sociality.

Opposite top:
The existing Queenslander, built by a neighbour's father in the 1920s, has undergone a series of sensitive restorations.

Opposite below:
A new pavilion sits along the southern site boundary, framing the garden, with the existing house to the east.

Above:
The design of the new pavilion is a refined interpretation of the timber construction of the old home.

The lived experience

Owners Andrew and Kate Jensen purchased their high-set, weatherboard bungalow in Morningside from their neighbour who had grown up in the home; her father had built it himself in the 1920s. There was a promise by Andrew and Kate to retain the original Queenslander house, with aspirations to sensitively update it to embrace the way of life in the subtropics, as well as seeking a direct connection to their yard for the couple's three children.

Although the original home has undergone a series of sensitive restorations and contemporary insertions have been added, it is the siting strategy by their architect Kieron Gait that has reformed the way the family lives. Rather than attaching an extension to the rear of the existing house, a detached pavilion containing kitchen, dining and living spaces runs along the southern boundary of the site. The distinction between the various daily activities is amplified by this separated living space, with the outdoor journey of retreat to the bedrooms as a clear expression of the definition between private and public zones of the house – something that could only occur in the steady Queensland climate.

Driven by the care taken to craft and assemble the existing house, the new pavilion design is a refined and elegant interpretation of the timber construction of the old home. Although artfully composed, it is a robust building that can be used by the family and their friends in any number of ways. 'From September onwards, it turns into a pool pavilion for the kids, with water and towels scattered everywhere,' says Andrew. Walls peel away to the east and north, creating a shaded verandah-like space that captures cooling breezes. The addition of this new building has shifted the hierarchy of spaces in the home, redefining the garden as a year-round hub of activity.

Opposite:
Open to the garden, the shaded verandah-like space captures cooling breezes.

Above:
Exposed studs and bracing are reminders of the home's past in spaces with contemporary insertions.

Following:
At the rear of the house, the ground has been built up into a new landscape to suit children's play.

Above:
The exposed frame in the new pavilion contrasts with the weight and warmth of the kitchen joinery.

MORNINGSIDE RESIDENCE

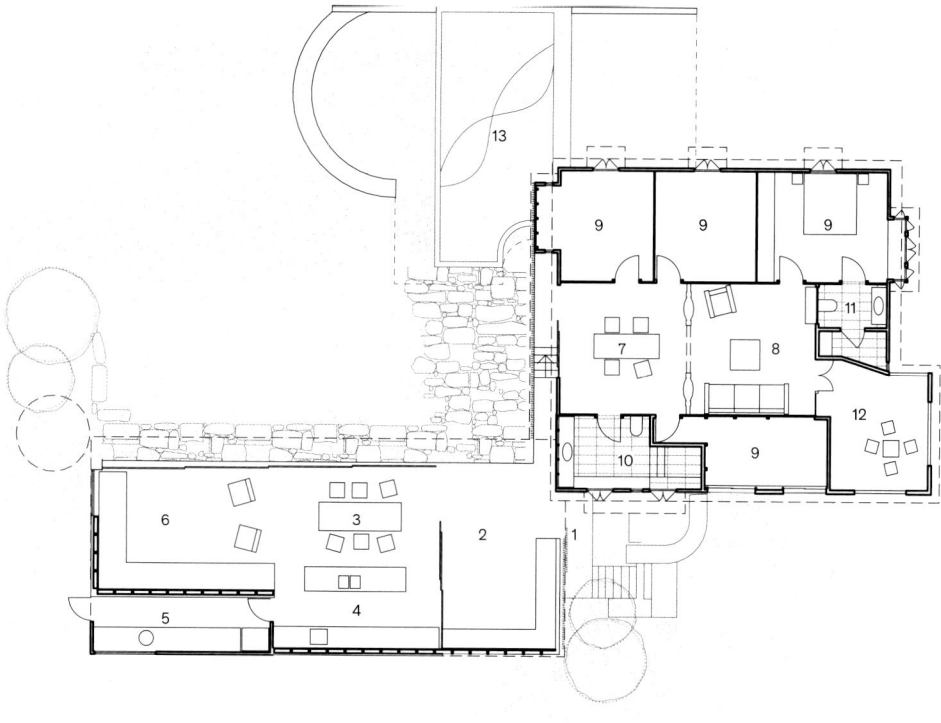

Plan

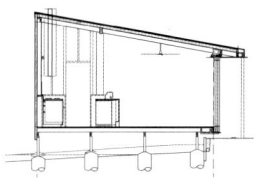

Cross section

1 Entry
2 Outdoor room
3 Dining
4 Kitchen
5 Pantry/laundry
6 Living
7 Craft
8 Family
9 Bedroom
10 Bathroom
11 Ensuite
12 Verandah
13 Pool

Architect — Kieron Gait Architects
Project team — Kieron Gait and Leah Gallagher
Builder — A.H. Done Builders
Engineer — NJA Consulting
Landscaping — Arborescence Tree Services
Certifier — Brisbane Certification Consultants
Photographer — Christopher Frederick Jones

1:250

One Room Tower

West End, Brisbane
Phorm Architecture + Design in collaboration with
Silvia Micheli and Antony Moulis

Completed – 2018
Project type – New build (secondary dwelling)
Total site area – 405 m^2
Internal area – 65 m^2 (extension) and 170 m^2 (existing house)
External area – 170 m^2
Number of residents – 2
Number of bedrooms – 1
Number of bathrooms – 1

One Room Tower is built on the land of the
Turrbal and Yuggera peoples

Location plan   1:5000   0 10   50m

The architectural setting

The project of densifying the established garden suburbs of Australia's major cities is an urgent task that promises to deliver a more sustainable and equitable built environment. In Brisbane, which has been a dispersed metropolis since the British settlement was founded in the 19th century, the development of compact, smaller-lot housing lagged that of other Australian state capitals, with the first signs of urban invention appearing in the 1990s and subsequently shaping development and planning policy in the first decade of the 2000s.

One Room Tower by Phorm Architecture + Design, in collaboration with Silvia Micheli and Antony Moulis, is a replicable model for suburban intensification that has been achieved by adding a new, independent but linked building in what was the backyard of the existing detached cottage. In this research-informed urban proposition, the relationship between the buildings and street is reimagined, recalibrating the way the site is occupied and experienced today and anticipating how this might evolve into the future.

This is a collaborative architectural enterprise, within the practice of Phorm Architecture + Design, extended and augmented through the dialogue with Micheli and Moulis, both academics at the University of Queensland. This future-focused mode of architectural practice overlays practice, building, teaching and research to advance urban design and planning in the subtropics.

Previous:
One Room Tower is a new, independent but linked building in the backyard of an existing cottage.

Opposite:
The new structure, a singular volume, contains highly flexible eating, bathing and sleeping spaces.

Above left:
The pavilion has a strong presence and actively participates in the life of the street, engaging passers-by.

Above right:
The detached addition acknowledges the timber-and-tin character of the surrounding neighbourhood.

The lived experience

Proudly perched in the backyard of an existing Queenslander house, One Room Tower intentionally belongs to its owners Antony Moulis and Silvia Micheli, as well as its dynamic West End community – both physically and metaphorically. Expanding and contracting the size of the existing home as required, One Room Tower was designed as a neutral and flexible space. With its prominent street presence, the pavilion actively participates in the life of the street. As a discreet building, it can function independently from the main house and genuinely invites public activity – take out the front fence and you can imagine that one day it might be transformed into the local coffee spot.

Although One Room Tower often functions as the public part to a private house – a place to host dinner parties, workshops or children's parties – it can also be used as guest accommodation. For Silvia's Italian parents, it's a home away from home. As you ascend through the levels of the tower, the public ground plane dissolves into a private sanctuary.

The standalone pavilion claims the entire garden of the existing house, but it strategically avoids its erasure. It simultaneously embeds you in nature and protects you from it – as Silvia says, 'The pavilion participates in the garden.' Openings are placed to celebrate the pockets of planting and borrow landscape views from the neighbouring properties. At the top of the tower, 'you feel like you're in the trees with the kookaburras'.

Opposite:
The pavilion embeds occupants in nature, claiming the entire garden of the existing house.

Top:
Inside the tower, spaces are defined by changes in materials and ceiling heights.

Bottom:
Strategically placed openings offer landscape views and create the feeling of being in the treetops.

Top:
Atypical and inexpensive materials are used, such as pool fencing and cargo net as the balustrade.

Bottom:
A breezeway stair and social court mediate between the original dwelling and the pavilion.

ONE ROOM TOWER

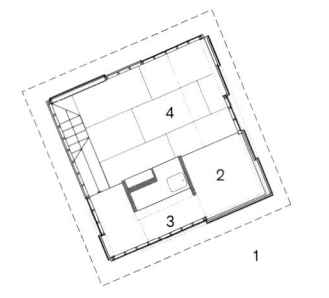

Ground floor

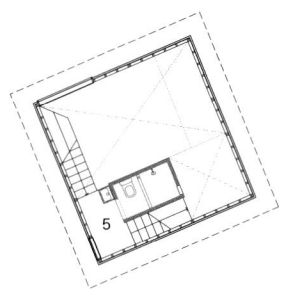

First floor

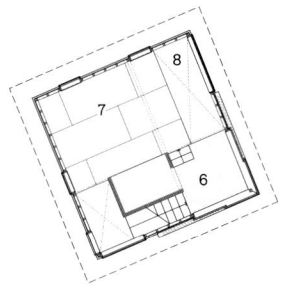

Second floor

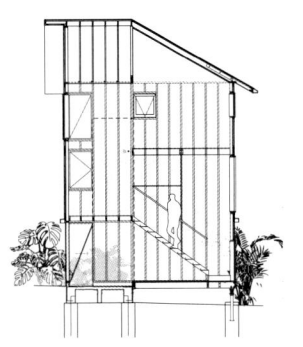

Sections

1 Courtyard
2 Entry
3 Kitchen
4 Garden platform
5 Wetroom
6 Balcony platform
7 Loft platform
8 Void

1:250

Architect — Phorm Architecture + Design in collaboration with Silvia Micheli and Antony Moulis
Project team — Paul Hotston and Yohei Omura
Builder — GTC Constructions
Structural engineer — Westera Partners
Town planner — Urbicus
Photographer — Christopher Frederick Jones

Channel Street Studio

Cleveland, Redland City
Anna O'Gorman Architects

Completed – 2020
Project type – Alteration and addition
Total site area – 911 m²
Internal area – 30 m²
External area – 17 m²
Number of residents – 4
Number of bedrooms – 4
Number of bathrooms – 3

Channel Street Studio is built on the land of the Quandamooka people

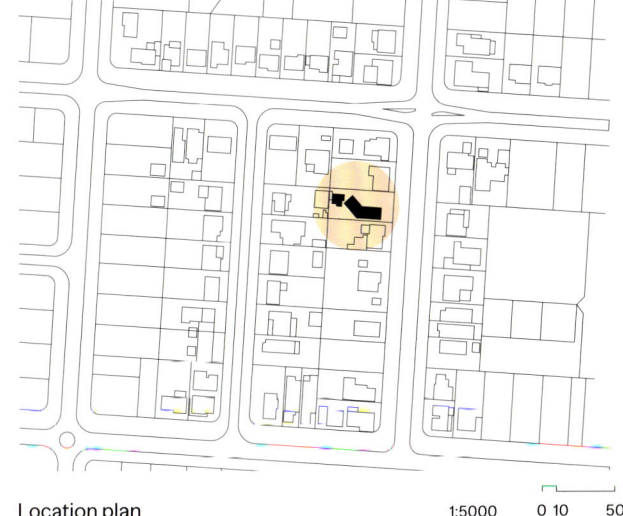

Location plan 1:5000 0 10 50m

The architectural setting

The architect's own home is writ large in the histories and theories of architecture, with local, national and international houses standing as landmarks in the trajectory of discipline and practice. In Australia, the opportunity for young architects to build independently, early in their careers, is a distinguishing characteristic of the culture and these foundational residential works are often realised by a venturous architect-owner.

In parallel these defining works are the result of commissions from close family members or friends and many are the outcome of an after-hours conversation over dinner, or at the sideline of a kid's soccer game, that shapes the ideals of an emerging architectural practice. In Queensland this latter pattern of practice has produced several noted works, including Elizabeth Watson-Brown's timeless Ngungun House (see page 294), a seaside escape on the Sunshine Coast for the architect's sister and brother-in-law and their young children that was completed in 1999.

Foregrounding Queensland examples of the architect's own home and studio are the 1996 Studio Vista by Alice L.T.M. Hampson Architect (see page 294) and the 1963 Railton House and Office in the Brisbane suburb of Spring Hill (see page 294), designed by John Railton for his family. At the Channel Street Studio by Anna O'Gorman Architects, this early career moment is captured in a deft work of adaptive re-use that combines work and life through the reimagining of a carport as a flexible studio and entertaining space for Anna's emerging practice.

Previous:
Channel Street Studio is a suburban utility building that activates the garden while retaining privacy to the main house.

Opposite:
A carport has been reimagined into a flexible studio and entertaining space for the main dwelling.

Above:
The new studio sits behind the original 1960s home on the Moreton Bay foreshore.

The lived experience

Suburban family life is a juggle between the needs of all household members, young and old and those in-between. The amount of dwelling space required for various activities expands and contracts over time, often leading to the demand for multifunctional and flexible spaces. In the case of the Channel Street Studio, architect Anna O'Gorman saw potential in the detached carport at her own family's 1960s home on Queensland's Moreton Bay foreshore. After years of lengthy, daily commutes to Brisbane's inner suburbs for work, Anna decided to make the leap and start her own architecture practice, so the space she immediately required was a studio. However, Anna saw an opportunity for this studio to be more than just a working space. 'In the future, I imagined that I would move my practice out of the studio and the space might be transformed into a parent's retreat or a secondary living or entertaining space,' she says.

Perched at the western end of the block, the original carport has been enclosed by operable louvres and translucent sheeting for access to natural light and fresh air. The studio opens out directly to the backyard via double-hinged glass doors, and the addition of a small bathroom and kitchenette allows for this suburban utility building to activate the garden into an entertainer's dream. As a separate building, the Channel Street Studio functions as an additional public zone to the domestic space while retaining privacy to the primary dwelling. 'On the weekends, we spend most of our time in the garden, with just our family or with friends. The studio transforms from work space to family space – it's part of how we live day to day.'

Opposite:
Double-hinged glass doors open out onto a small patio and an angled wall acts as a screen to the main home.

Above left:
Operable louvres and translucent sheeting enclose the original structure, giving access to light and fresh air.

Above right:
The addition of a small bathroom allows the studio to be used as a standalone secondary dwelling.

Following:
An open-air kitchenette strengthens the connection between the studio and the garden.

Above:
Although currently functioning as the owner-architect's studio, the space is designed to be more than just a workspace.

CHANNEL STREET STUDIO

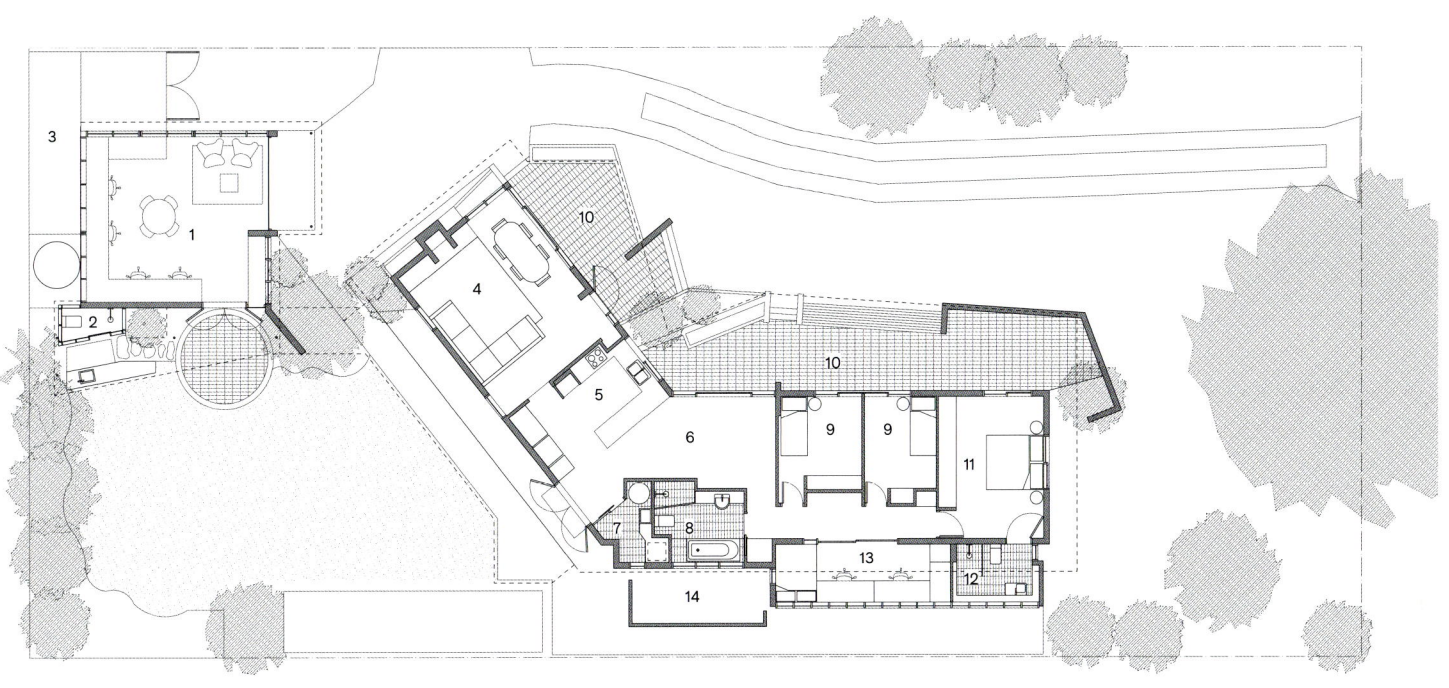

Plan

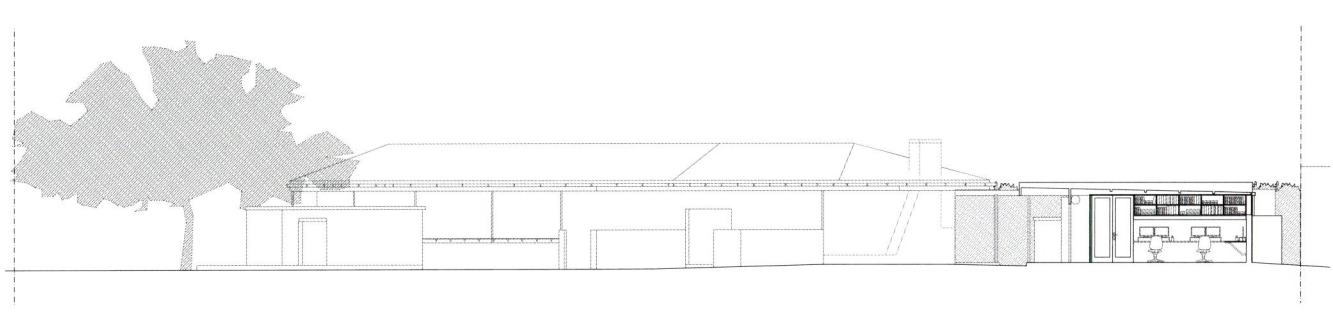

Longitudinal section

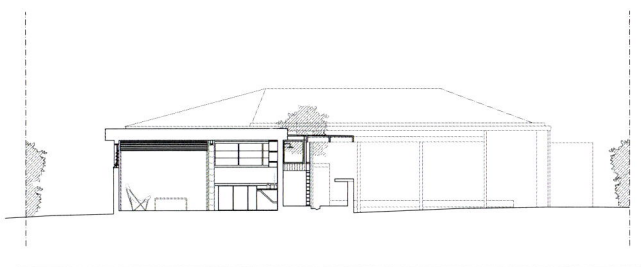

Cross section

1	Studio	8	Bathroom
2	WC/shower	9	Bedroom
3	Shed	10	Terrace
4	Lounge/dining	11	Main bedroom
5	Kitchen	12	Ensuite
6	Sunroom	13	Study
7	Laundry	14	Fern garden

1:250

0 ——— 5m

Architect — Anna O'Gorman Architects
Project team — Anna O'Gorman
Engineer — Brisse
Photographer — Christopher Frederick Jones

Pictorial endnote

3 House (2020) in New Farm, Brisbane, by Burton Architects and Channon Architects. Photography: Christopher Frederick Jones.

Alinghi Residence (2005) in Agnes Water by Grose Bradley BVN. Photography: John Gollings.

B&B Residence (2018) in Paddington, Brisbane, by Hogg and Lamb. Photography: Christoper Frederick Jones.

Banney Residence (2016) in Red Hill, Brisbane, by m3Architecture. Photography: Michael Banney.

Clayfield House (2004) in Clayfield by Owen Architecture (addition to a Mervyn Rylance-designed house). Photography: Jon Linkins.

D House (2000) in New Farm by Donovan Hill. Photography: Jared Fowler.

Dragon House (2001) in Sunshine Beach by John Mainwaring Architects. Photography: John Mainwaring.

Dunbar (2000) on North Stradbroke Island by Jennifer Taylor and James Conner. Photography: Christopher Frederick Jones.

Garden Bunkie (2018) in Lutwyche, Brisbane, by Reddog Architects. Photography: Christopher Frederick Jones.

Grant House (1996) in Sunshine Beach by Gerard Murtagh. Photographer: John Gollings.

House for the Central Coast of Queensland (1983) in Rockhampton by Don Gazzard and Associates. Photography: John Gollings.

Kitawah (1911) in East Brisbane by Robin Dods, with conservation and extensions by Conrad Gargett. Photography: Christopher Frederick Jones.

Carpenter Hall House (1986) in Eildon Hill by Russell Hall Architects. Photography: Toby Scott.

Chapman House (1995) in Noosaville by John Mainwaring Architects. Photography: John Mainwaring.

Clare House (1991) in Buderim by Clare Design. Photography: Reiner Blunck.

Clarke MacLeod House (2001, extension 2015) in Taringa by Chris Clarke. Photography: John Gollings.

Dyer Street House (2018) in Chapel Hill, Brisbane, by James Russell Architect (addition to a 1959 Vitaly Gzell-designed house). Photography: Toby Scott.

EJ Hayes House (1947) in St Lucia, Brisbane, by Edwin Hayes and Campbell Scott. Photographer unknown. Hayes and Scott collection. Fryer Library, UQFL 278, Box 1.

Fifth Avenue House (1992) in St Lucia, Brisbane, by Bud Brannigan Architects. Photography: John Gollings.

Fulcher Residence (1964) in Bardon, Brisbane, by Peter Heathwood. Photography: Christopher Frederick Jones.

Langer House (1950) in St Lucia by Karl Langer. Photographer unknown. Australian Institute of Architects collection. John Oxley Library, State Library of Queensland image no. 6523-0001-0593.

Malouf Residence (1967) in Holland Park by Bligh Jessup Bretnall. Photography: Richard Stringer. Australian Institute of Architects collection. John Oxley Library, State Library of Queensland image no. 6523-0001-0430.

Mocatta House (1966) in Yeronga by Robin Gibson. Photography: Richard Stringer. Australian Institute of Architects collection. John Oxley Library, State Library of Queensland image no. 6523-0001-0468.

Mooloomba House (1995) on North Stradbroke Island by Andresen O'Gorman Architects. Photography: John Gollings.

Newmarket House (2004) in Newmarket, Brisbane, by Owen Architecture. Photography: David Sandison.

Ngungun House (1990) on the Sunshine Coast by Elizabeth Watson-Brown. Photography: Michael Nicholson.

Ogilvie House (2004) on the Sunshine Coast by Kerry Hill Architects. Photography: Jon Linkins.

Pettit and Sevitt two-level Split Level House 2H (1973) on the Gold Coast. Photography: Max Dupain. Collection: Museum of Applied Arts and Sciences. Gift of Mr Ron Sevitt, 1994.

Pie Residence (1986) in Peregian Beach by Geoffrey Pie. Photography: Richard Stringer.

Plywood Exhibition House (1958) by Peter Heathwood and John Dalton, displayed at the Brisbane Exhibition (1958–1963) before being moved to The Gap. Photography: L & D Keen. Australian Institute of Architects collection. John Oxley Library, State Library of Queensland image no. 6523-0001-0606.

Railton House and Office (1963) in Spring Hill by John Railton. Photography: Christopher Frederick Jones.

Ravenscraig II (1965) in Surfers Paradise by Geoffrey Pie. Photography: Gabriel Poole. Australian Institute of Architects collection. John Oxley Library, State Library of Queensland image no. 6523-0001-0024.

Studio Vista (1995) in Hamilton, Brisbane, by Alice Hampson Architect (addition to a 1930s Mervyn Rylance-designed house): Photography: Jon Linkins.

Sun and Shadow House (1978) in Fig Tree Pocket by John Dalton. Photography: Dianna Snape.

Tent House (1990) in Eumundi by Gabriel Poole. Photography: Reiner Blunck.

The Courier Mail Tent House Commission (1992) displayed at the Botanical Gardens, Brisbane, by Gabriel Poole. Photography: Courtesy of Elizabeth Poole.

Architects & designers

Anna O'Gorman Architects
annaogorman.com

Atelier Chen Hung
a-ch.com.au

Bark Architects
barkdesign.com.au

Bligh Graham Architects
blighgraham.com.au

Blight Rayner
blightrayner.com.au

Brit Andresen Architect

Cavill Architects
cavillarchitects.com

Claire Humphreys
clairehumphreys.com.au

Clare Design
claredesign.com.au

CultivAR Architecture
cultivar.net.au

James Russell Architect
jrarch.com.au

Jesse Bennett Studio
jessebennett.com.au

John Ellway Architect
jellway.com

Kevin O'Brien Architects
koarchitects.com.au

Kieron Gait Architects
kierongait.com.au

Kim and Monique Baber
baberstudio.com.au

KIRK
kirk.studio

Lineburg Wang
lineburgwang.com

ME
mearchitect.com.au

m3architecture
m3architecture.com

Nielsen Jenkins
nielsenjenkins.com

Owen Architecture
owenarchitecture.com.au

Phorm Architecture + Design
phorm.com.au

Richards & Spence
richardsandspence.com

Steendijk
steendijk.com

Stephen de Jersey Architect
sdejarchitect.com

Twofold Studio
twofoldstudio.com.au

Twohill & James
twohillandjames.com

Vokes and Peters
vokesandpeters.com

Zuzana&Nicholas
zuzanaandnicholas.com

Photographers

Alicia Taylor
aliciataylorphotography.com

Benjamin Hosking
benhosking.com.au

Christopher Frederick Jones
cfjphoto.com.au

David Chatfield
davidchatfield.studio

Dianna Snape
diannasnape.com

John Gollings
gollings.com.au

Peter Bennetts
peterbennetts.com

Peter Hyatt
hyattgallery.com.au

Scott Burrows
scottburrowsphotographer.com

Sean Fennessy
seanfennessy.com.au

Simon Devitt
simondevitt.com

Toby Scott
tobyscott.com.au

Tom Ross
tomross.xyz

Artwork credits

Page 30 *Teacher's Union Building in Spring Hill* by Michael Barnett.

Page 31 William Robinson, *Creation Landscape: Water and Land,* 1991, oil on canvas, 183 x 732 cm. Private Collection, UK, courtesy of Nevill Keating Pictures.

Page 35 *Peter Cook: Tower Projects 1983–1984.* John Oxley Library, State Library of Queensland. Record no. 21108124880002061.

Page 46 (Left) *Me by Me 1* by Lewis Miller; (Right) *Cloud, Old Gulch, Lord Howe Island* by Peter Anderson.

Page 47 (Left image) (Left) *Heron Island Suite #17*, edition 12/30, by Judy Watson; (Right) Untitled by Cynthia Nanala (Warlayirti Artists).

Page 53 (Left image) *Mina Mina Dreaming* by Judy Watson Napangardi; (Right image) *Yam Leaf* by Janet Golder Kngwarreye.

Page 71 *The Unobtainable* by Joshua Parry.

Page 97 (Left image) Bruce Reynolds.

Page 118 (Top image) (Left) *Anson Bay* by Tracey Yager; (Right) *Straddie* by Denis Brockie.

Page 119 (Left) *I found modernism in the pages of a magazine #1* by Gareth Donnelly; (Right) unknown.

Page 154 Sandra Okalyi.

Page 161 Jai Vasicek.

Page 172 (Top image) *Mododa'e diburi'e hijë'oho (Tail-feathers of the swift in flight),* bark cloth textile work, by Sarah Ugibari, Ömie Artists.

Page 218 (Top of image) *Pool VIII* by Jordy Hewitt; (Right) Laura Patterson.

Page 224 (Left, below ceramic plate) Daisy Hamlot; (Middle top) Tim Johnson; (Middle bottom) Gemma Smith; (Right top) Vivienne Binns; (Right bottom) Jonathan Kopinski.

Page 225 (Bottom of stairs) Jonathan Kopinski.

Page 226 (Left, top of stairs) Janet Venn-Brown; (Centre, Yuendumu dot paintings, left to right) Peggy Napurrula Poutson, Paddy Japaljarri Stewart, Bessie Nakamarra Sims; (Canvases to right) Gordon Hookey.

Page 287 (Left image) Ian Smith.

Page 289 Michael Barnett.

Page 290 (Left to right) Unknown; Robyn Schuurmans; Shane Thompson; Mark Hiley.

Acknowledgements

We would like to thank the collaborators who have been an integral part of this journey: Mary Mann, Paulina de Laveaux, Rachel Carter, Harriet Empey, David Malouf, Brit Andresen, Michael Keniger, Silvia Micheli, Ashley Paine, Lucy Bland, Natalia Pullen, David Chatfield, John Gollings, Brian Donovan, Timothy Hill, James Du Plessis, Andrew Yeo and Nancy Underhill. Thank you to the homeowners and their families who have generously shared their houses and their experiences, and to the architects, photographers and institutions we have worked with.

First published in Australia in 2022
by Thames & Hudson Australia Pty Ltd
11 Central Boulevard, Portside Business Park
Port Melbourne, Victoria 3207
ABN: 72 004 751 964

First published in the United Kingdom in 2023
By Thames & Hudson Ltd
181a High Holborn
London WC1V 7QX

The New Queensland House © Thames & Hudson Australia 2022

Text © Cameron Bruhn and Katelin Butler 2022
Copyright in all texts, artworks and images is held by the creators or their representatives, unless otherwise stated.

25 24 23 22   5 4 3 2 1

The moral right of the author has been asserted.

All rights reserved. No part of this publication may be reproduced or transmitted in any form or by any means, electronic or mechanical, including photocopy, recording or any other information storage or retrieval system, without prior permission in writing from the publisher.

Any copy of this book issued by the publisher is sold subject to the condition that it shall not by way of trade or otherwise be lent, resold, hired out or otherwise circulated without the publisher's prior consent in any form or binding or cover other than that in which it is published and without a similar condition including these words being imposed on a subsequent purchaser.

Thames & Hudson Australia wishes to acknowledge that Aboriginal and Torres Strait Islander people are the first storytellers of this nation and the traditional custodians of the land on which we live and work. We acknowledge their continuing culture and pay respect to Elders past, present and future.

 A catalogue record for this book is available from the National Library of Australia

ISBN 978-1-760-76246-9

British Library Cataloguing-in-Publication Data
A catalogue record for this book is available from the British Library

Every effort has been made to trace accurate ownership of copyrighted text and visual materials used in this book. Errors or omissions will be corrected in subsequent editions, provided notification is sent to the publisher.

Front Cover: La Scala by Richards & Spence
Back Cover: C House by Donovan Hill
Photographed by David Chatfield

Design: Studio Bland
Editing: Harriet Empey
Research Assistant: Mary Mann
Printed and bound in China by C&C Offset Printing Co., Ltd

FSC® is dedicated to the promotion of responsible forest management worldwide. This book is made of material from FSC®-certified forests and other controlled sources.

Be the first to know about our new releases, exclusive content and author events by visiting

thamesandhudson.com.au
thamesandhudson.com
thamesandhudsonusa.com